Still Talking Blue

MAINSTREAM *SPORT*

STILL TALKING BLUE

A COLLECTION OF CANDID INTERVIEWS WITH EVERTON HEROES

BECKY TALLENTIRE

MAINSTREAM
PUBLISHING

EDINBURGH AND LONDON

First published in Great Britain in 2001 by
MAINSTREAM PUBLISHING COMPANY (EDINBURGH) LTD
7 Albany Street
Edinburgh EH1 3UG

ISBN 1 84018 664 X

This edition, 2002
Reprinted 2004

A catalogue record for this book is available from the British Library

Typeset in Gill
Printed and bound in Great Britain by
Cox & Wyman Ltd

Dedicated to the memory of Brian Beedles and Gordon Watson.
Good men and great Evertonians.

CONTENTS

FOREWORD

by Alex Young

I first encountered Becky when she invited me to be included in the *Talking Blue* series. I enjoyed that very much. I liked her approach, which made me feel at ease, and her cheek, which made me laugh. Her writing is lively and original and the format offers the fans a voice and a chance to finally ask the questions that have bugged them for years. I think it's only right that the players have been so forthright and honest with their replies, it's the very least they could do to salute their astonishingly loyal fan base.

Our paths crossed again when Becky co-authored Holy Trinity – Kendall, Harvey and Ball – a book with a difference as all the proceeds go to the Former Players Association. Blueblood was set up to help alleviate financial and medical suffering of heroes who wore the Royal Blue for the sheer love of it, and little else. Too frequently, those old warriors fall on hard times and need some financial or medical support. I'm a patron of the charity, and it has my full support and backing. The work they have done so far is tremendous and they've brought some sunshine back into the lives of those former heroes. I'm privileged to be associated with Blueblood and it's my absolute pleasure to write this foreword to introduce you to *Still Talking Blue*. While I have your attention, this is the ideal platform for me to pass on a message to Evertonians the world over. Thank you for the love you showed me from the very start. I first came to Everton in November 1960 and was accepted from the word 'go'. There's no place in the world quite like Goodison Park when packed to the rafters with its passionate supporters. Many of the readers of this book won't even have seen me play, but their fathers may have told them stories about the olden days.

Evertonians are the most loyal and faithful supporters I've ever encountered and the respect they show to their former players is exceptional. I'm a very proud man to have been a part of the Everton family – thank you for having me.

Enjoy your book.

INTRODUCTION AND ACKNOWLEDGEMENTS

Welcome to *Still Talking Blue* – my pride and joy

During the writing of this book, I was privileged to spend a great deal of time with these Everton Legends and I couldn't help but notice there was a common denominator – they were all absolute gentlemen. Their questions were all submitted by the fans and, taking into consideration the nature of Evertonians, there was no stone left unturned, no holds barred and no questions shirked. Each question was asked as written, and every last man took it in his stride and in the nature it was intended. From a bygone age when football was played for the love of the shirt and scant financial reward, these men are our heroes and they have every right to be.

While I'm on my orange box, I'd like to take this opportunity to thank a few people who've cheered and encouraged me along the way:

Paul Tollet, for worrying about me. Alex Young for being such a gentleman – it's no wonder everybody loves you. Sharon Malins (sadly a Kopite) – thanks for coming to find me, it's as if it were yesterday – minus the bow tie. Mikola Williams, my online PA, *confidante* and jester, you've really had me cackling into my cauldron, I don't know what I'd have done without you. Pere Blanche and Nick Beedles, for always being so wonderfully supportive and generous, I'll never forget it – even when I'm in Acapulco. David France, for adding me to your splendid collection of 'Evertonia'. Howard Kendall, for sharing your secrets with us. Louise Irving, refuse to go quietly, I have more faith in you than I have in myself. Sal Green, cameraman, friend and photographer – hold the salt. Mike and Ed Loftus, who would have believed it? I'm so happy to have found you both again. Stoo Roberts, Colin Berry and Kenny Fogarty for always making me laugh. Billy Williams, my magnificent proofreader – take a bow, you did me proud. My Nanny, Alice Gray, who once danced with Dixie Dean, and of course my good old Mum and George, who are still humouring me. I'll get my act together one of these days, I promise. The members of the Toffeenet and Evertonia mailing lists and subscribers to Toffeeweb, WSAG and Bluekipper, whose ridiculous recall of trivia gave me the idea for the book in the first place.

It seems a bit unfair, but the truth is that the pleasure was indeed all mine. I don't know whether to laugh or cry.

THEY ASKED THE QUESTIONS

Mick Abrams is exiled in Newcastle upon Tyne and started supporting Everton because of the effect they had on his dad. If we won he was the happiest man alive but if not, then he'd be utterly dejected – a trait he appears to have passed on. His hero is Graeme Sharp for scoring some of the best goals ever by an Everton player.

Ian Ainsworth attended his first game against Coventry in 1970. His claims to fame are: being mistaken for Dave Watson at 'Waggy's' Testimonial dinner, having a personal tour of Goodison Park by Brian Labone and sitting next to Andy Gray at a company conference in 1987 where he was a celebrity guest.

Robin Ashford is a Southerner who's decided to come clean and admit that in 1984, when he was eight, Gary Lineker came along and caused him to fall in love with the Blues. He gets to watch around 15 games a season, listens to all the others, wears his shirt with pride, pretends to be Big Dunc when he plays and is always full of cautious optimism about the new season.

Mike Benson is an accountant and has been an Upper Bullens season ticket holder since the dark days of the early '80s when names like Biley and (Mick) Ferguson graced the team-sheet. In his eyes, the best player to wear a blue shirt is a toss-up between Trevor Steven and Graeme Sharp. Mike lives in West Derby, with his wife and young son, Sam (who is also an Evertonian but doesn't know it, yet).

Tim Bentham queued all night for a '95 Cup final ticket and his first match was against Arsenal in '91, when Cottee scored then admitted he was offside. Tim lives in London, his hero is Barry Horne and he never leaves the house without his lucky scarf.

Jon Berman has spent a lifetime watching his beloved Everton. One of the authors of *Everton Greats – Where Are They Now?* he is married with two daughters and spends his spare time trying to convince them that Everton are better than shopping. His favourite ever player is Alan Ball.

Colin Berry has been Blue for longer than he can remember, despite his grandad taking him to watch Phil Thompson's testimonial. He is based in Liverpool, works in the computer games industry and once met Neville Southall on the beach while on holiday in Llandudno.

Clive Blackmore met Bob Latchford at Hightown Squash Club, saved a penalty from Russell Osman and almost bummed a fag from Johnny Morrissey, but lost his nerve at the last minute. He works as an information officer for Worldbank and is based in Washington DC.

Rob Bland has been an Evertonian since he was mesmerised by the mercurial skill of Duncan McKenzie on Gerald Sinstadt's *Kick Off* in the '70s. Seldom seen without some form of Everton attire, he lives in Morecambe.

Ian Bonnar, an Evertonian from birth, grew up in Formby and had to endure the Colin Harvey years at high school. He has recently surrendered his season ticket for the bright lights of London and is a journalist and web-developer, living in the shadow of Upton Park.

Phil Bowker is from a rugby league family and watched the 1968 FA Cup final to see what football was all about. Because he was only eight, he thought 'Bromwich' was a stupid word, so naturally became an Everton supporter. Such logic typifies all the work he's done in the IT industry since 1979, hence the need to keep moving. He is living in Brussels this year, or at least until he gets rumbled.

Stuart Brandwood saw his dad cry for the first time when we beat Rapid Vienna – his karmic payback for enduring the '70s. His hero is Kevin Ratcliffe, he lives in Netherton and would like to thank his mum to whom we owe the victory of the '95 Cup final for sewing herself into her lucky tartan skirt.

Charlie Brewer was indoctrinated from an early age and could recite the Everton team with positions and main characteristics from the age of three – much to the amusement of his dad's mates. He is now based in Seoul, South Korea, and runs a banking and finance IT consultancy.

Tony Brown lives in Wigan and was 11 years old when he attended his first match in 1984 versus Spurs as a mascot (yes, his mum still has the coin they used to toss up). A season ticket holder since 1985, he admits to crying when his hero, Nev, told the crowd he loved us all at half-time against Coventry in 1998.

Mike Burke is a London-based barrister and has supported Everton since his first gasp of breath. His darkest day was when the forces of evil triumphed and the heavens rent – Everton 0, Liverpool 5. His finest hour was in 1985 when God smiled down on this sceptred isle – Spurs 1, Everton 2.

Simon Burke is a silver-tongued trumpet-playing idle layabout occasionally earning a living as a musician. Originally from Rossendale but currently residing in Toxteth, Simon looks like a haggard version of David O'Leary.

Rob Burns watched Everton v Doncaster in the FA Cup third round and never looked back. He knew all of the players by the end, sang Everton songs all week lying on his top bunk, ironed the programmes, attached the ticket stubs and hung them on his wall. Every time he went to Southport he was twitching with excitement – as he'd once seen Paul Bracewell there in his sponsored blue Ford Capri.

David Cairns attended his first game against LFC with his uncle, a die-hard red. Giddy with the sheer magic of the occasion, he was hypnotised by both Alan Ball's white boots and his goal – we won 1–0. And so it began. Unlucky Uncle Terry!

David Catton moved away from his home city as an 18-year-old in 1962. Nowadays he mostly goes back to watch Everton – which he has done through thick and thin for almost 50 years. Highlights? – any game in which Alex Young played.

Paul Checkland has lived in Maidstone, Kent, for nine years and supported Everton since the age of four when his dad first took him to Goodison. He still has his first season ticket for the old Goodison Road stand that cost £8 in 1962.

Andy Cheyne was born in Wallasey and grew up in Cronton (where, in the '90s, it was rumoured without any sense of irony that Everton were going to build a stadium on an old slagheap). Such is his devotion to the Blues that he's modelled his entire life on his beloved Everton and become a chronic under-achiever. He now lives in West Berkshire.

David Chow (pronounced Daveed – the French way) has supported Everton ever since arriving in England from Hong Kong in 1985. His all-time hero is Big Nev and Daveed's heart could be heard breaking that miserable day in December 1997 when Neville packed his gloves and moved on.

Paul Christopherson lives in Nottingham and works as a design engineer. Fortunately, his first match was EFC 6, Chelsea 0 when Bob Latch scored the fourth and sixth to achieve his 30 goals for the season. Vows were made that day, for better or for worse, and so began the addiction.

Neal Clague would like to thank his dad for taking him to see Everton v Bolton in the '70s on the weekly day-trip boat from the Isle of Man. Neal lives in Douglas and, believe it or not, exports kippers for a living. He declares his favourite player as Tricky Trev because of that goal against Sunderland.

Patrick Clancy is the eternal student and has been supporting Everton since he became fascinated with his Uncle Ged's EFC tattoo as a child. Apart from watching the Blues, his hobbies include skateboarding and listening to ridiculously loud music.

Andy Clarke is an IT consultant living in Essex with his wife and two boys. His godfather who stood on the Street End in the '50s converted him to the Royal Blue faith, and his first match, aged nine, was a 2–0 victory over Stoke City in January 1973. He fondly recalls his away trips on Barnes Travel throughout the '80s.

Tony Cocoran is the chairman of the Dublin branch of the Everton Supporters Club. Although he hates the way football has become so mercenary now, he still only has eyes for the Blues. In an open and honest public confession, he would like to cleanse his soul and admit that he financed his jaunts to England in the late '70s by selling (then illegal) porn magazines and condoms in Dublin's fair city.

Jim Conboy met his wife on ESCLA train to Ipswich away in December '84 (we won 2–0). His worst moment was being in the Boys Pen at Anfield watching them murder us 5–0 sometime in the '60s and his most imminent project is to discover how many Evertonians are living in Hesketh Bank.

Iain Cooke is a computer programmer at the Bank For International Settlements based in Basel, Switzerland. Born in China, he became an Evertonian when he first visited the UK in 1976 because his brother was a rabid Red and he wanted to annoy him. He soon realised it was his calling.

Sean Corr was born and bred in Monaghan, Ireland, and now works in Dublin as a software tester. His first live Everton game was a friendly in the late '80s versus Drogheda United, marred by Dave Watson stealing his pen after giving his autograph. His favourite ever player is Kevin Sheedy.

Mike Coville lives near New York but still manages to get home once or twice a season to see his 'Blueboys'. His magic moment was watching Dave Hickson, with blood pouring down his face, score the winner against Man United, and his most treasured possession is the *Daily Post* FA Cup final souvenir of 16 May 1966 celebrating the 3–2 victory over Sheffield Wednesday.

Roy Coyne is a retired nurse and has followed the Blues since the '50s. His best ever game was the '66 Cup final with Jimmy Gabriel at the corner flag looking at his watch. But even sadder than seeing Spurs beat us 10–4 was watching Dave Hickson run out at Anfield wearing a red shirt.

Still Talking Blue

Ste Daley is from Speke on Merseyside. He once spent a whole day taking photos of himself in the Whistling Dixie mascot outfit after finding an unlocked door during a pre-season.

Gary Davis is an astrophysicist and professor of physics at the University of Saskatchewan, Canada. When he adopted the Blues in 1984 he didn't realise it would become an endurance trial of Herculean proportions.

Tom Davis sells packaging products from his Dallas mansion but was born and raised in Walton, L4. Still playing amateur 'footy' in spite of his age, Tom has been a Blue since 1961 and spent his honeymoon watching the 1989 Cup final. He still gets to see his beloved Everton at least once a year.

Michael Dudley first sat on the crowd barriers in the old Goodison Road ground section with his dad, a season ticket holder who had been watching Everton since William Ralph scored his 60th goal. Michael missed all the good stuff in the '80s when he moved to the States to become a professor but is now more fanatical than ever keeping in touch via the Internet and by phone calls to his good old dad.

Mark Edwards dines out on the fact that his parents bought Alex Young's old clubhouse in Aintree. Brought up in full Everton legend, his first match saw Big Bob's record-breaking thirtieth goal against Chelsea. Mark and his wife Anna are season ticket holders in the Street End.

Steve Fairclough was born and raised in Wallasey, but moved to Toronto in 1982. His greatest time as a Blue was when he returned to live in the UK (for 18 months) to witness, first hand, the 1986–87 season. His therapist agrees that this helped rid him of the trauma of living through the '70s. His all-time hero is Mick Lyons.

Lee Farrell is the only Blue in a family of unfortunate Reds and lives just outside Glasgow. His first game was versus Southampton at Goodison in 1983 and his hero is Peter Reid.

Peter Fenton is too young to remember the glory days but does remember beating Swindon 6–2 and at the end of the match hearing D:Ream's 'Things Can only Get Better'. Peter was full of optimism for the future. Oh, how wrong he was.

They Asked the Questions

Tony Field was born to shout for the Blues and vote Labour. One of his finest memories was at Molineux when Peter Knowles thought it would be a good idea to kick Alan Ball, but gave up the game for good after a serious battering, simultaneously from Jimmy Gabriel and Brian Labone.

Ray Finch used to walk to Goodison as a five-year-old from St George's Heights where he lived with his Nan. His best moments were the '85 Cup-Winners' cup semi and meeting Alan Ball at a testimonial for Portsmouth keeper Alan Knight. He enquired why he never 'came home' and Alan Ball turned away as his wife replied that was the one thing he couldn't bear to be asked.

Bernie Flood says the surge of joy on the North Bank, Highbury, was unbelievable when Adrian Heath scored the winner in the FA Cup semi-final in 1984 against Southampton. After so many years of near misses and failures we had finally made it – Everton were back.

Kenny Fogarty was born in Liverpool in 1966. He left England's green and pleasant land in 1991 in search of work and has been unable to find a job well enough paid to lure him back since. He is a systems programmer at IBM Finance Systems, living in Amsterdam in his swanky apartment. His all-time hero is Neville Southall.

Ged Fox hates Rod Belfitt, Bernie Wright and Clive Thomas. He spent his formative years in Halewood and moved to the capitalist south in 1982 to work for an investment banking and asset management company. His heroes are Bally, Latch and Sharp.

Gary Fulton thought he'd died and gone to heaven when he saw the hallowed turf at Goodison for the first time in 1981. His first game was Howie's first in charge and he went on to hero-worship Graeme Sharp. Working in Cheshire as a caster in a pottery, Gary once met Barry Horne at an *NME* Brat Bus gig.

Jonathan Gard is as mad as a March hare. He looks like Robin Williams and is so small he can get bottles of champagne down his pants and still walk normally. Good to go to town with, Jon supports Everton but doesn't know why.

Nicholas Gard was born in Halewood, raised in Montreal and now resides in Kirkland, Washington, where he is employed as a Consulting Ecotoxicologist (definition provided upon request). His most thankless task is trying to explain his devotion to uncomprehending Americans and his proudest accomplishment was teaching his elder daughter to say 'Everton' as one of her first words.

Simon George is a Brummie. His first match was at Aston Villa when we were beaten 6–2 and his claim to fame was being on the season video that year in the most awful purple coat ever made. He took a big slab of the pitch back home to Birmingham after the Wimbledon game and his favourite ever player is Joe Parkinson.

Keith Giles is originally from Aintree but now living in Perth, Australia. He hasn't been back yet because he's a student and a bit short of cash but stays up all night listening to the radio or watching Everton on TV and wants to know if that counts.

James Goddard has been an Evertonian since he was six, inspired by the magic of Gary Lineker. His worst moment was the 1989 Cup final with Stuart McCall scoring twice, taking it to extra time and still losing to Liverpool. A software developer working for BT, he lives in Ipswich.

Tim Gunnion believes that Bobby Latchford walks on water and his son's first words were 'Graeme Sharp'. Raised in brutal Bootle, he is now based in Frankfurt and cites his heroes as Trevor Steven, Andy King and Andy Gray. The worst day of his life was when son number two turned to 'the dark side' with the searing words 'You can't have a match if you're in the same team.'

Rob Hamilton is from Melbourne, Australia, and has been an Evertonian since 1984 when his dad decorated the house with streamers for the Cup final. An early source of fascination was John Bailey's big hat and when not studying or listening to heavy metal, Rob is working hard to save up to go and see the Blues again.

Joe Hannah already had Blue blood on joining the Merchant Navy at 16 – thanks to his dad. He sailed the seven seas until he fell in love with an Australian girl, which was when he jumped ship and married her. Joe has lived in Sydney for 30 years and is a grandfather of five, but his first love is still Everton.

Stephen Hardy became a Blue despite his father playing in the same school team as Roy Evans and being a season ticket holder at Anfield. His first game was against Forest in 1978 and his favourite memory is the QPR Championship game in 1984–85. His favourite player of all time is Trevor Steven.

Frank Hargreaves is amazed how enthusiastic his two sons are over Everton. Little do they know what life as a Blue has in store for them, wondering if the club will ever get its act together and conduct itself in a manner befitting its magnificent support. Frank lives in hope that he may one day see Everton serving up football of the highest scientific order.

Kevin Hazard was doomed to support the 'dark side' but his Red father was away at sea when a cousin smuggled him into Goodison Park. He was hooked before even entering the ground as he stood outside the Blue House with a bottle of lemo and a packet of salt-and-vinegar crisps.

Jonne Hellgren began supporting Everton after the '86 Cup final when a mate of his told him to watch the game as 'the team in red were supposed to be really good'. He rang back after the game and said he preferred the blue ones. His magic moment has to be the '98–'99 Anfield derby, and seeing us win. Hopefully, it wasn't a once-in-a-lifetime experience.

Paul Holmes was at the head of a queue entering the Dartford tunnel, listening to Everton, 2–0 down to Wimbledon in 'that game'. He swore to God that if we survived he would move back home and never take the Blues for granted again. He now lives in Hoylake.

Mark Hoskins grew up in Navan, Co. Meath, and became a Blue on FA Cup final day 1984. He decided to support Everton because of his unnatural dislike of Elton John, the nicer shirts, and his love of the Scouse accent. After that there was no looking back. He still has a picture of Amo on his bedroom wall.

Steve Houghton blushes to admit that his first hero was Steve

McMahon. Born a Blue, his funniest goal was John Bailey's from his own half when we beat Luton 5–0 and it bounced over Jake Findlay's head, and his most bizarre moment was Inchy beating a man by crawling through his legs. Neville Southall is his favourite player of all time – the epitome of a legend.

Andy Howarth lives in Los Angeles, where he runs a small pest control company. His first game was in the early '70s against Burnley, which we won 1–0 from a Dave Clement penalty, and his most memorable Everton experience was witnessing the FA Cup win against Man Utd in 1995.

Gary Hughes has spent a ludicrous amount of money following Everton around the country and 2001–02 is the 20th anniversary of his first game. Highlights include: Ratcliffe's ironic 25-yarder at the Kop End and Gary Stevens deflected bobbler in the very same place.

Wayne Hughes started attending Goodison in the 1976–77 season and invaded the pitch when Big Bob scored his 30th goal. His most treasured possession is a fully autographed picture of the 1969–70 team and favourite moments include the Watford Cup final and Sharpie's goal at Anfield.

Julian Jackson is based in Hong Kong working as chief producer for a sports website. His prize possession should be a signed menu of the Everton team circa 1976, but he swapped it for the bumper book of jokes. His claim to fame is that a fairly famous model once dumped him because he came home for the '95 Cup final and didn't invite her.

Steve Jensen emigrated in '87 and is a manager for Australia's largest property development company. He has only been back home once since then (during the close season – big mistake) but stays up until all hours watching televised games. His most treasured possession is a photograph taken with Alan Ball in 1997.

Colin Jones would like to take this opportunity to thank his dad for his Blue blood. Arthur played right-back for South Liverpool, Runcorn and Marine and graced the hallowed turf at Goodison (and Anfield) for Liverpool County FA. Meanwhile, Colin waited by the car park at the Park End to get Joe Royle's autograph at every home game for years; he may still be there.

They Asked the Questions

Kenny Jones still fills up when he recalls the day Tony Kay was banned, then he remembers the '66 Cup final, and everything comes back into perspective. His first game was on a wet sodden Saturday back in 1963 against Newcastle and his long list of heroes include: Bobby Collins, Alex Young, Roy Vernon, Westy, Jimmy Husband, Bob Latch, Tony Kay, Alan Ball and Jumpin' Duncan McKenzie.

Mike Jones still has some of the pitch in his garden from the great escape against Wimbledon and laughs as he remembers the trees shaking as Barry Horne scored that goal. He once wished Bakayoko good luck in Arabic before he scored in the Southampton game and often lies awake wondering why Pat Nevin used to warm up by saving shots in goal.

Peter Jones has an early memory of winning a case ball autographed by all the Everton first team including Albert Dunlop and Bobby Collins – his first favourite player. He fatefully took it to school, where it impressed everyone and they took it out for a game at playtime. Tragically, the next time he looked there was not a name to be seen.

Colm Kavanagh is an overworked newsagent in an outer suburb of Ballykissangel. He yearns for a return to the glory days, as the posters of successful Evertonians on the shop walls are looking very faded. His all-time hero is Mike Lyons and he once had his hair cut beside Joe Royle at the barber's in Walton Vale.

Dan Keats was brought up in the Home Counties, where everybody else in the playground was a Liverpool fan (naturally) and he wanted to be different. His cause was helped by the fact that we beat Watford in the FA Cup the following year. His hero was Tony Cottee because he had cool hair.

Dave Kelly likes his heroes to sweat blood for the Blue cause, consequently, his all-time favourite is Colin Harvey but he only earns that accolade after a multiple photo-finish involving Tony Kay, Kevin Campbell, Peter Reid and Alan Ball. He is waiting patiently in Blackburn to be paid after *The Echo* featured his top-ten sad ex-Blues in the 'Pink'.

Tony Kennedy still hasn't forgiven his sister for going to the '66 Cup final and not taking him with her. Born in 1950, his first full season attendance was in 1960–61 and his greatest moment was clinching the championship against Fulham in 1963.

Mark Kenyon was born in Liverpool in 1965. His first game at Goodison was against Stoke City in 1974, we won 2–1 with Joe Royle scoring both. Mark moved to Minneapolis in 1999, where, in his spare time, he coaches Under-13s on how not to play 'soccer' by showing them Everton videos of the last five years.

Mike Kidd is an Associate Professor of Law at the University of Natal, Pietermaritzburg. An Evertonian since the early '70s as a result of a rather tenuous family connection, his first and only game was the last one of the 1996–97 season: Everton 1, Chelsea 2. This was a very important and emotional pilgrimage for Mike, but the next time he takes the trouble to visit, he hopes we can be bothered to win.

Steve Kirkwood's great-grandfather was Danny Kirkwood who played for Everton as right-half in the Championship-winning side of 1890–91 (when Everton were still at Anfield). Steve's favourite moments were the Highbury semi-final v Southampton and playing for the Everton Internet side in 1999 and 2000 – the only time he'll ever get to wear the blue shirt.

Tony Kuss is an Irishman residing in Melbourne. He became an Everton fan aged six when he saw his oldest brother cry after Liverpool lost to them. This pleasurable sight was enough to turn Tony's heart Blue forever. He has never had the pleasure of standing in Goodison Park but holds consolation in the fact that when he does, he will be mature enough to fully appreciate where he is and what he is experiencing – Everton FC – the greatest football team on earth.

Alistair Laignel is based in Jersey but would like to stress that he's not a tax exile. A fan since 1967, his best memory is sneaking out of work just in time to see Andy Gray's clenched fist salute on TV when Everton beat Watford in the FA Cup final of 1984.

Gary Lambert recalls April 2000 only too well. It was one week before the home game v Liverpool that he noticed a weird look cross Nick Barmby's face as he warned him that we 'do' our lovable friends from across the park. It all made sense soon after.

They Asked the Questions

Alex Langley lives in Leeds and carries a stone from Duncan Ferguson's garden with him at all times. His first game at Goodison was the opener against Coventry back in 1972 when we lost 4–1 and he's not missed many games since, including Europe, friendlies and pre-seasons.

Dominic Lawson is from a long line of Blues and his gran knew William Ralph Dean when he lived in Laird Street. His best Everton memory is the '84 Cup final, and he now spends most Saturdays on the M6, travelling to and from Goodison, waiting for Walter's slow-burning revolution to come good.

John Lloyd is a practising historian. Born in Liverpool into a family of Blues, he watched his first game at the age of four. A regular attendee at Goodison until 1963, when he left Liverpool for vocational reasons, John is currently based in Scotland, having worked as an academic at the University of Stirling.

Lyndon Lloyd was born and raised in South Africa, lived in the UK for 15 years and emigrated to San Francisco at the turn of the millennium. An implementation designer for an e-business agency, he cites dancing in the centre circle of Goodison in the pouring rain after the 1998 escape as his most memorable day.

Tony Lloyd was taken to see Alan Ball and Brian Labone playing in the reserves at Goodison when he was six years old and is past caring whether this is true or not – it's what he remembers. Being brought up in Oxford led to a brief flirtation with Oxford United, but the crowd's tendency to sing a particularly awful rendition of an awful song from an awful musical, soon brought him to his senses.

Paul Longke loves Colin Harvey, Johnny Morrissey, Sharpie and Big Dunc. He misspent his youth hanging around the café in West Derby that the players used to frequent after training and is still basking in the warmth of asking Tommy Wright how his injured leg was.

Jim Lynch first went to Goodison on the day that Gordon West made his debut, 3 March 1962. His claims to fame are working with Billy Dean during a holiday job with Littlewoods, keeping a clean sheet at Wembley and not being short-listed for the job as Everton Chief Executive.

Stewart MacLaren has been an Evertonian since 1976 and names Duncan McKenzie and Bob Latchford as his first heroes. The '84 FA Cup final v Watford marked his first live experience of watching the Toffees and his favourite memory was the 3–1 triumph over Bayern Munich at Goodison. Alex Young and Andy Gray are Stewart's favourite all-time players and he endeavours to keep the spirit and pride of Everton alive from his new home in sunny Spain.

Richard Marland was raised in Maghull with Gordon West as a neighbour but now lives in Waterloo, Liverpool. The success of the '80s clinched his utter devotion and he's been on board ever since, having held a season ticket since 1985–86, the season he finally started work.

Simon Martindale is based in Bristol. In early Merseyside childhood, his cruel 'Red' dad told him there was no such team as Everton. His first game was a home defeat by Queens Park Rangers and, to add insult to injury, he dropped his first toffee from the Toffee Lady in the Gwladys St 'trough'.

Rob Marwood's favourite player was Gary Lineker, but he was promptly replaced by Tony Cottee. His worst moment was the game against Coventry in the 1994–95 season when we lost 2–0 at home, because that was the day it really sunk in just how crap we were.

George Mason moved from Formby to Florida – and who can blame him? A quality assurance manager in Clearwater, George has been supporting Everton since the '50s and has witnessed the magic of all the great players: Bobby Collins, Roy Vernon, Alex Parker, Brian Labone, Tommy Ring, Alex Young, Tony Kay, Alan Ball, and even supported Liverpool (for one game only) when Everton transferred Dave Hickson.

Neil McCann has lived in Thailand since the mid '90s. He regularly attended matches during the glory years of the '80s and still manages to get to a few games every season. His greatest memory was the FA Cup win in 1984 and his lowest ebb was losing the league title in 1986 at the Manor Ground, Oxford.

Ciaran McConville is based in Dublin. Working as a manufacturing technician, he has followed Everton since the mid-'80s and tries to get over for three or four games a season. His first game was Liverpool v

Everton at Anfield in 1994, financed by his first official pay cheque.

Jamie McDonald moved to London in 1989 to start a career in the city. A season ticket holder for 24 years, he paid a steward to drive him back to London from the Blue House after that Coventry game. His hero is Peter Reid and most treasured possession is Alan Harper's shirt from the '85 Cup final.

Kevin McFadden began watching the Blues in the early '60s as a young lad. He's been to many games over the years, but give him the '84 FA Cup final any day! He lives in Waterloo, and occasionally chats with Gordon West who lives nearby.

Dominic McGough was born and raised within earshot of Goodison, from a long line of Blues. Departing Liverpool in '84 by getting on his bike (as Norman Tebbit suggested) he went to live in London and Brussels. Dom returned to the North West in 2000 in order to continue the instruction of his son Kieran in all things Blue.

Andy McGrae has moved to Cambria, Illinois. Unfortunately most of his life has been spent watching Everton escape relegation, and the Wimbledon game goes down as the best he's ever witnessed. His claim to fame is being made to cry by Big Nev, at the age of seven, after asking for his autograph and being told to 'bugger off!'.

Paul McIver has been on board since the Charity Shield of 1963 when we stuffed Man Utd 4–0. Alan Ball is his hero and his most enduring memory is the 1995 Cup final, sitting with his sons, Kevin and Graeme, on either side.

Damian Mckay fondly recalls being at the back of the Street End at the Bayern Munich game and watching a St John Ambulance man making his way up to a girl who had fainted. Just as he reached her, Tricky Trev stuck away the 3rd, cue pandemonium and his hat went one way and his bag the other. In direct contrast, his worst moment was trudging out of Wembley in '86 and hearing the cheer as they lifted the cup.

Ray Mckay is proud to announce that his hero is back where he belongs; yes, it's Big Dunc. His first game was an FA Cup tie against Shrewsbury in the early '80s, and his most treasured possession is a picture of Duncan and Michael Ball with him in the middle, taken at the lottery seller's player of the year bash at Goodison.

Neil Mckeown was sentenced to trudge through life basking in the twin shadows of dashed dreams and perennially false dawns in the early '80s. His most treasured possessions are a signed photo of the '85 squad – signed in blue pen so you can't make out the names – and a framed copy of the *Football Echo* from the night of the Wimbledon game. It reads 'Safe!'.

Terry McWilliams emigrated to Canada in the summer of 1970 and named his son after Alan Ball. He will never forget the euphoria of the '66 Cup final or the utter dejection of '68.

Roy King Miaa moved to Kristiansand, Norway, in 1980, ostensibly for two years. His most enduring Everton memories include the FA Cup final of '66 which resulted in a broken toe due to his father's celebrations at Temple's winner, and the European Cup-Winners' cup of November '95, which comprised a 17-hour car trip from Norway to Rotterdam. He spent the game standing in the rain outside the stadium, whilst his mates got to watch it for free having been dragged in by the Everton stewards.

Andy Morris didn't miss a game last season home or away, including friendlies. His hero is Big Nev and his proudest moment was the day he was mascot in front of 13,000 in 1982. Introduced to the Blues by his grandfather at the age of six, he now runs the Widnes branch of the EFC supporters club.

Dave Morris was brought up just outside Ellesmere Port, where every random bike ride as a kid ended up with a trip past Dave Hickson's house – this part of the ride was always conducted at the speed of one of those dawdles in velodrome events before they break for home. Dave's most poignant game was a humdrum 3–1 win over Sunderland in October '82; it was his Pa's last match and the first for his son Roland.

Kate Mottram was born in Birmingham but was converted to Everton by a group of Scouse relatives, led by her dad. Her first match was the semi-final against Luton in 1985 where a strange man threw her in the air after Mountfield's winner. Her hero is Peter Reid.

They Asked the Questions

Neil Mulhern is studying Politics and Media at Queen's University Belfast. He started supporting the Blues in 1984, having bought the Le Coq Sportif shirt in London whilst on holiday. His first game was the 1986 Charity Shield and his favourite moment was Amokachi's double strike to kill off Spurs in the FA Cup semi-final in 1995.

Mark Murphy remembers being perched on a stool his dad had made in the Bullens Rd enclosure watching his first game, Colchester United in the FA Cup in the late '60s. When Alan Ball scored, a strange man threw Mark in the air in celebration. We won 5–0, and from that moment on he's been Everton daft. His most treasured possession was the autographed picture of Mike Lyons' goal against Leeds from the middle pages of the programme, until he lost it in a fire.

Kenny Myers graduated through the ranks of the Boys Pen, then Gwladys Street proper before leaving Liverpool for California in 1971. He still gets home for at least four or five games a year, which always includes one of the derby matches.

Dermot Nealon is too old and disillusioned to have a hero. He lives in Dublin and started following EFC in 1970 when they visited Dublin and thrashed Shamrock Rovers 5–0. One of the highlights of his life came in '88 when we had just signed Cottee. Everton visited Drogheda and he got into the after-match 'banquet' and met all the squad. Colin Harvey was manager and made sure all the lads signed a book he brought along.

Ted Neeson declares his earliest recollection is the '68 FA Cup final, which resulted in a passionate dislike for Jeff Astle. Having spent his formative years sailing the seven seas in the Royal Navy, the salty sea-dog eventually settled in Manchester – the nearest place to Goodison he could find work. His favourite player is Stuart McCall.

Darryl Ng works as a banker for a financial institution of some repute in Singapore. Recently married, he has been an Evertonian since they wore 'those nice royal blue jerseys' in the Charity Shield of 1986. His first match was a 4–1 thrashing by Aston Villa in 1999 and his first-born son will be named after Trevor Steven (although it's not clear whether Mrs Ng was aware of this at the time of going to press).

Stan Nuttall moved to the States in 1968 and resides in the San Francisco Bay area. His most memorable moment – besides being at the 1966 FA Cup final win – was coming on as a second-half substitute for Jimmy Gabriel in a local game in California.

Michael O'Connell is a postman but he'd rather be an artist. An Evertonian since the FA Cup final in 1968, Michael drinks Bushmills and claims to be the only Evertonian living in Galway.

Joe O'Reilly first travelled with his dad from Dublin while Gordon Lee was manager. After the game they went to the souvenir shop, where he tried to buy a scarf but was too small to be noticed by the staff. A security guard spotted his dilemma and took him through a side door into a small office. In walked Gordon Lee who gave him the silk scarf he still has to this day.

Mike Owen lives in Childwall and his first match was a 0–0 draw at home to Blackburn, on Saturday 6 April 1963, leaving a six-year-old bitterly disappointed because we had two goals disallowed. Mike never played for Everton despite writing to Alan Ball and asking for tips. Alan replied and advised him to practise, eat lots of fruit and go to bed early. Mike still practises and eats lots of fruit but rarely goes to bed early.

Jason Palmer is a tutor at Pontypridd College. His best Everton moment was listening to the Bayern game on the radio at home; the crowd were so loud he swears he could have been there. He looks like a member of the boy band Hanson and his best ever player is Kevin Ratcliffe (because he's Welsh).

Reg Pearson used to follow his brothers week in, week out, begging to be taken to the match only to be told to go home. One week in 1969 against Leicester, they relented and he nearly died. He was astonished at how big the players were and still wipes a tear from his eye as he declares the pitch has never been the same shade of green since that happy day.

Phil Pellow spent most of the '70s and '80s working in London and the Middle East, then returned, prodigal-son-like to his native Waterloo. Founder of the fanzine *Satis?*, he now resides in Pellow Mansions with Steve, Alex and Angela, a cat called Josh and a bald spot.

They Asked the Questions

Ed Pepper is a Southerner, but went against his natural Man United supporting instincts after listening to 'that game' against Wimbledon in '93. His claim to fame is that by yelling from his seat in Lower Bullens at exactly the wrong moment he is responsible for Andrei Kanchelskis's worst touch in the professional game.

Marko Poutiainen is a software engineer living in Oulu, Finland. He had affection for Everton since his teens, but not until that Wimbledon game did he realise how much the club meant to him. A pioneer of the Everton Internet community, Marko started the first Everton-related website and gathered the flock for the mailing lists.

Mike Prenton has been an Upper Bullens centre-line stalwart for 27 years, more in hope than expectation. His two greatest moments of sheer joy among many would be Inchy's header in the '84 semi and Trevor Steven slotting it home to sink Bayern Munich. His schoolboy hero was Andy King and his favourite ever player is Tricky Trevor.

San Presland's first match was EFC v Man United in 1966 and she was shocked to see it was in colour! San won loads of money on 'Who Wants to be a Millionaire', lives in New Brighton and once had a double-page centrefold in the *Footy Echo* when she wrote a football simulation/prediction at their request.

Paul Preston is old enough to cite Alex Young as his hero and works as a professor of contemporary Spanish history at LSE (London School of Economics). Paul began following Everton in 1959 and his magic moments include Derek Temple's goal in the 1966 Cup final and Danny Cadamarteri's against Liverpool in 1997–98.

Stefan Pun is from Singapore, the hot and humid island nation in South-east Asia. He works as a sports editor for a website and has been a Blue since 1985 when he watched his first ever Merseyside derby on the television. The club continues to give him many a sleepless night.

John Quinn is fading fast, living discreetly in Tewkesbury and desperately hiding from many financial institutions. His only claim to fame was that he man-marked Tony Kay in a Business Houses match one Saturday in the '60s just after his release from prison – 9–1.

Osmo Tapio Räihälä (b. 1964) is a Finnish composer living in Helsinki. His life changed dramatically on 26 November 1977 when he was converted to Evertonia by Bob Latchford's hat trick. Räihälä gets inspiration to compose his work from Everton and this is reflected in orchestral pieces like 'Hinchcliffe Thumper – tha' bloody intermezzo' and 'Barlinnie Nine'.

Phil Redmond is a social worker from Warrington who hates everyone and everything. He has a ridiculous memory for football-related trivia, is the editor of *When Skies Are Grey* and has a cat called Pebbles. He sincerely believes that a football-type Armageddon is just round the corner and that Man United will end up in a super league of one – playing themselves.

Andy Richardson's worst moment was watching the team disappear in Schiphol airport to board what should have been his flight – if only he'd arrived on time. A Street End season ticket holder, his favourite memory is of Latch scoring his 30th against Chelsea – 6–0. Working for computer support at BT, Andy is a biker, lives in Hackney and always arrives at The Netley looking windswept and interesting.

Antony Richman is a bank manager. A former season ticket holder, he is now based in Johannesburg and is a founder member of the Everton Football Club Supporters Club of South Africa (EFCSCSA). His most enduring moment as an Evertonian is being in the lavatory when Paul Rideout scored the winner in the '95 Cup final.

Dave Richman emigrated to South Africa in 1974 aged 13. He's now married with two children, works as a quantity surveyor, and is legendary for suffering horrendous injuries from playing football with the kids. Founding member of the imaginatively titled 'Everton Supporters Club of South Africa' and editor of the fanzine *Gwlad Tidings* for EFCSCSA.

Paul Rigby would like to pay tribute to his wife Val; she knows what the Blues mean and has never once uttered 'well, it's only a game'. Born and raised in the Dingle, his dad and grandad put Paul on the road to Evertonia, a journey which has never wavered in spite of him now living in Connecticut, USA.

They Asked the Questions

Rob Rimmer is from Aintree. His most treasured memory is almost falling from the front row of the Upper Bullens when celebrating the third goal against Bayern and realising it was all over.

Ian Roberts felt true inner contentment in Rotterdam when Kevin Sheedy scored the third. He was first taken to watch Everton play Chelsea at Goodison by an auntie in April 1968, aged three. He is married to Sharon, with a daughter, Lucy, and has recently relocated from Vauxhall Road to Wallasey.

John Roberts didn't start supporting the Blues until his best mate at university convinced him that rugby was crap. A sailor, John never misses a match when he's on dry land.

Stuart Everton Roberts has been a regular match-goer since 1981. His finest moment was the 1995 FA Cup semi final v Spurs and favourite player of all time is Kevin Sheedy. He changed his name by deed poll.

Sean Rostron is a local government worker from the Wirral. A season ticket holder for years, his first game was a 2–1 home defeat by Chelsea on 29 March 1969. His favourite player of all time is Graeme Sharp, on the strength of one goal.

Pete Rowlands was born and raised in New Brighton and now lives in London, working for a medical charity. The finest game he attended was Bayern Munich at Goodison and his favourite player of all time is Neville Southall. He is dedicating all his spare time to brainwashing his son, Jack, into supporting the Blues whilst patiently waiting for the glory days to come round again.

Mike Royden is a history teacher in South Wirral and author of several local history books. His first game was against Blackpool in November 1962 and his magic moment, meeting Alex Young and asking him if it was a penalty in the '66 final. 'No question about it!' came the reply he'd waited 32 years to hear.

Carl Sanderson made his debut against Chelsea in 1973 when we won 2–0. It was his ninth birthday and his dad told him to stamp his feet as hard as he could when we scored. He now runs the mathematics department in a secondary school in Cheshire. He firmly believes that the future's bright – the future's Royal Blue. Nil Satis Nisi Optimism.

Brian Sayle has been watching the Blues since 1983 when his dad dragged him along to Goodison Park. His favourite player is Andy Gray and he can remember playing in his school team and trying to head the ball when it was on the floor having seen Andy manage it with ease at Notts County.

Lol Scragg is residing in Arbroath making computer games for a living. His first game included Bob Latchford's 30th league goal and he was arguably the only person to miss Sharpie's screamer at Anfield past Brucie the Clown as he was in the bloody bog at the time.

Gagandeep Sethi hails from Twickenham and became a Blue for the lack of a local team to support in a big rugby area. Currently studying in Minnesota, and modelling in Minneapolis to pay for it, he first fell in love with Howie's team of '84 and hasn't looked back.

Rob Sharratt travelled from Australia to Goodison for the Coventry game just to help keep the boys in the Premier League – and it worked. A Gwladys St season ticket holder until he emigrated in 1968, his first match was Christmas 1962, a 2–2 draw at Hillsborough.

David Shepherd was born into a family of nomadic football atheists, and started supporting Everton in late 1968. A regular attendee of Goodison Park, he writes lyrical match reports for Blues fans exiled overseas. His first of many Everton heroes was Alan Ball, and his ambition is to live long enough to see Everton beat Leeds at Elland Road in a league game.

Ari Sigurgeirsson started following Everton when they went to Iceland in 1969–70 to play Keflavik FC. After that his wish for years was to own a white pair of boots like a certain Mr Ball. His all-time hero is Sheeds and he has visited Goodison twice so far, once in '86 when we beat Southampton and again in '98 to a 0–0 draw with the Kopites.

Colin Smith can recall his first match in 1974, away against Plymouth in the FA Cup fourth round, which we won 3–1. His worst moment was losing to Oxford, April '86, and realising we'd blown the league. He has numerous heroes and they include Duncan McKenzie, Gary Jones, Southall, Ratcliffe, Reid and Sharp. And apart from Derek Hatton in a hotel in Bratislava, he hasn't met anyone famous.

Martin Smith went to watch Everton in the late '70s as a five-year-old but his first concrete memory is of Bobby Latchford's penalty in the 6–0 defeat of Chelsea. Having been a regular since the late '80s it would appear that his attendance at the match is something of a jinx. Thankfully Martin has now relocated to New Jersey so the Blues can look forward to more success.

Colin Smyth always stuck up for the underdog so started supporting Everton in the late '70s. Ironically, his first game was that 2–6 home tonking on Boxing Day '77 by Man Utd. He once saw Graeme Sharp fishing on the canal and his hero is Bob Latch.

Mark Staniford is the editor of *Speke from the Harbour* fanzine and occasional journo, when pressed. The first game he went to was the 6–2 drubbing in the late '70s at Elland Road and he's been hooked ever since. His most valuable possession is the shirt that Trevor Steven wore in the 1985 Cup final. Mark lives in Allerton, works in accounts, is a season ticket holder in the Paddock and married to the lovely Bernadette.

George Lee Stuart first ascended the Park End stairs to the real theatre of dreams as an awestruck four-year-old in 1960. Now a university lecturer in Lismore, Australia, his hobbies are catching up on sleep, tidying up toys and lately he can be seen pushing his aged body around a football field after an eight-year absence, as well as coaching the university third team.

Mark Tallentire is a football journalist working for *The Guardian*. He is also the brother of the author and took her to see her first game at Goodison Park in 1969 against West Ham – a 2–0 victory with goals from Alan Ball and Jimmy Husband.

Dave Tickner lives in Liverpool and has been watching Everton regularly since 1959 when Bobby Collins was signed. Needless to say he has seen far more lows than highs over the years, but the highs have been much higher than the lows were low. He once saw Alex Young walking down London Road but, simultaneously, lost the power of speech.

Paul Tollet proclaims his heroes are Alex Young and 'Tricky' Trevor Steven. His first game was in 1969 and he has followed the Blues regularly since 1974. Finest moments include Wembley '84, Andy King's goal, Bayern Munich, Duncan McKenzie and the Utd supporters' faces after the '95 Cup final.

Matt Traynor was born at home, half a mile from Goodison Park. The first game he remembers was the 6–0 drubbing of Chelsea, but his favourite has to be the semi of '95, and stuffing the 'dream final' down the media's collective throat. Now living in London, he is an economist with London Transport.

Steve Tynan has settled in Aldershot after spells in Bahrain, Malta and Liverpool. His first trip to Goodison was in 1967 and for some reason he keeps coming back. Married to Paula and a father of three, he credits his dad, John, for his love of all things Everton and his hero is Bob Latchford.

John Walton is himself an Everton legend; he was the little skinhead ball boy in the opening titles of *Match of the Day* when Andy King scored against Liverpool at Goodison. Sadly he never made the full team due to a cocktail of wine, women and song. He now looks after the engineering side of the JW Marriott Hotel in Dubai.

Pete Warner is the father of Catherine who recently made her debut as the Toffee Lady and he hopes she doesn't eventually blame him for the legacy. His first match was versus Blackpool in 1960 and his hero is Alex Young.

Richard Ward was a school contemporary of Joe Royle at Quarry Bank. He cried with despair at half-time during the '66 Cup final and again with joy at Rotterdam. Roy Vernon is his all-time favourite player, and he categorically states that the team of the early to mid-'60s including Gabby was the most exciting he has ever seen.

Alan Welsh was named after Alan Ball and his sister Jo, after Joe Royle. He still has a card from his second birthday signed by the 1970 Championship-winning squad and his hero is Andy Gray. Alan once bumped into Colin Harvey in the Prestatyn Nova Centre and sat on the seafront talking about the Blues for what seemed like ages but was probably only ten minutes.

Billy Williams is the finest German-English translator on the face of the planet, a chain-smoker and a heavy drinker – both of which sins are attributable to watching the utterly shite Everton teams of the '70s week in, week out. He traded Wavertree for the bright lights of Cologne in 1990.

Karl Williams is a season ticket holder and travels to every home match from Kinmel Bay in a van with a group of about 15 lads. Working as a computer analyst he has been hooked on all things Blue since the day his dad took him to witness the 5–0 walloping of Notts Forest in December 1984.

Nick Williams lives in Warrington and follows the Blues around the country because he can't think of anything better to do with his life. During the week, he acts like an E-Commerce manager for a bank, but is secretly worrying about whether Super Kev will be fit for the weekend.

Phil Williams is a bean counter in Chester. His hero is Mike Lyons and his first game was at home to Coventry City in the late '70s when Coventry wore that lovely chocolate away kit. His favourite moment was Graham Stuart's winner against Wimbledon in '94.

Keith Wilson now occupies the best seat at Goodison Park, Upper Bullens Row E – right opposite the players tunnel. He has been watching the Blues since the early '60s and witnessed every one of Latch's 30 goals that glorious season.

Mark Wilson is reputed to think of Everton more frequently than other notable subjects (including Buffy the Vampire Slayer) and spends his life wandering up and down the country in search of that elusive 100 per cent away record.

Neil Wolstenholme is a fourth-generation Blue exiled in London and finds common ground with his Arsenal supporting in-laws by reminiscing happily over the famous Michael Thomas goal at Anfield. Struggling to earn a living as a management consultant and freelance writer, he spends his free time singing Everton songs to his young son in the bath.

Mike Wood was born in Liverpool but now works in Zurich, looking after a bank's databases. His first game was against Spurs in 1964 – a 2–0 win with the memorable chant of 'Don't say Brown say hopeless', aimed at Bill Brown (from the Hovis advert, for the younger readers). Since leaving the UK in 1976, Mike has managed about five games a season.

Jeremy Wyke has supported the Boys since his brother took him to his first match in '79 when Joe Royle scored two for Norwich in his last game at Goodison. His all-time Blue heroes are Big Nev and Sharpie and Jez plays (a bit) like Pat Van den Hauwe, with the flair of Tricky Trev, and topped off with Paul Bracewell's hair.

Adam Yates didn't think we'd make it as Coventry equalised in '98, and when the whistle blew he couldn't celebrate because his feet had gone completely numb with stress. He once met Big Nev at a book signing and his finest moment was watching the League Trophy being paraded around Goodison in 1985. It felt like we were going to win everything forever.

JOHN BAILEY

Born 1 April 1957
July 1979 – October 1985
£300,000

Gordon Lee knew John Bailey from their days at Blackburn and wanted him to be included in Everton's blueprint for success. The clubs couldn't agree a fee and 'Bails' became the first ever player to be sold at tribunal. After much deliberation, they arrived at a figure of £200,000 with a further £100,000 to follow after he had played 60 games. Being the tough-tackling, fearless full-back he is, he played them all in his first season and the bill was settled. Howard Kendall came in as manager and he couldn't believe his luck.

> He was worth his weight in gold on the pitch, in the dressing-room, as a comedian and a story-teller. When Pat Van den Hauwe arrived as his replacement, I broke the news by telling him he had the best contract in the world – £300 a week and Saturdays off.

John Bailey, take my hand and meet your people.

Soon after he arrived he slammed in a couple of goals for us, but the team he joined was on the wane. Ask him how he felt to be near the top of the league for a few seasons, yet only just escaping relegation the next? *Kenny Fogarty, Amsterdam, Holland*
When I joined, we'd qualified for Europe so I was in the UEFA Cup in my first season. I got my place through Mike Pejic, and a lot of other players got cleared out, including Martin Dobson and Dave Thomas. We hit a slump and ended up near relegation, which resulted in Gordon getting the sack. I was ever-present in every game and I established myself as Everton's left-back, but, unfortunately, the team didn't progress the way we would have liked. It sorted itself out eventually but that season was a bit strange.

On a personal level, I was very pleased with my performances and I won the player of the year award, but as a team it was quite disappointing at the end.

Does he come from Blue heritage and who was his boyhood hero? *Dominic McGough, Ellesmere Port, Wirral*

As a youngster, I was brought up as a Red like all my family and, this might hurt a lot of people, my hero was Emlyn Hughes. I loved his attitude on the pitch because he was a 100 per cent winner. I used to study his actions in the tiniest detail and I even did my tie-ups like him. I do a great impersonation of Emlyn, but I have to be on a football pitch and I need a ball.

When I moved to my first club, Blackburn, I was still a Liverpudlian, but once I put the Blue shirt on at the press conference that was it. I reacted to what I saw, the club, the fans and the entire set-up. I was an Evertonian from that moment on and I'm still one to this day.

I remember seeing John a couple of times walking back from the game along Everton Road in the vicinity of Breck Road. Did he have family around there? *Michael Dudley, Long Island, New York, USA*

I still have family there. Sadly, my brother's passed away now but my sister-in-law lives in Breck Road and I've moved back to Everton Road where I live with my sister. I regularly have what I call a 'walkabout' and a few lagers down Breck Road and I've got a lot of very good friends down there.

What was Gordon Lee like? *Rob Hamilton, Melbourne, Australia*

I hold Gordon Lee in very high esteem. I knew him from when he was manager at Blackburn and I was a young apprentice. He was a very strange fella, but I appreciate him and owe him everything for bringing me to this great club.

Gordon only knew about football. You could ask him about anything that was going on in the world; wars, politics, deaths, hurricanes, and he wouldn't know a thing, but he could name you every player in the entire four divisions of the league and give you their characteristics; he was a football fanatic. Andy King used to roast him, he called him Dracula and used to take the mickey out of him so badly it was mortifying, but I loved him and he loved Everton, he gave it 100 per cent and it was a shame it ended the way it did.

Gordon Lee – plank of wood or underrated? *Ged Fox, Wickford, England*

John Bailey

I think he was underrated. He might have come across as a plank of wood but his knowledge of football was second to none and there are still many people in the game who respect him to this day. He goes to so many games, even now you see him midweek and at the weekends watching people. He must do scouting reports for dozens of clubs because his knowledge of the game is fantastic. He was a great manager, things just never happened for him here, but what a person to have on your staff for running teams down and sussing them out. He was fantastic.

He'll probably want to forget it, but after the 5–0 Derby defeat he went out in Anfield for a few drinks and took a lot of stick. Was this his lowest point of his Everton career? *Mike Benson, West Derby, Liverpool*

It was the cheapest point of my career, actually, because I didn't have to buy a drink that night. You've got to be strong in victory and you've got to be equally strong in defeat. You've got to go out, hold your head up high and say: 'So what?' These things happen and worse things will happen in life, but you take it on the chin. I always said I didn't care if I scored an own goal or a hat trick of own goals, I'd still go out and face the music. I'll have a drink and face the Reds and anyone else. Don't forget, I enjoyed a pint as well and I'd take the good with the bad because that's the kind of person I am. If they want to give me stick, then so be it. I just didn't like it when my wife was about. They could give me all the stick they wanted in front of my friends or my brothers, but not in front of my wife.

Did the Kevin Brock back pass achieve the same legendary significance among the players as it did in the supporters' folklore? *Andy Cheyne, Hampstead Norreys, England*

We talk about that when we have reunions and meet each other at matches. I was injured and watching from the stands that day. That back pass was very significant, it earned us a replay and we won. From then on, I think we got beat once in about nineteen matches, we got to the League Cup final replay and won the FA Cup – it was quite a turnabout. I don't know what happened, but God just seemed to look down on us and smile. We responded and everything started happening and now it's part of our history.

You scored goals in your fourth and fifth games for Everton and then you didn't score for five years. What happened in between? *Paul McIver, Culcheth, Cheshire*

I didn't get over the halfway line! If you saw my two goals, you'll know they weren't exactly the greatest. I scored the fluke from my own half against Luton and the goal after that was away against Stoke and that wasn't intended either; it was a cross. My goals were great accidents and nothing more. I was an attacking full-back, but I assisted in more goals than I scored and I've got to take a bit of credit for that. I didn't take penalties, which most full-backs do, and I wasn't the greatest striker of the ball, although I was a great passer.

What was his worst injury and how did he sustain it? *Paul Checkland, Maidstone, England*

Touch wood, to this day I've never had a bad injury, I was either too quick or quick enough to jump out of the way. My worst injury on my legs was a scrape of my Achilles at Newcastle, but that was just wear and tear, fluid and old age and bits of bone. The worst I ever got was when I pulled my finger out of joint and I've still got three screws in there to this day. It happened while I was trying to tug back a player on a training pitch by his bib, which is typical of my career really.

Who would be your first Everton eleven? *Jonne Hellgren, Tornio, Finland*

Big Neville, Tommy Wright, Brian Labone, Kevin Ratcliffe and Ray Wilson. Bracewell, Reid, Sheedy, Steven in midfield, but that's a close call with Kendall, Harvey and Ball, they were magnificent.

I know Dixie's legendary, but I have to put Sharpie and Andy Gray upfront because they were tremendous. What about Latch though? I'd have him in there somewhere, too. Maybe I'd have to have him on the bench, but Andy and Sharpie were awesome, to get them up front as a full-back was something else. They were all great players and that would be my dream team.

Does he remember his fifty-yard 'screamer' against Luton, when we won 5–0 and did he really say 'Not even Pelé could do that' after it went in the net? *Kenny Fogarty, Amsterdam, Holland*

I did say that later on and I still say it now, but only because it was the joke afterwards. I remember it to this day, Jake Findlay was in goal, David Johnson made the forward run and I tried to put him in over the top but I over-hit it completely. I turned away in disgust and I can't repeat what I said to myself, then all of a sudden I heard the crowd roar and the ball was nestling in the net. I didn't actually see it until I watched *Match of the Day* later on that night. From that day on, the crack in the dressing-room was always: 'Even Pelé tried that from the halfway line and he couldn't manage it.' We had some good laughs over that one.

John Bailey

Did he ever practise that superb ability to pass into space for forwards to run onto? *Phil Pellow, Waterloo, Liverpool*

I had a nice left foot, but I couldn't kick with my right to save my life, that was just a standing foot. However, if a player moved I had the natural ability to drop it into his path over the full-back or the centre-back, which was probably the main feature of my game. I had good distribution and that was a very good question, I'm glad you asked it.

Which player was the easiest to wind up? *Nicholas Gard, Seattle, USA*

I was the easiest to wind up and the players used to call me Gnasher because if anyone said the wrong thing, or I didn't understand the question in the first place, I'd just go mad. Neville was always there, but he always got his own back, he was so dry it was unbelievable. Most of the lads were on their toes, Andy, Trevor, Peter Reid, Gary Stevens but if you caught Neville he would always get his revenge by cutting your socks off or putting your clothes in the bath or something stupid like that.

My dad (a little round Scotsman called 'Mac') worked for many years as a commissionaire in the players' lounge and he reckoned you were the friendliest and most down-to-earth of all the players. *San Presland, New Brighton, Merseyside*

It's how you've been brought up and where you come from. I belong to a working-class family from the heart of the Everton area of Liverpool and we're very down-to-earth. I went through my career going to restaurants with people asking me what I was doing there. I'm only a human being and I have to eat.

I've mixed with ambassadors and royalty and I've mixed with the lowest of the low. I'm just one of those lads who came through secondary school with no airs and graces. I can chat with the best and I can chat with the worst. I've always gone through life with a smile on my face and if I make people happy, then I'm happy too. I remember Mac, he was a good man and if he had a laugh then I'm glad about that. I had a chat with all the commissionaires whenever I got off the bus. I was full of nervous energy and I was buzzing. That's the way I am and I give full credit to my parents for that.

That goal against Luton – did you teach that trick to Beckham? *Mike Prenton, Leeds, England*

I wish I could, I wish I had his wallet. No, that was the biggest fluke ever, but it was a goal and it's got my name beside it in the history books. I always remember seeing poor Jake, the goalkeeper, in Majorca on holiday and we had a few laughs and a few drinks over that. You don't teach anybody that, it was a total accident, but there are not many who score in their own goal at Goodison Park, either.

Who does he think is the best winger that he came up against and did he ever piss off any of the refs with his jokes on the pitch? *Jon Berman, West Derby, Liverpool*

Chris Waddle was a difficult winger and I don't know if anybody will remember a player called Colin Powell, who used to play outside right for Charlton when I was young. He always gave me a nightmare time and I was forever getting booked when I played against him. I was only young and still learning the game, so it was probably down to my inexperience but he was the hardest man I ever played against. For opposition in the '80s it would be Steve Coppell and Chris Waddle.

As for the refs, I always took the mickey out of them. We had a great banter and I loved the refs then. These days they're so strict and take themselves too seriously. In my day you could have a great crack with them and you knew where you stood, there was a line you would never cross and even the refs would crack a few jokes themselves.

When the ball would go out of play or go dead for injuries, I would have a running commentary going with them and with parts of the crowd, especially over at the Paddock side and Gwladys Street. I loved it. I probably did piss a few off, but it was all in fun. I think that's what the game's all about and I wish I could see a lot more of it now. The problem is there's so much money around that it's all gone serious and businesslike now.

You used to walk round town with the silver tracksuit on. Was that how you felt about EFC or were they just your best clothes? *Mike Prenton, Leeds, England*

I think that was just a sign of the '80s, the bad taste Elton John era. Adidas sponsored us then and we would go to the factory and choose what we wanted, so we ended up with a lot of outrageous gear, flip-flops and stupid coloured tracksuits. I remember that silver trackie, it had a hood on it too. I was a bit of a poser then, so it was ideal because it stood out and that was the reason I wore it.

Please ask him if he ever gave St John the kicking he so richly deserved for making him cut his thumb on that bucket. *Colin Smyth, Ormskirk, England*

John Bailey

No, I didn't really get the chance, I'll tell you what, it was bloody sore. I was doing an interview for the Milk Cup final. The interview finished and I picked up the bucket and drowned the Saint but it was all in jest, as usual. The plastic was split and I sliced my thumb. I should have had it stitched, actually, but I just stuck it together with a plaster and kept the plaster on right through the final, so it went septic.

Heysel. The reason for our demise or are we just sad and bitter that it all just seem to slip through our fingers? *Frank Hargreaves, Anfield, Liverpool*
It's something we can't really talk about on Merseyside because it's a sore point, almost as sore as my thumb. A lot can be said about it, but it can't be said. All I know is it was very sad. We knew we had a great squad and could have gone on to better things; we'd already conquered Europe in the Cup-Winners' cup all we had to do was go and win the European Cup. We would easily have done that because we were the best team in England. The supporters knew and we knew. I don't like talking about it because we had our chance taken away and that's what's so sad about it all.

If he were playing today would he prefer full-back or wing-back? *Phil Pellow, Waterloo, Liverpool*
I played as a wing-back, an attacking full-back. I was unique at that time and before me there'd only been Ray Wilson and Terry Cooper. My strongest point was getting forward and attacking. I wasn't the best defender in the world, which later cost me my place, but if I was playing today I could fill that wing-back role quite easily.

I remember something on FA Cup final day about a twenty-stone kiss-o-gram. Would you care to relate the tale? *Tony Field, Loughborough, England*
I got a beautiful kiss-o-gram for Howard for the Milk Cup final and she was an absolute darling. She came on the coach and kissed everyone and we wouldn't let her off the bus. Then it was the FA Cup final. We were making our way to the team coach from Bellefield after we'd finished our training session when all of a sudden this twenty-stone woman appeared from nowhere, she was an absolute dragon. I've still got the photograph in my hall of her picking Adrian Heath up in front of all the lads. I got a twenty-stone moose from the Gaffer in return for getting him an absolute babe. It just doesn't seem right.

Howard once said he was as mad as a hatter. When he met Freddie Starr did he find a kindred spirit? *Phil Pellow, Waterloo, Liverpool*

Freddie was unbelievable that day (1984 FA Cup final). I was rooming with Andy Gray, who looked like Freddie Starr and we woke up to hear laughs and giggles. The lads were hanging out of the windows and there was Freddie and all the cameras on the lawn. He's a local lad, brought up the same way as me with no airs and graces. You get what you see with Freddie and he was on form that day.

I think Michael Barrymore was on the other channel with Watford but Freddie was a different class. The lads enjoyed it so much, all our nerves were settled and we didn't know we were playing in a Cup final even when we walked on to inspect the pitch and salute the crowd. He came on with us and the fans recognised him straightaway, even in the dressing-room he was making us laugh. It was better than any manager's team talk in the world.

I asked Andy Gray why he looked like crap in front of the *Grandstand* cameras whilst they were in the hotel on the morning of the 1984 FA Cup final. What is John Bailey's excuse? *Lol Scragg, Arbroath, Scotland*

I don't know what your point is unless you're calling me an ugly bastard or something. We had just woken up at the time, but maybe I did keep Andy awake all night by talking in my sleep. I used to take a sleeping tablet the night before a match, so I always had a good night's kip, but if I kept him awake I've got to hold my hand up. Having said that, Andy is an ugly bastard in the morning, anyway, and I can vouch for that because I've slept with him a few times.

Ask him to describe the greatest day of his life. *Peter Fenton, Derby, England*

That would be the 1984 FA Cup final because that was by far the greatest day of my life. From the moment I was woken up in the morning by Freddie Starr in the garden of the hotel, right through to the end of it. It was a fabulous day and to actually walk up those steps and receive my medal, I can truly go to the grave a very, very happy man.

I assume that the 1984 FA Cup final was the highlight of your Everton career. What was the low point? *Ged Fox, Wickford, England*

Collecting my boots from the boot-room and saying goodbye to the lads and

John Bailey

Howard and the coaching staff. I remember somebody trying to interview me for local radio, I couldn't even speak and there were tears streaming down my face. Driving away from Bellefield was really hard. I was off to Newcastle, but I'd never felt so devastated in all my life. It's making me sad now, just thinking about it.

That bloody hat at Wembley. Why did you wear it? There can be no excuses. Neil Wolstenholme, Muswell Hill, North London

The reason I wore it is because it got shoved into my hands on the steps. To this day I wish I had a pound for every person who's asked me that question because I'd be a multimillionaire. I've had letters from the fella who made it, who wore it and gave it to me, but, unfortunately, when I came off the pitch I gave it to a steward to hold while I got interviewed for the television and I've never seen it again to this day. But now, I think I know the fella who may have it. I was with him at a function a few weeks ago and he wouldn't hand it over to me. I'd love to have it in my possession because it would probably raise an awful lot of money for charity. He might read this, change his mind and let me have it back one day. Sometimes, people upset me because they say I put it on to be a clown. I wasn't a bad player, I won FA Cup and League Championship medals; I wasn't just a joker.

Can he tell us the story of the ambassador's wife when the team were on a Far East trip? Joe McBride reckoned it was the funniest thing to have happened, but then he would as he was very young at the time. Jon Berman, West Derby, Liverpool

That might be the story where we locked her in the toilet. We got invited to the ambassador's residence in Japan and it was all very formal. Mr Moores was there, God rest him, and they were all wearing dickie bows and on their best behaviour. Anyway, the wife went to the toilet and for some reason the key was on the outside of the door. Someone happened to lock her in and lash the key down the garden into the undergrowth and they had to get a joiner and a locksmith to get her out. It didn't go down well with the management, although I think they knew who was responsible. The Gaffer still gives me a look now and again when the question comes up. Billy Wright got locked in the toilet, too, that night.

Derby day at Anfield in 1981 and Bailey connects with a corner and sends a screamer into the Everton goal. How did he feel after that and did his family (who were all Reds) give him merciless stick? Kenny Fogarty, Amsterdam, Holland

That was another cheap night out for me. I went into the Sandy Brown Hall of Fame, along with Micky Lyons – I played in that game, too, when he lobbed Georgie Wood. I just wanted the ground to open up and swallow me. I got terrible letters, people telling me I'd always been a Red, which was absolutely ridiculous, no one scores an own goal because they want to. I went out for a drink with my two brothers that night and we had the cheapest night out of my life. I held my head up, I wasn't the first person to score an own goal and I certainly wasn't the last, especially in a derby match, and you have to take the good with the bad. Even Emlyn Hughes has scored own goals! But I did get a lot of stick, more so off the Evertonians than the Liverpudlians, so that annoyed me and it was very upsetting.

Does he feel regret at missing out on the later stages of the '80s glory train or pride at being part of its inception? *Neil Wolstenholme, Muswell Hill, north London*
I feel a little bit upset for missing out, but I didn't have to leave Goodison Park. My days were numbered when Pat arrived, but Howard didn't want me to leave because he knew I was valuable in the squad, around the players and in the dressing-room. I was a great part of the squad, but he knew my ambitions and I needed first team football. I could have said no to Newcastle United, I wasn't pushed out of the door or anything like that. I could have stayed, played out my days on an easy contract, picked up easy money and bonuses and played in the reserves, but that wasn't for me and I moved on.

When they went on to another League Championship, another FA Cup final and all the other stuff, I was sad because it could have been me. So I was just sad and I was sad for the fans, missing out on the European Cup. If we had been in Europe I'd have still been there. But there was no way I was going to stay in the reserves, it wasn't right.

How much did it hurt when Howard Kendall let him go? Any hard feelings? *George Lee Stuart, Lismore, Australia*
It hurt me very much, there was no way I wanted to leave Everton. I loved Everton then and I still do now. There were no hard feelings, we sat down and had a good talk, man to man. Howard and I didn't always get along, we had our fall-outs and I was no angel. I've kicked the door a few times and thrown a few cups, and he's thrown a few cups at me, but to this day we remain very best friends. He's a father figure to me. We go on holiday every year to Majorca and he's been a big influence on me. He's looked after me, my career and he's a big part of my life.

Newcastle. Did he play with Gazza and Beardsley? How did the Toon feel losing players like that and how does the back room at Goodison feel at becoming a selling club? *George Lee Stuart, Lismore, Australia*

I did play with Gazza and Peter at Newcastle, it was a great club. Gazza was young and it was when the good clubs started watching him. I had the honour and the privilege to play with him when he was coming to his peak. I even recommended him to Howard at one time. Peter Beardsley was another fantastic player and we got him eventually too.

Newcastle had to sell at that time. I think we finished seventh the first season I was there, but it wasn't good enough. They knew they had to sell their best players and over the years that became a bit of a trend with them. They did challenge for the Premiership that year with Keegan, but they seem to have slipped away again. They even managed to get Shearer, but they're still a mediocre side.

Everton have got great players now, but, unfortunately, we're in the same predicament as Newcastle, we're not challenging and we don't look as if we're contenders to do anything other than cups and we can't even seem to do that now, either. If that's the case and there's no money in the pot, we have to sell our best players and that's exactly what we will do. I'm not on the staff, I'm the same as you, just a supporter, so I don't know what happens behind the scenes, but I see what's in the papers and hear things on the street. I think we'll continue losing our best players until we hit a run of luck.

What happened to Bubbles the chimp? *Mike Jones, Dubai, United Arab Emirates*

What a great question! I got that in Toronto, me and Ratters bought a couple, but he bought his for the kids, I bought it for myself like the big kid I am. I took Bubbles on the lap of honour when we won the Charity Shield. I've still got a photograph of that, too. I eventually gave him to my neighbours, Sylvia and Ken Roberts. They were very good friends of mine who looked after me through bad times. They were like a mum and dad to me. I think they've still got Bubbles hanging about somewhere in their bungalow in Southport.

Who were the biggest piss-artists in the mid-'80s team? *Ged Fox, Wickford, England*

We were a great drinking squad. Besides myself, there was Reidy, Andy Gray, Sharpie, Sheeds and Trevor Steven. Oh yes, Everton were fine drinkers. Derek Mountfield was a bit quiet so we used to have him holding the kitty. Big Nev was a teetotaller, but he was always there with his tea until the bitter end.

He never went to his room, he would order a pot of tea and stay there all night with us. The team spirit was unbelievable and they were a great set of lads. I love them to this day, they're fabulous.

Pat Van den Hauwe. Savage or Lily Savage? *Mike Prenton, Leeds, England*

He came across as an animal, but I roomed with Pat and I loved him, he was a great fella, but he was worse than me for liking a bevvie. He could drink and he loved a nark. I never actually saw him fight because he was all say and no go, although I know what people are saying when they ask about him. He was a fantastic player, he'd have to be to take my place. He was 100 per cent aggressive and he had a mean streak, even in a social environment. I was a bit wary because he didn't like people staring at him and you'd always feel trouble was just around the corner. I had to calm him down and talk to him on a few occasions. He was very strange, but he did his job on the park and that was what mattered most.

How did he rate Pat Van den Hauwe as a left-back compared to himself at his peak? *Mike Benson, West Derby, Liverpool*

He could play with both feet and was a natural great defender, which I wasn't, and he was better in the air than me. It needed a good player to shift me and Pat was good, he was a Welsh international and proved he was a great player when he went on to win championships and caps and to become a folk hero with his attitude and his aggression. He hasn't been seen for a while, or at least since he made a few comments about Kevin Ratcliffe that I, for one, didn't agree with. He said a lot of bad things to a newspaper to make some money. I hear he's somewhere in South Africa.

Snobs or The Continental? *Jon Berman, West Derby, Liverpool*

The Continental was the nightclub the Everton and Liverpool players used to go to. I think Brian Tilsley from *Coronation Street* owned it. It was the 'in' place and full of posers and women. So if you wanted to be part of the 'in crowd' then that was the scene after midweek matches on a Tuesday or Wednesday night, and we were always there. We'd get the next day off after a match so we could have a nice lie-in the morning.

What's his view on the ever-increasing number of foreigners coming into the game? Good, bad or indifferent? *Colm Kavanagh, Co. Wicklow, Republic of Ireland*

You have to wonder if they're coming here for the money because there are that many bad players who've done nothing at all, like Asprilla and all those who played for Newcastle. They're just cheating supporters out of money. On the other side of the coin, there have been some great pluses and some fantastic players who've come across. Look at Liverpool, they've done the Treble and there are only about two British players in the whole squad. If they're genuinely coming here to win trophies and to boost our game, which I think they are – even our national team are starting to turn around a little bit now and I think that might be because of the influence of foreign players – then that can only be good news. So my answer has to be there's two sides to that argument: you are going to get the cheats, as we've seen, and will continue to get, and there's going to be the pluses. It might all change again in the future because it looks like we're going to get a lot more foreign players, looking at the spiralling transfer fees.

The board situation at Everton – did it ever get talked about at player level? *Frank Hargreaves, Anfield, Liverpool*
Everything was going along smoothly in my day so nobody asked anything. We got our bonuses in our wage packet for winning trophies, got our allocation of tickets and everyone was happy. I don't know what's going on these days, I really don't, but if the manager's got anything about him then none of the unrest should get through to the players. They shouldn't know about anything going on behind the scenes.

If he could re-run a match which one would it be? *Richard Ward, Hook, England*
I'd re-run the Milk Cup final when Alan Hansen hand-balled for a penalty. It was definitely hand-ball, as we've seen on replays a hundred times since. We should have protested to the referee a lot more than we did. I think there were only a couple of the lads who went to him. I could go through loads of games and pick out moments, but that was the main one because not only was it a Cup final, it was against Liverpool and it was a penalty. To say that it just hit him on the arm is ridiculous. I've spoken to the ref since then and he admits it was hand-ball, although in his TV interview afterwards he said it was ball-to-hand. There's no such thing as ball-to-hand in the penalty box. So if I could re-run that moment I'd be on top of the ref and right in his face.

Is football taken too seriously these days? Are we in danger of forgetting that it is a game as well as a profession and a business? *Neil Wolstenholme, Muswell Hill, north London*
Well, it is a business, it's still a game, but it's really big business, too. Players are

requesting £100,000 a week now. Even £50,000 a week is absolutely ridiculous. We were on £250 a week and winning trophies. You've got agents and even negotiators and something's got to give. It will all explode soon because the wage structures are going crazy. Average players are getting ridiculous money and driving round in top-of-the-range cars at eighteen. Schoolboys are getting paid fees of thousands of pounds and somebody's got to sit down and sort it out. Ultimately, it's the supporters who've got to pay, they've been paying fortunes over the years and it's not right. I've got no kids, but God help the ones who have and they have to take them to a game and kit them out. It must cost a fortune.

Honest opinion on the way the club is managed on and off the field nowadays? *Colm Kavanagh, Co. Wicklow, Republic of Ireland*
In the '80s we were so successful that nobody was asking questions like they are now as we're in a bleak spell and things are looking grim. There's the question of the stadium move and the lack of success of the team. In my day we had Jim Greenwood as secretary and Sir Philip, who's still involved now, and he was a tremendous servant to Everton and a wise man. I'm glad he's on board. In the '80s it was run professionally, but we've hit a slump because of on- and off-the-field activities and I can just hope that somebody will come along with a cash injection and sponsorship and hopefully it can be sorted out.

Has he thought of using his experience in a coaching role, say with youngsters, for example? *Phil Pellow, Waterloo, Liverpool*
I have done the coaching with Howard at Sheffield United and at Everton. Unfortunately, when Howard came back to Everton the last time there was no place for me and I've been out of work ever since. If a job does come along, I'd be up for it. I love being involved in the coaching side, but not with the really young kids, I like to be with the lads between 13–18 because you can get through to them and I'm quite comfortable to get amongst them and have a go.

If he could change anything what would it be? *Neil Wolstenholme, Muswell Hill, north London*
I would have changed a lot of things in my personal life, but you can't do that. I'm fit and well and I'd like a job, but in general I'm happy with life. I'd like to see Everton doing a hell of a lot better than they are, financially stabilised and with a far better squad, but in the meantime I keep smiling and keep being happy.

John Bailey

Do you look back on your time at EFC fondly? *Rob Hamilton, Melbourne, Australia*

I look very fondly on my Everton days. I still watch videos and I still do the after-dinner circuit and question-and-answer sessions about those glory years. I look forward to nights like that, reminiscing and answering questions from the past and meeting old friends. It's great to talk about it and be remembered, like I am now. I have fantastically happy memories and I'll take them with me to the grave because I'll die a very happy man. I look forward to the future, but I like to keep one foot in my past . . . My lucky left foot.

JIMMY GABRIEL

Born 10 October 1940
March 1960 – July 1967
£30,000

Johnny Carey could spot a talent and there was none more so than the fresh-faced lad he brought down from Dundee. Only 19 years old, and checking in at £30,000, the blonde bombshell was to become the most expensive teenager in British football history.

> When I first arrived at Everton, it was a bit of a weight on my shoulders because £30,000 was a hell of a lot of money in those days. A few of us signed around the same time and we got on great, there was Tommy Ring, Bobby Collins, Roy Vernon, Micky Lill and myself. Once I got to know the other players and mixed in with them a bit, we shared the pressure and they helped me along.

It was money well spent and the marauding midfield dynamo went on to make a formidable reputation for himself. He sported the Royal blue for 300 games in a career that spanned seven seasons. Rough, tough and feisty, there was always something happening when he was wearing the number 4 shirt. You could bet your life on it.

Jimmy Gabriel, your audience awaits.

Who did he support when he signed for Everton and who does he support now? *Kevin McFadden, Waterloo, Liverpool*
As a kid I always supported Dundee. I played for them and was transferred from there to Everton. Now I support Everton.

As an exiled Scouse Evertonian living in Scotland I would ask Jimmy if he remembers the North End club, as one of his shirts

is proudly displayed on the lounge wall? *Lol Scragg, Arbroath, Scotland*

I do remember North End, I had one season there before I went to Dundee and what a great season it was. We won the League Championship, about four different cups, and I think we got beat by Paddy Crerand's junior team in the Scottish Junior Cup. The guys who played for Dundee North End really looked after me, gave me good advice and helped me more than anybody to go on and have a really great career. That was a fabulous year for me.

He played with some greats, including the Golden Vision. Who was the best Evertonian he played with and why? *Mike Coville, New York, USA*

It's hard to say. Alex Young was a fantastic player and he was so wonderful to watch, silky smooth yet strong. He scored and made goals, had it all and did everything with class. Roy Vernon was as sharp as a needle, he could play deep in the midfield, forward in midfield, upfront and was a captain in every sense of the word. I felt he almost single-handedly won the league for us. Brian Harris was brilliant too. They were all good and great to play with. I'd also like to mention Tony Kay because he had a huge input with us winning the League Championship. I really feel that if Brian Harris or myself were playing alongside him, Everton would have been a real powerhouse for years to come because of his influence. Unfortunately, he didn't play for much more than a year and that was a real shame for Everton because he would have been huge. I often wonder what might have been.

How was Harry Catterick as a boss? Did he calm you all down or instil fire in you? *John Quinn, Tewkesbury, England*

Harry had a couple of different ways of dealing with players. He kept his finger on the pulse, if he thought we were getting too loose he would be very strict and if we were losing confidence he'd help us regain it. He was always solid and we could pretty much do whatever we wanted on the pitch if it would help our game. He was only interested in results and performance.

He was only capped twice for Scotland. Why? He was worth more than that! *Mike Coville, New York, USA*

It must have been me who sent that question in! I was a wee bit unfortunate in that when I got my first cap for Scotland we played down in Wales and it was a mud bath. For some reason, they had picked quite a small forward line, I think Alex Young played, too. We got a bit stuck in the mud that day and never really got going. We got beat 2–0 and as soon as that happened they just thought that we were no good, especially the boys who were making their debut. So they went off to find another lot. I was unfortunate at that time because Paddy Crerand and Jimmy Baxter were playing for Celtic and Rangers respectively and they brought out a rule that no Anglo-Scots would be selected for the team. I think that lasted two or three years, but it was enough to let Paddy and Jimmy establish themselves and get control of those positions. Even Dennis Law and Dave Mackay suffered because they weren't selected either. I was playing well then and I think my performances would have got me into the national team, but they wanted to encourage the best Scottish players to stay in Scotland.

Does he remember nutting Paddy Crerand at Old Trafford? And if I'm not mistaken, he got away with it! *Tom Davis, Texas, USA*

No, I can't remember that, I don't think I would nut him. Maybe I clashed heads with Paddy, but I love the bones of him and would never do that. He played for Scotland and I loved to play against him. We had a good rapport and I always seemed to get on with the Manchester United players. Bobby Charlton was great too. I really liked him. But I would never have intentionally have done that to Paddy unless he'd done it to me first.

I'd like to ask Jimmy if he enjoyed those games he played upfront. I particularly remember the FA Cup fourth-round replay against Leeds midweek at Goodison when he wore the number nine shirt and came racing onto a through ball and lashed it into the roof of the net at the Gwladys St End. *Tony Kennedy, Loughborough, England*

I remember the goal, it was a thunderbolt. I was playing alongside Roy Vernon and I was really excited because, whether they admit it or not, every midfielder wants to secretly be a centre-forward. That's the glory position and playing in a cup tie was great. I remember Roy knocked me a through ball and I chested it past their young centre-back. I was just on the edge of the penalty area and I smacked it in with my left foot and it flew right into the top corner of the net. It was a fabulous goal but it wasn't placed, I just hit it as hard as I could. I remember Roy got a scrambly in the second half and we did them 2–0. We didn't like Leeds and we wanted to wallop them whenever we could.

Who was the real hard man of the 1963 Championship-winning side: Tony Kay, Dennis Stevens or himself? *Dave Kelly, Blackburn, England*

It was probably me. Tony was a strong player, but I was like the policeman. My job was to make sure that, whatever the atmosphere of the game, it was working in our favour. If we were being out-skilled, then I would turn it into more of a rough-and-tumble by making a few hard tackles and getting them excited. We usually ended up playing rough with West Ham. If we were playing a skilful game and were winning I would try to calm everybody down and keep the game going so we didn't lose our temper. If there was any real bother, then I would go and sort it out. In general, the guys could look after themselves, but I was expected to keep my finger on the pulse.

Tony was never frightened of anything, he just went in, and Dennis was a great little player, a clever inside-forward who could score goals. I liked working with him, he'd let me go forward and sit in for me. I got a lot of help in policing from Roy Vernon too. He was the skipper and he'd say things to get me mad then unleash me and I'd hammer in a few tackles. He was clever at pulling my strings.

Could you ask Jimmy whom he rated as an opponent in his playing days? *David Catton, Sheffield, England*
When I first came down to England I was playing at right-half, so I was against the inside-forwards. There was an unbelievable amount of brilliant players I competed against every week – George Eastham, Johnny Haines, Bobby Charlton, Jimmy McIlroy, Jimmy Greaves, Ivor Allchurch and Derek Kevin – they were either big monsters or fast as lightning. You were facing superstars every week and it was so difficult.

I was always reasonably comfortable on the ball, but it took me over a year to get tuned into the defensive side of my job. I knew how important that was and how I had to change every week, depending on the opposition. You could look back to those days and pick every one with a number ten on his back, and the names that would come out would take your breath away. The talent they had back then was unbelievable.

The question I would like to ask is whether he spent one summer doing a lot of upper-body weight-training? I recall there was one season when, for the first few weeks, his physique looked absolutely unreal. It also appeared to affect his playing – change of centre of gravity, perhaps? *David Catton, Sheffield, England*
I never did any weight-training, I just let myself go a bit, got heavier, and it looked like muscle but was just body fat. I lost a step, and maybe I looked good, but I wasn't as fit as I should have been. There wasn't a lot of dieting or looking after ourselves like they do today. I wish there had been. I was one of the first Everton players to go on a diet. At one time, if players started putting

Jimmy Gabriel

on weight that was it, a couple of years later they weren't playing any more. I knew I'd put on weight, and it affected me, so I found a way to control it and kept it steady after that.

I recall seeing you play at Molineux in the mid-'60s in a cup match. Bally hadn't been with us long and Peter Knowles gave him a bit of a kicking. You and Brian Labone kicked Knowles up in the air and he was very quiet after that. Did you realise that you were probably responsible for Peter Knowles giving up footy, which he did very soon after that match, and finding God? He became a Jehovah's Witness after that. *Tony Field, Loughborough, England*

When you're on the pitch everybody's your enemy. We were at war, and although it's supposed to be a bloodless war, we all know it's not. If Brian and I felt that Peter needed working on to get the result, then that's what we did. We only did what was necessary to ensure a win for Everton. So, I'm not going to do a Pontius Pilate and wipe my hands clean on that. I did give him a couple of kicks, but my legs were there for him to kick me if he could.

Was Richard Gough one of the physically toughest defenders he's ever seen? *Neil Wolstenholme, Muswell Hill, north London*

He was one of the toughest around, but Dave Watson was my favourite tough guy because of what he put out game after game. He would go out there and play with injuries and he never let anyone know about it. We knew because we were on the staff, but he was a fine man. So if you want to talk about somebody as hard as nails then Dave Watson was that man, and what a great servant to Everton.

I'd like him to rate some of Everton's centre-forwards in order of skill and effectiveness as team members. *David Catton, Sheffield, England*

There were some great Everton forwards, but I have to say that Vernon and Young were the best that I played with in an Everton team. Whenever I received the ball I almost instinctively knew where either of them were, and my choices were either to play a target pass to Alex's feet, chest or head, or to play a through-pass to Roy's penetrating run. Alex Young had the touch, Roy Vernon had the pace, and the rest was easy. Both of those players brought something special to Goodison Park at a time when the fans needed to believe that their team could be winners of trophies and still play entertaining football.

Roy and Alex spearheaded our winning challenge for the 1962–63 League Championship by scoring the goals we needed to get the job done. I know other strikers were top quality, none more so than Bob Latchford. Then there's Fred Pickering, who scored a hat trick on his Goodison debut, but for me Young and Vernon are forever on my mind when I mentally revisit my days as an Everton player.

Did you have a Jack Charlton-type black book for certain players? *Tony Field, Loughborough, England*

No, never, but there were certain players you could frighten with your first tackle, and after that they would leave you alone to play quite nicely. There were others, and if you woke them up you had a battle on your hands, so you didn't disturb their slumber. After a game I would wipe the slate clean. I got my cheekbone broken by a centre-forward's elbow and you remember that. You'd wait for your moment and then remind them that they couldn't get away with things in this life. But I didn't have a book, or even mentally keep a black book. Players would change, they would evolve and gain confidence, adding another dimension to their game so you had to concentrate on shutting them down and not settling old scores. You had to go in there with a clean sheet and just take it as it came.

I'm sure Jimmy could not have forgotten scoring against Liverpool as a makeshift centre-forward in the 1963–64 season. Was that one of his best-ever highlights? *Tom Davis, Texas, USA*

The game ended up 3–1. I only scored once, but I made the other two for Roy Vernon. When I think back to my days at Everton, that game against the old enemy keeps coming up, and it's definitely one of my better moments.

I loved to play with Roy Vernon, it was perfect, we fitted one another like a glove. I was good in the air, could get up and flick balls down and Roy was like lightning, getting in behind defenders and scoring, so we were laughing. That day, I was getting picked up by big Ron Yeats and I decided to switch places with Roy, but Ron didn't come with me and I ended up with a smaller guy marking me instead. The ball came to me, I jumped and headed it and Roy stuck it in the back of the net. I scored with my lucky left foot as well, so we were 2–0 up. Then it went 2–1, we broke them down and Alex Scott hit a free kick. I remember jumping up early on Big Ron so that he carried me up. I nearly got a nose-bleed I went so high, but I was able to head it back down and Roy just banged it in the net and that was the end of their comeback.

Jimmy Gabriel

Another thing I remember is Mike Meagan hitting a ball to me and I knew I was going to get crunched by Big Ron. I was right, the next thing I was flat on the floor with Ron on top of me and I must have gone six inches into the surface of the pitch. It was tough to play upfront with all those big lads hammering you, but it was fun.

What was it like playing in front of over 60,000 supporters at Goodison Park? *Mike Coville, New York, USA*
It was absolutely magnificent, I'd never seen a crowd like that. I'd been part of a big crowd watching Dundee v Rangers, but that was when I was a boy. Dundee v Motherwell had 136,000, but I'd never been playing on the park. They were fantastic and were all Everton supporters – there might have been some supporting the other team, but they were totally drowned out. You couldn't really hear the individuals, all you could hear was a buzz, like white-noise around your head. It lifted you and made you play to your limit. It used to make my hair stand on end.

Who was his most consistent teammate in his Everton career? *Jason Palmer, Merthyr Tydfil, Wales*
That would have to be Brian Labone. Every week, we knew what we would get from him and he was as solid as a rock. He was an excellent centre-back and captain. He had everything going for him and rightly got selected for England.

There was always hatred between Everton and Leeds. On one occasion, it really boiled over, culminating in Sandy Brown getting sent off and the players being taken off the pitch early by the referee for a cooling-off period. Even a long-time Evertonian, Bobby Collins, was 'programmed' to hate us. Why did we always have these battles? *John Quinn, Tewkesbury, England*
Bobby Collins introduced me to my wife, Pat. When I arrived at Everton, I was lonely and homesick, so Bobby set us up on a blind date and we've been together for almost 40 years now.

I don't know why Leeds and Everton had that, but I think it came from them rather than us. They were jealous because we were a big club and they thought they were going to bring us down. We beat them to send them down to the Second Division, so it could have been that, or maybe because Bobby Collins inspired them. I know there were a lot of guys at Leeds who were little quiet players, not good enough for other teams and probably wouldn't have been good enough for the First Division if Bobby hadn't taught them how to go look after themselves.

Sometimes, that's what you have to do. You should never try to injure people, but you need to be able to take care of yourself out there. Leeds were a weak team and a year after Bobby arrived they were very strong. Part of that was to do with the brilliance of some of the players, like Giles and Bremner, all these guys coming to the fore and becoming men, but it had a lot to do with Bobby's determination to make everybody play hard.

I know that every time we played Leeds it was a battle, but sometimes it wasn't in our best interests to go into a battle. In that game, in particular, if the referee had been half as strong as he should have been then half of the Leeds players would have been off because the tackles they made were terrible. The one on Derek Temple was unbelievable, the defender had both feet in the air, over the top of the ball. He kicked Derek right into the crowd and Derek was limping from that point on. Sandy Brown got booted and the referee saw the retaliation and he got sent off. We couldn't believe the referee was allowing the Leeds fouls and at the same time penalising us, we didn't know whether to declare war on Leeds or to play our way back into the game. As I recall we fell between both of these choices. Aided and abetted by the referee, Leeds managed to divide us and we had no chance of bouncing back after that.

I blame the referee totally, he was horrendous, he lost control of the match and he couldn't direct the play after that. It should have been a good game of football and a competition, but instead it became a total mess because it was mishandled. I think that was the last really bad game Everton and Leeds played against one another. That drew a line under it and we started to play better after that.

Any thoughts about why Catterick dropped Fred Pickering for the 1966 FA Cup final? *Mike Coville, New York, USA*

Fred had proved in training and in previous games he hadn't been fully fit. Harry didn't want to play someone who might not perform as well as somebody who was fully fit, there was too much at stake. He wanted a team to go out there and win the Cup, so he played Mike Trebilcock and, of course, he went on to score twice and win it for us. So it was a great move on Harry's part, but Fred was devastated. We all felt for him, being told so late on that he wasn't going to play, but he certainly would have done if he had been fit and he would have scored a hat trick. He'd been great for the team all the way through the championship, so it was a real shame. But as a manager, Harry made the right decision at the right time.

I'd like to know his thoughts about the 1966 FA Cup win against Sheffield Wednesday (I know I keep on going on about this game

but it was one of the most exciting I have ever seen!). His performance in the first half was not that good, nerves? *Mike Coville, New York, USA*

You're right, I wasn't as good. The problem was that I couldn't figure it out because they changed their style of play and that took us by surprise. I liked to go into games and, after about two or three touches, figure out what was happening so we could start working in the right areas. But I was puzzled in the first half.

They came at us in a different formation and it caught us out, it was something we hadn't seen them do before. We didn't have Fred upfront either, we had Mike Trebilcock, and he was more of a floating player, so it was a bit awkward in the first half. In the second half, they scored and went 2–0 up, but our first goal was the main thing. The ball was thrown up the back, it went to Ray Wilson, to Colin Harvey, to me, I flicked it to Brian Harris and he hit it first touch to Derek Temple. He headed it across to Trebilcock, and he smashed it into the back of the net. It was the sweetest of goals and something we needed. I don't think a scrambled goal would have done it, but a goal like that where you cut them to ribbons set them back on their heels. It got us on our toes and then we were after them like a dog after a snake.

Did he think that we should have had a penalty when Springett brought down Alex Young? *Mike Coville, New York, USA*

Yes, we should have, and I was taking the penalties that day so I wasn't the one up in the air shouting 'penalty' because it was such a big thing at Wembley. Nobody had ever missed one at that time. John Aldridge was the first to do that in the '80s at the Liverpool–Wimbledon final, but that wasn't so much a miss as a brilliant save.

Cast your mind back to 14 May 1966. Can you recall going on a mazy run in about the 88th minute? What did it feel like holding out the Wednesday players by the corner flag and looking at an imaginary wristwatch? To us on the terraces it seemed as though you were there for about five minutes, but I suppose it was only about thirty seconds. After Derek Temple had put the ball in the back of the net I didn't think the day could get any better, but that little cameo really put the icing on the cake. *Rob Sharratt, Narara, Australia*

The first time I'd seen somebody do that was in the '60s when I came to England. It was Jimmy McIlroy and he was playing for Burnley at the time. Towards the end of the game, he got the ball and held it, but he didn't just stick his backside out, he did it with such skill. He got the ball and he would pull it and twist it and turn it, I was fascinated and so impressed. In the Cup final I thought I should head to goal and try for a fourth, then it flashed into my mind about Jimmy McIlroy and I headed off to the corner flag and started messing about.

What was going through his mind in the 90th minute at Wembley in 1966 when he was holding the ball close to the corner flag with desperate Sheffield Wednesday players surrounding him? *Dave Kelly, Blackburn, England*
If I'd have been a Sheffield Wednesday player I'd have booted me up in the air, but they didn't. I wasn't trying to take the mickey out of them, because they were very worthy opponents, I was just trying to waste time. But I so wanted them to try and get it because I was going to do a Jimmy McIlroy.

Was the 1966 FA Cup win his greatest moment playing for the Blues? The Everton support was tremendous, especially when we were 2–0 down. What impact did the crowd have on the players and the result? *Mike Coville, New York, USA*
If the crowd goes quiet on you, you tend to go quiet as a team, especially when you're used to big crowds. It must have been gut-wrenching for them when we went 2–0 down, they must have thought we'd lost with half an hour to go. When we scored that really good first goal it lifted their spirits and they knew we would do it again. We got the second goal shortly after, and the third which was an absolute cracker from Derek Temple. Colin hit a long ball forward and there was a mistake by the defender, who miscontrolled it, so Derek had a long run and a lot of time to think about what he was going to do. He smashed it and nobody has ever hit a ball cleaner. The goalkeeper just missed it with his fingertips and it went inside the post and into the corner of the net. It was a fantastic goal to win with.

The crowd at Goodison always kept us going, and because of them the team never quit. How can you quit if somebody's shouting for you? How could you give up when they're roaring and singing and yelling for you? We had crowds of 60,000 and they wouldn't let us give up, but we needed them to be there.

What do you think of the modern-day system of rotating players? If that system had been vogue in your day I suppose your Everton career could have been extended, or were you one of those

players who needed to play every week? *Rob Sharratt, Narara, Australia*

It would have been hard for any of us to understand why we had been left out and we all wanted to play every week, but if you've been brought up in the rotation system, I don't think it's a bad thing to skip a game to give yourself a break. If you look at the clubs that are doing it, they're playing a huge number of games where the intensity is really high. The players have to deal with television watching their every move and there's more pressure on them than there was in our day. That pressure can get too much, and rather than have the players lapse in form it's better to let them sit out a couple of weeks and let them come back refreshed. Players are reasonable about these things now, they understand it's for their benefit and they'll fall in line. I think it's the way of the future.

How did he feel having to leave EFC for Southampton? What was his relationship with Howard Kendall, who was brought in to replace him? *Paul Preston, Muswell Hill, north London*

Harry said that if I wanted to play at the back with Brian Labone then he would move me there. John Hurst wasn't really settled in yet, and hadn't really made the position his, besides, Harry liked me playing there. I didn't want to do that, though, I wanted to play in the midfield so I decided I should move. I saw it as a new start and I gave it my best shot.

With Howard, I was really proud that they brought in who I thought was the very best midfield player at that time to take my place. I got on great with Howard. He had showed such great promise at Preston, he was so good and to have him put on the number four shirt was very flattering. I knew that you could never own a shirt, just borrow it for a while, but I knew I was leaving it in safe hands.

We didn't really know each other because Howard knocked around with the good guys. We got split into two dressing-rooms. Harry put the good guys in the one and who he thought were the bad guys in the other. I was with the bad guys, along with Johnny Morrissey, Alex Young and a few of the others, but all the new signings got put in the good dressing-room. Labby was in there with Ray Wilson, Howard and all the nice people. It was funny, we had great fun and we used to laugh about it.

I wished him all the best and I was confident that he would be great. I sent him a telegram before his first game, to take the sting out and so he knew that I wasn't angry with him. If you hand over your shirt to somebody who deserves to be wearing it, you should be happy for the club and not sad for yourself.

I went to the Southampton v Everton game after Jimmy's transfer. When he came onto the pitch, a couple of Evertonians ran to him and put blue scarves round his neck. I seem to remember him walking towards the Evertonians, behind the goal, with his hands in the air. Was this true or is the romantic in me taking over again? *David Tickner, Bowring Park, Liverpool*

That's true. The guys came and put the blue scarves on me and I walked towards the fans to thank them and let them know how much I missed them. I thanked them for their appreciation. It was a happy–sad moment for me. I was happy that they'd recognised me and remembered me, and I was sad because I couldn't be with them any more. I had to move on. I remember that, it's one of my best memories. I really appreciated it because I always loved the Everton fans. The game went on and I scored for Southampton. We beat Everton 3–2. It was a poignant moment and something I'll always remember.

He played in the same defence at Southampton as the late John McGrath, a character-and-a-half. Please get him to recount a tale about John's exploits. He was a lovable rogue by all accounts – unless you were the centre-forward he was marking at the time, of course. *Dave Kelly, Blackburn, England*

John was a great fella. He was tremendous in the air, towering above them all. I liked playing at the back with him because when he went for the ball I knew exactly what was going to happen. It was simple, he would win it or miss it, and I could tell before he even made his tackle if he was going to win it or not, so I could prepare to get in there and win the second challenge. I thought he was talented, but he got a bad rap from Bill Shankly when we played Liverpool. John went up a bit late and flipped their centre-forward, who came back over the top of him and hurt himself. Shankly called us an 'alehouse team', so he got the name of being an alehouse player, and it wasn't right.

John was a character. He had a really strange routine before the match. We would arrive about 45 minutes before the game and get ourselves ready in the usual manner. John would arrive about an hour and a half before the game. He'd go in the shower and massage oil all over his body, then he'd go back into the shower and do the same again, with a different type of oil. This was his routine. It's a wonder his strip stayed on him because he was so slick. One day, we were already on the pitch and the ref blew his whistle to get the captains together. John came running down the tunnel like a great big, slick grease ball. He came flying out onto the turf and he had these great big boots on. He decided as a centre-back he didn't want to play football, he wanted to put these big boots on so he could smash the ball away. He wouldn't encourage himself to play as he was capable, he wanted to be a centre-back. Every time Hughie Fisher and I saw John on the pitch, we had to laugh at him bouncing around like a lunatic and with the fans cheering him on like mad.

I recall an incident when Southampton played the Arsenal. The story goes that McGrath and Bob Wilson collided at the edge of the box, none of the namby-pamby rolling about you see nowadays. McGrath just sat up and said to Wilson: 'You've broken my fucking leg.' Is this true? *Tony Field, Loughborough, England*

I think that happened down at Southampton. You just jogged my memory with that, but I'm not sure if that was McGrath or Hughie Fisher. I think it was Fisher, you know, because I remember I carried a wee grudge against the Arsenal goalie for that, I thought it was a rough challenge. Nobody could get close enough to McGrath to break his legs, he would just plough through them – beside which his legs were like tree trunks, you wouldn't have been able to break them with a mallet!

Can you ask Jimmy if he ever wanted the Everton job when he was caretaker manager? Did he realise Everton were in free-fall at the time or did he think that it could be turned around and not end up in the mess we are in now? *Gary Fulton, Northwich, Cheshire, England*

That was such a difficult time for Everton and for me, it was all so unexpected. I was scouting a player at Stoke City, I went to pick up my tickets and I was asked to phone home as there was a message waiting for me. It was one of the board asking if I would go back, which I did. I was wondering what it was all about. Howard hadn't talked to me about packing it in or anything, he was as solid as a rock. So I went back and they said they wanted me to take over the team and I realised that Howard and Colin must have gone. I assumed Colin had walked with Howard or he would have taken over – he had far more experience than me.

Colin phoned me that night and asked me what was going on. I said that I'd assumed he'd walked out. At that point, I would have liked to tell the board that Colin had much more experience than me but by the same token, it's always exciting to be in charge of the team you love. I put it to Colin that we work it together, and he was fine with that.

Bringing me in made it really difficult for the players. Colin had been coaching them and suddenly the guy from the reserves turns up to manage them. It was a bad mistake by the directors. I'd taken over from Colin for one game and we won 3–0, but it was hard for the players to take anything seriously because as a reserve team Coach you're very much in the background. The lads played as well as they could, they played their hearts out, but the chemistry wasn't there and the breaks weren't going our way.

Would you take the manager's job again if the call came? *Ray Finch, Havant, England*

No, I'm a coach and I enjoy coaching more than managing. You've got to be the type of person who likes to manage because all the cogs of the wheel are coming into you. I like to have a specific job and get on with it. As a manager, you've got to worry about all kinds of things and you never get any real time to sit down and work with your team because you're worrying about newspapers and fans and all that. When you're a coach, you just get on with it. You know what you want to do, how fit you need to be and what type of football you want to play. Anything else is a distraction.

Did he genuinely believe that the first two seasons with Joe Royle would be the start of something big? *Osmo Tapio Räihälä, Helsinki, Finland*

Yes, I did and I liked Willie Donachie, his first-team coach. It seemed as if Joe had made some good decisions and we'd gone and won the Cup and played some really good football, especially at the semi-final when we beat Tottenham 4–1 and really played them off the park – we murdered them. We beat Man United 1–0 and then went for the Charity Shield and beat Blackburn 1–0. So it seemed that whatever Joe touched turned to gold. We only just missed out on going to Europe due to Arsenal's late goal but things were looking good. I don't know what happened, but Joe fell out with one of the reporters and different things started happening. It was disappointing. I honestly did feel that when we won the FA Cup we were on our way to the big time.

He said at the time that Richard Dunne was one of the best prospects he had ever seen. What does he think went wrong? *Paul Preston, Muswell Hill, north London*

I don't think anything went wrong. He's just a young lad who's not reached the age where he can be as good as he's going to be. To be a centre-back you've got to be like Brian Labone, and he was about 26 before he reached his peak and then he kept it going for ten years. You can have all the talent in the world, but you have to learn lessons when you're playing centre-back and it takes a long time to study the game. Once Richard Dunne has learned those lessons he'll be excellent because he's got pace, power, height, two good feet and good technique. It's down to him to keep playing and learn the game, I think he'll be outstanding when he's about 25. That's when you'll see the best of him and it will be until the end of his career.

When he was reserve-team coach who was the best kid he had on his books? *Colin Smith, Princeton, New Jersey, USA*
We had a number of very good players, but for some reason they couldn't quite make the next step. For some it was physical, that they weren't quite strong enough or quick enough, but technically they were always very good players. Some of them were too individual and never could get the idea of playing in a team. There were different things that held them back. I personally really liked Gavin McCann, I can remember arguing with the powers-that-be that we had to keep him. You never know if it's going to come right for young players, but if it does for Gavin, he's going to be special. I always had that feeling about him. Everton were thinking about letting him go when he was in the reserves, and I managed to get him kept on and he's become a great player. I've watched him play for Sunderland and he's been fantastic. I see he's been picked for the England squad now and it doesn't surprise me one little bit.

What went wrong with Andrei Kanchelskis at Everton? *Osmo Tapio Räihälä, Helsinki, Finland*
When Andrei first came to Everton he had a sparkle about him, so maybe that was his time. I think Andrei is best suited to a team that's higher up the league. He was an excellent player, he had tremendous pace and power, he was a great finisher, but it's difficult for a guy coming from Russia trying to fit in. I think if we'd kept higher up the league then he would have been fine, but he got a bit disappointed and dropped his shoulders. He had to realise that it was him who was putting us up there in the first place so if he dropped his shoulders then it would run through the team. I think the trouble the team had in getting results got to him because he went to Fiorentina and Rangers and did well for them. He probably thinks more now rather than going on instinct; that dulls your sparkle. Once you start thinking it's backwards from that point on.

Why didn't Tony Grant make it? I can remember typing up an interview with Jimmy where he was waxing lyrical about Tony Grant. I think the heading of the article was: 'He's got the lot'. With all that talent how come he couldn't do it consistently at

Premiership level? Was it just the physical frailty? *Richard Marland, Waterloo, Liverpool*

I don't think it's a physical frailty. He's not the most powerful player in the world, but he's got pace and quickness, an agile mind and good body movement. I saw Tony play the other week for Man City against Bradford. I saw him getting the ball and passing it, getting it and passing it. Now, as a young boy, he would get and pass for sure, but he would beat people and go at them. He would take people on, and he's an unbelievable dribbler. It seems to me that as he's been pushed from pillar to post, from youth to reserves and so on, he's lost that dribbling thing. Now, he can't have completely lost the ability to dribble, but he just doesn't do it any more. He was so explosive and could easily get past two or three players, but for some reason he seems to have cast it aside in the top flight. I think he's got to get back to it and go at people whenever he has the opportunity. Once he does that he'll be back to the good prospect we all think he is. I'd like to get him on the phone and tell him he's not playing the way I know he can.

Can I have the white trench coat he used to wear on the bench when he was caretaker manager? *Neil Wolstenholme, Muswell Hill, north London*

I think I still have that somewhere. Yes, you can have it if you want.

Living in the USA he must be aware that soccer has not fully hit the American sporting psyche. Given Man United's recent collaborative marketing effort with the New York Yankees, what could Everton do to broaden their fan base, marketing, and revenue opportunities in the States? *Paul Rigby, Connecticut, USA*

They'd have to have a look around and see what would fit best. Every time Man United does something, they open the door and if you're willing to go through that door with them, there's usually a reward on the other side. They think long and hard before they do something and especially New York Yankees, they're another team who are very forward thinking and motivated. It would be in Everton's best interest to have a look in that area for the future. Football is starting to grow over here and it's really taking off, everywhere you look kids are playing soccer. It would be worth our while to approach a few teams and break the ice. Maybe swap a few players over for a bit of training, that sort of thing and just form a link. I just know there are so many good players over here and they're going to start going to England soon. We might as well get in early. A club that's ahead of the game would do that.

Jimmy Gabriel

Are your children Evertonians, and if not why not? John Quinn, Tewkesbury, England

Any time they hear the word Everton they say: 'My dad played for Everton.' They're not football fans because they've lived most of their lives in America. Although they understand the importance of it and being attached to a huge club like Everton, they haven't been brought up around it. But they've got kids of their own now, and they're into baseball.

What does he think of the present fees and the wages that the players are getting now? Mike Coville, New York, USA

We were getting huge amounts of money compared to the players ten years before us and now they're getting huge amounts more than players ten years before them. I think they get paid what they deserve to get paid. They're entertainers who go out there every game, put their heart and soul on the pitch for the fans and for the team, and give it all. They can be lambasted or they may be praised, and whatever the going rate is I think they should get it. Look at the basketball players in America, they're getting millions, $250 million for a five-year contract, so it's not a lot compared to that. If that's the going rate and they're the best players, then they should get it.

Does he scout for us in the USA? Neil Wolstenholme, Muswell Hill, north London

I'm one of the coaches at the University of Washington and I don't know how much scouting I could do, but nobody's got in touch with me and said: 'Jim, could you help us with this or keep your eye open for me?' There are some great players over here, the best players in the world are going to come from the United States in a very short time. There are fantastic athletes and they play good soccer now because they understand the game so much better. There are young kids coming up, and from what I see, they're phenomenal. Somebody at some time has got to start getting a scouting system going and getting old boys like myself to keep an eye out for talent.

If he could do it all over again what would he change? Phil Pellow, Waterloo, Liverpool

I'd definitely play more times for Scotland if I could. I love Scotland and I think I could have helped them. I'd also phone Tony Kay just before he was about to meet those guys and warn him what would happen. I'd make sure he was very clear on that one because Tony would have helped us tremendously. We'd have won a lot of championships and cups if he'd stayed longer. I might have stayed when Harry offered me to. I played with Bally and Colin Harvey in the midfield, and maybe it wouldn't have been so bad to play behind them and Howard after all.

What does he think of the proposed move to the Kings Dock?
Mike Coville, New York, USA

I'll never leave Goodison Park, my memories are all there. If they go to the Kings Dock then I'll go there and watch Everton when I'm home – I'll watch them wherever they play. If Goodison Park is not right for the club to progress and become as rich as Man United, then that's what we have to do. But my memories will always be at Goodison Park even if they knock it down and clear the site, it will always be alive in my mind. And that would be the same for all the players who ever played there, all the managers who ever managed there and all the fans who ever watched from there. I love the Old Girl.

ALAN HARPER

Born 1 November 1960
June 1983 – July 1988 and
August 1991 – September 1993
£60,000

Always a man with an eye for a good deal, Howard Kendall had spotted the perfect utility player, but he was on the wrong side of Stanley Park. A few carefully chosen words, a deposit of £30,000 and the promise of the same again after 50 games and Alan Harper was Goodison-bound. If you can only have one person on the substitutes' bench, then it's pretty damn handy if he can play in any position you care to name.

> I signed him three times in my career, once at Man City and twice at Everton. He was absolutely priceless because he could play all the full-back positions, sweeper and anywhere across the midfield. I didn't need to carry a spare player, only him. It was unfortunate at the time that we had such a great side and he didn't really have a regular place. He picked up his share of medals, though, and he thoroughly deserved them.

Run for your lives – it's Zico!

> The first person I met when I arrived at Goodison was John Bailey. Howard and the team were just about to go to Magaluf on the end-of-season trip. I bumped into Bails again not so long ago and he said exactly the same thing, this is eighteen years down the line. It's nice to see that some things are consistent in life, even if Everton isn't one of them!

He was a local schoolboy who joined LFC. Was he ever invited to join Everton and, as a 15-year-old, what would he have said if someone had suggested he'd end up playing on the other side of Stanley Park? *San Presland, New Brighton, Merseyside*

Only Liverpool showed any interest and came in for me. If anybody had even joked that I would end up playing for Everton when I was a kid, I would probably have gone mad.

It didn't take long for Howard to convince me this was the place to be. In fact, it only took about five seconds. He told me that if I really wanted to play I had more chance at Everton and he would give me that opportunity. Howard talked a good game and straightaway I knew what I wanted to do. Liverpool asked me to stay and offered me more money, but I wasn't interested in the cash, it was the thought of getting a game that appealed to me the most and I couldn't wait to sign up.

Being born a Red, it was all a bit strange when I first arrived, but I'm a Blue now. Most of my family still support Liverpool, but a few switched allegiance to follow my career. I'm not sure they thank me for it too often.

Did the players feel that the Oxford game was as much a turning-point as us fans do? *Osmo Tapio Räihälä, Helsinki, Finland*

There was a feeling amongst all of us that our luck was changing. We knew we'd turned a corner and we could go on from there. There was an element of luck too – remember Kevin Brock's back pass when Inchy nipped in and scored? You've got to ride your luck when it comes, which is exactly what we did. I keep hoping that our luck will change again soon. The sooner the better.

Best 'utility' man I've seen at Everton in my lifetime – unsung and underrated. How much was he earning the season we won the league? *Frank Hargreaves, Anfield, Liverpool*

I arrived at Everton on £250 a week.

Did he ever imagine he would become a league champion so quickly? *Osmo Tapio Räihälä, Helsinki, Finland*

I never thought it would happen so fast, it was such a young side too. From what I'd seen in training I had every faith in the team, but I thought it would take a few years to reach the top while we got to know each other. We didn't need time to gel, we all got on great from the word go. As chance would have it, Howard had collected and inherited a brilliant bunch of lads, so I always knew we had the potential, but it all happened so fast, especially considering we had a bit of a sticky time early on.

Alan Harper

He scored one of my favourite goals, the one knocked on by Gray and Sharp, which he buried past Grobbelaar. I think this was the first time we'd come back against them for ages. It was a turning-point in a way, because it showed we could compete. How did it feel? *Clive Blackmore, Washington DC, USA*

That was just the most brilliant feeling ever. I came on as sub that day. We were getting beat 1–0 and Sharpie missed a penalty. The game was going off and there were about ten minutes left. I can see it now, the flick-on and the pass across. I just hit it and it went in. Since Grobbelaar got done for bribery I've sometimes thought he might have let it in, and it's been playing on my mind for years.

Did the fact that Liverpool finished second to us during both our Championship-winning seasons and your not being able to get a game with them pre-'83 make you smile a little more? *Steve Fairclough, Toronto, Canada*

It did make me smile, not because they let me go, that was my choice, but just because they were one of the best sides in Europe at the time next to us, so it was especially nice to beat them.

What did you think of your nickname 'Zico' and how did it come about? *Steve Houghton, Battersea, south-west London*

I had many nicknames and that one is probably the most printable. It originated at Chelsea when I scored from outside the box. The following game was at Goodison and they started chanting 'Zico'. I was looking around to try and figure out what they were on about and then it dawned on me, and when I realised I was absolutely made up.

Go on, just for us, describe that goal at Chelsea! *Mike Prenton, Leeds, England*

Nev rolled it to me outside the box and I just shot from there. No, I'm just messing. I can't remember who passed it to me, but it was either Trevor or Gary. I was in the middle of midfield and I thought I would just hit it. The goalkeeper was Tony Goddard, who used to be at West Brom, and it flew over the top of him. No one was more shocked than me, I'd never hit the ball so sweetly in my life. They hit the crossbar, too, that day, so it was a bit of a strange game.

When he scored that screamer at Stamford Bridge were his eyes open? *Jim Lynch, Brentwood, England*

Probably not. I just punted it and in it went.

After the 1986–87 season you were presented with a trophy by the lads in The Winslow as the best all-round player. Did you consider this an honour? *Steve Fairclough, Toronto, Canada*

Yes, I did, because they were the people who went to all the games. It was a great honour that they thought I was good enough to win it and I was really pleased and proud.

How did he feel when he scored the own goal of the century at the Bernabeu when Everton played Real Madrid in a friendly? Were Everton inhibited by the ground/atmosphere/opposition? *Dave Morris, Glasgow, Scotland*

I thought that was a great goal. Not many people can say they scored at the Bernabeu, you know, so I was quite pleased, although I don't know how happy Bobby Mimms was. It was such an awesome place, but we did play a really young side that day. A few of the regular lads were out injured and we had a game the following week, so they didn't play. In spite of the result it was a great occasion and such an experience, and I still think it was a good goal.

How badly did the European ban affect the morale of the squad? Did it mean winning the Championship in 1987 was a touch anticlimatic as there was no place in the European Cup? *Colin Berry, Wavertree, Liverpool*

It was difficult knowing that we wouldn't be going into Europe and it had been such a long time since Everton had been there. The European ban was really upsetting because we had a great squad and we could really have gone on from there. We certainly wouldn't have broken up so quickly.

When Howard left it broke everybody's heart and then it all dissolved, lads were going off here and there and it was never the same again. I thought we could have gone on and on because we were so good and so young. We had years in front of us when we could have dominated English and European football.

Just before Alan scored our first goal against Sheffield Wednesday in the '86 FA Cup semi-final he flattened Glynn Snodin. The ball was returned to Harper over the prostrate Snodin's head and he slotted nicely over the advancing keeper.

Alan Harper

Did he think the referee was going to blow up and disallow the goal? *Gary Hughes, Whiston, Merseyside*

No, because I didn't foul him so it wasn't a free kick. The only thing I saw was Martin Hodge coming at me and I thought: 'Uh oh, it's time to hit it now.' Snodin ended up on the floor because he tripped over my leg.

Did you really mean to chip Martin Hodge? Who cares anyway, we love you for it and all went bonkers! *Paul McIver, Culcheth, Cheshire*

Of course I meant it! I had no choice other than to chip him. My family were at that match and they were right behind me when I scored. Before the game they had a few drinks and decided to have a bet on me scoring the first goal. They phoned me in the hotel and I told them I wasn't playing, so no one bothered to put the bet on. They could have made a few bob on me that day.

Was there a position you didn't play in 1986–87? Given that you redefined the term 'utility player' was it something you consciously worked at, or did you just find it easy to switch positions? *Steve Fairclough, Toronto, Canada*

I didn't play upfront. I don't think I could because it's so scary, and I didn't play in goal, so the only shirts I didn't wear were one and nine. I didn't mind where I played because I didn't really have a favourite position. As long as I was getting a game it made absolutely no difference. I was used to playing in different positions from when I was a kid and I found it easy to adapt. I was just happy to get on the pitch. I got 34 games on the trot in midfield once when Reidy was out injured.

Which players were his best mates off the pitch? *Osmo Tapio Räihälä, Helsinki, Finland*

Howard was into the 'team-spirit-building' exercises and I don't know if people paired off as best mates as such. We all got on together and did everything as a team. We socialised, played golf and formed cricket teams, and we were a unit on and off the pitch.

What's your favourite Everton moment? *Mike Prenton, Leeds, England*

That has to be John Bailey scoring at Goodison against Luton when it bounced over the keeper and into the net. He always says that was deliberate, honestly, he does.

Wasn't he frustrated when he would come in for someone injured, say at right-back, play some stormers and then get moved when the injury cleared? *San Presland, New Brighton, Merseyside*

When that happened I knew I was going to get a game somewhere else so it didn't bother me or affect me at all.

Bluekipper.com think you look like Plug out of the Bash Street Kids. Do you agree? *Paul McIver, Culcheth, Cheshire*

Yeah, I do. When I was at Liverpool Sammy Lee christened me Plug and still calls me Plug when I see him even now, so that's a fair shout!

You appeared to have a special bond with Big Nev. True? *Mike Prenton, Leeds, England*

He was my room-mate so we were close and really good friends. In training, I liked going in goal and he liked going out, so that's why we ended up swapping round. If you look at the size of him next to me we must have looked ridiculous when we were together. The good thing about Nev was that he didn't drink, so when we roomed together he used to wake up early and make me a cup of tea.

Did the players really get on as well as it seemed? *Mike Prenton, Leeds, England*

As corny as it sounds, the answer is yes. What a bunch of lads, every single one was brilliant. We all enjoyed each other's company and there was a big family atmosphere. If somebody was dropped or injured everyone would rally round and help them out. It was magic in those days, there was a fantastic team spirit.

What was it like to always be the twelfth man? *Osmo Tapio Räihälä, Helsinki, Finland*

It was never a problem to me because I always thought I was one of the best twelve players at the club and Kevin Richardson felt the same. Now they have five subs kitted out on the bench, but back then there was only one, so it was special because some of them didn't even get a shirt.

You seemed to carry a lot of respect amongst the players. Was it your pre-match keepy-ups? *Mike Prenton, Leeds, England*

Probably, yeah. I was the best and no one could beat me, although Adrian Heath always claims he could. In fact, we still talk about it now, but I'm sticking to my guns on this one. I was the keepy-up king.

Alan Harper

Could you ask Alan if he realises that Everton never lost a game in which he scored? *Billy Williams, Cologne, Germany*

I didn't know that. I only scored four, though, so I can't get too carried away.

What did he think of the Lineker season as opposed to Andy Gray? *Frank Hargreaves, Anfield, Liverpool*

They were such different people in personality and as players. You can't knock what Gary did because he scored plenty of goals, but we changed our style of play to accommodate him and never won anything. Andy Gray was a great character on and off the pitch. He was robust and different class. Him and Sharpie were just awesome together.

Would you ask Alan if it helped motivate him when the crowd picked on him? *Stuart Roberts, Guildford, England*

I didn't really pay much attention to it and it never bothered me. Every player tries to give 100 per cent and it's annoying when you don't play well. It's still the same now, but I hope the players who get a bit of stick can take it in their stride, work hard and do a better job. I don't believe any player goes out there with the intention of playing badly. Anyway, you shouldn't be listening to the fans, you should be busy concentrating on what you're doing.

Please tell Alan that I keep saying that we would never have won all those things in the mid-'80s without him. Howard signed him three times, twice at Everton and once at Man City. What are his thoughts about Howard as a man and as a manager? *Osmo Tapio Räihälä, Helsinki, Finland*

I thought he was great. He was good to me, he helped me a lot, but most of all he gave me a chance. He was a magnificent man–manager who knew how to handle players and get the best out of them. He was hard but fair, and I think that's a great quality in this game. I always had the utmost respect for him and I still do, both as a man and a manager.

Why didn't Warren Aspinall make it big time? *Osmo Tapio Räihälä, Helsinki, Finland*

It boils down to the individual and the way you go about things. Warren was an easy-going and happy-go-lucky lad who wasn't the hardest trainer. There have been a few like that, but you've got to have a bit of luck as well, sometimes, and it's a case of being in the right place at the right time.

Does he remember the roars whenever he used to save Big Nev's penalties in the warm-ups at away games? *Mick Abrams, Newcastle upon Tyne, England*

I can still hear them now. We had a cup game against Stoke and Nev and me were taking penalties at each other. Everyone else had gone in, but the crowd were laughing so much that we stayed. We got a right old bollocking when we came in because the Gaffer wanted to give us his team talk. That was the day Howard opened the windows in the dressing-room and told us to listen to the Evertonians singing for us. He said there was no way we could lose, we had to win it for them. When we went out the crowd were going berserk and it certainly did the trick.

Looking back, does he feel his career went well as he was able to contribute to a great team, or would he have preferred to have been a regular in a weaker side? *Neil Wolstenholme, Muswell Hill, north London*

Oh no, my career has been smashing. I've been so lucky and a lot of people can only dream of winning what we did. I'd have hated to play in a weaker team, we always ran on the pitch confident that we would win every pass, every tackle and every game.

Did he ever resent the fact that he was the designated jack-of-all-trades and was never fully recognised for all his efforts, whereas Paul Power played just one season for us and won player of the year? *Darryl Ng, Singapore*

Paul had a great year and you can't knock that. Labels like 'jack-of-all-trades' and 'utility player' never bothered me as long as I felt I'd contributed to the team. I thought Paul Power deserved to be player of the year because he had a fantastic season.

As a supposed long-time drinking buddy of Howard Kendall, in the boozing stakes, who had the most hollow legs? *San Presland, New Brighton, Merseyside*

The whole team seemed to have hollow legs. Peter Reid and Mark Higgins could certainly drink a few. I think we tried to outlast each other. We were frightened to go to bed because it was more than your life was worth to throw the towel in, so we all stuck together and it was all done as a team-building exercise. At least, that's what Howard told us.

Ask him to name his all-time best Everton team and where

would he have played in it? *Steve Kirkwood, Crowthorne, Berkshire, England*

Southall in goal, then a back four of Stevens, Van den Hauwe, Ratters and Bailey. Steven, Reid, Brace and Sheeds in midfield. Upfront Andy Gray and Sharpie and Inchy as sub. I wouldn't be in it; I'd be there as a fan.

Exactly which medals did he win with Everton during the glory years – my records differ? *Billy Williams, Cologne, Germany*

Two Championships, one European Cup-Winners' cup, FA Cup winners and losers, Milk Cup losers – remember the one nobody wanted to win? Four Charity Shield, and I think that's it.

How many nicknames did he have? A lad he recently coached at Burnley said Neville Southall called him 'Bones'. Please set the record straight. What are your nicknames and why? *Gary Hughes, Whiston, Merseyside*

Nev used to call me Bones because I was so thin at the time. There was Zico and there's one I haven't got a clue about which is Mooncat – I suppose the lads in the Gwladys Street will know about that, but I don't. The one I get called most of all is Bertie. I still get called that now and I answer to it. That came from Roy Evans at Liverpool. I was always moaning and he called me Bertie after Albert Tatlock. Colin was reserve-team coach at Everton when I was at Liverpool and he heard them calling me Bertie. He started it off when I got here and it stuck.

I assume he's still involved in coaching the youngsters. If so, how good is Steven Schumacher? *Richard Marland, Waterloo, Liverpool*

He's a Schoolboy International and he has all the attributes to be a good player, but he needs some luck and to work hard. All kids need to work on their weaknesses. He's played for England since he was about 14, so if they keep picking him then he could be getting somewhere, but there's a lot of work involved early on.

Does he enjoy working with the youngsters on what appears to be a very tight budget? *Dominic McGough, Ellesmere Port, Wirral*

I work with the lads aged 15 to 17. It keeps you young teaching the kids and they're all good lads. They enjoy it and if they want to play for Everton they will, I don't think money has got an awful lot to do with it. The proof of that is the Under-19s and the reserves, who are really successful.

Are there any real talents amongst the kids? Is anyone on the brink of being ready for the first team yet? *Richard Marland, Waterloo, Liverpool*

There are loads of talented kids, but thinking of the first team, that's really hard to say. It depends on what Walter Smith wants. I see talented players but I don't see any breaking into the first team just yet.

I've heard that Martin Keown really hates Chelsea. Did Alan ever have a pet-hate team? *Steve Kirkwood, Crowthorne, Berkshire, England*

I used to hate going to Highbury to play Arsenal. It was a lovely stadium but I just couldn't get myself round it at all.

Is there any hope of the club matching the excellence of its youth scouting and coaching with excellence of facilities in the near future, and do our current facilities embarrass him? *Neil Wolstenholme, Muswell Hill, north London*

I'd like to think that in the future there'll be an influx of money and we can get everything sorted out and back where we belong. It doesn't embarrass me because the facilities don't make the player. All you need is a bit of grass and a ball. The facilities help, but the kids just want to be on a football pitch. We won the Under-19s league and we haven't got any facilities, so what does that tell you?

We hear a lot about behind the scenes, such as the academy site left to rot, the reserves being scrapped, etc., so what is his view of the coaching structure in place at the club? *Mick Abrams, Newcastle upon Tyne, England*

The coaching is great from the young ones upward. You don't win things with Rangers and then become a bad coach. Archie is Scotland's number two, Andy Holden runs the reserves, there's Colin Harvey, former player and manager. They're all successful football men and I think the set-up is great.

What does he think of players these days who are seemingly happy to sit on the bench every week and collect their wages? Has the hunger for success left the game? *Mick Abrams, Newcastle upon Tyne, England*

I think so. The money has made a big difference and they don't want to play as much now. Nothing can hurt them because they have so much cash – if they get fined it means nothing. You see a lot of average players now earning lots of money. They don't really want to play and they're happy to sit there and pick up their pay cheque. I'm not the type of person who would want to sit on the bench week in, week out. I wanted to be playing every single game.

Why did he sling his hook to Dublin with Steve Bird and his late father, Joe Bird, during the weekend of the '95 FA Cup final? Is he mad, or what? *Billy Williams, Cologne, Germany*

The people I went with are mad Evertonians and we couldn't get tickets for the game. We said we'd go to Dublin rather than stay in Liverpool because we wanted to go somewhere different. We flew over and it was full of Man United and Liverpool supporters, but we watched the game wearing our Dogs of War T-shirts.

The board situation at Everton – did it ever get talked about at player level? *Frank Hargreaves, Anfield, Liverpool*

No, never. It's got nothing to do with players and we were all too busy playing football and team-spirit-building to be bothered with any of that. All the behind-the-scenes stuff was sorted out by other people.

After having taken so much unfair stick from the Everton fans what is his take on the Nyarko situation? Does he have any sympathy for Nyarko at all? *Stuart Roberts, Guildford, England*

All players get stick, it doesn't matter who they are – just ask Duncan Ferguson. The fans have their favourites and they don't like others. You've just got to get on with it and not worry about what the supporters are saying. You have to get on the pitch and do your job. I can only imagine that Nyarko must be a sensitive lad.

Did he mind getting woken up early by Freddie Starr? *Alan Welsh, Warrington, England*

That was the morning of the FA Cup final at the hotel in Beaconsfield. He arrived and woke everybody up doing his German walk and telling jokes. He was a mad Evertonian and he wanted to join in the fun. Some of the lads get up early and some like to lie in bed till midday. Andy Gray was normally a late riser and he wasn't too happy about it.

If you could re-run one moment of your career what would it be? *Antony Richman, Johannesburg, South Africa*

I made my debut at Goodison against Stoke and was standing in the tunnel waiting to go on to the pitch. 'Z-Cars' started playing on the PA and I heard the crowd roar. I hadn't played in front of a big crowd before and it was the loudest noise I'd ever heard. Those few seconds were so precious and magical and certainly the most exciting of my life. If I could bottle a moment and save it forever, then that would be it.

DAVE HICKSON

Born 30 October 1929
May 1948 – September 1955 and
August 1957 – November 1959
Apprentice

I was only 14 when I got the call to come to Goodison. I finished school at half past three, jumped on the bus and arrived about an hour later. The players had just finished training and the first people I saw were Joe Mercer and T.G. Jones. It quite took my breath away because they were idols of mine and from that moment I knew I belonged here.

While I was learning my trade I played for the Cheshire Army Cadets and Dixie Dean was the manager. He really took me under his wing, he spent a lot of time nurturing me and he got me a place in the England Army Cadets team when I was 16. I made my debut for Everton against Leeds on 1 September 1951, just short of my 22nd birthday. We won 2–1.

As tradition dictated, Everton took this valiant and determined warhorse and handed him the revered number nine shirt. There was nobody quite like him, untouchable in the air, strong and fast and with two good feet. Our radical blonde was an amalgam of spirit and damage and thought nothing of spilling blood for the royal blue cause.

We had to look after ourselves on the park because it was a very physical game back then. I would give them three chances, and then I'd let them know I was playing.

They don't make them like that any more.
Can you believe your eyes? It's Big Davey Hickson, the Cannonball Kid.

I tend to think of him as a heading specialist, but he scored a fair number of goals with both feet. What were his best footballing abilities? *David Catton, Sheffield, England*

I always thought of myself as an all-round player. I could always score, but I preferred to make goals, I used to love that. I managed to get quite a few, but it was important the people I played with scored too. In our promotion season, John Willie Parker got 36 and I clocked 29, so that wasn't bad – 65 between us!

Who did you support when you were young? *Michael O'Connell, Galway, Republic of Ireland*

Man United, I'm sorry to say. I was born in Salford and came to Ellesmere Port when I was a baby. I used to go back to visit my Gran and we liked Man United. I would follow Everton and Liverpool from a distance, but mainly the Blues because I knew Joe Mercer. I admired him enormously, he was one of my heroes and came from Ellesmere Port, too.

How much did the two years in the army hurt your career? *Steve Fairclough, Toronto, Canada*

My National Service lasted over two years, that's a long time out of a short career and it did hurt. It was so close too, because Theo Kelly, the Everton secretary, tried his best to get me out of it, but it had already been signed and sealed, and so off I went to Egypt. I was 18 at the time.

While I was away Everton got relegated and the worst part was knowing that I might have been able to get into that team and try to do something to save them.

The majority of Everton fans are too young to have witnessed relegation. What was it like to be relegated? *Tim Gunnion, Frankfurt, Germany*

It was bad. We went down to the Second Division in 1949, I came out of the army in 1950 and we came back in 1954. I became part of the new team to come through to try and get them back up again. Nobody likes that feeling at all.

Does he feel a bit aggrieved at not winning much in his time at Everton? *David Chow, Manchester, England*

I do and I don't. I didn't win much, but what I hope I did was help to get Everton back into the First Division. That was the most important thing and it was my main achievement. The feeling of bringing a team back up is brilliant, and there's nothing can compare to it.

Dave Hickson

I once went as twelfth man to Charlton, and at that time you didn't get on the pitch, it was a case of wheeling skips, but I got a feel for the First Division and I liked it, I knew that was where we belonged.

Who was the player of his era that he admired the most? *Mike Coville, New York, USA*

Tom Finney was the man I admired most and he was my hero, but I used to love playing against Billy Wright, he was great. John Charles was one of the top players of his day and one of the best I played against.

Does he remember scoring a magnificent 20-yarder against Liverpool in the so-called Merseyside Floodlit Cup? *John Lloyd, Stirling, Scotland*

I think we beat them 3–1. Laurie Hughes was centre-half that night, the man who eventually signed me for Liverpool when he became manager.

Just how did Malcolm Barrass manage to stay on the field during the '53 FA Cup semi-final at Maine Road when Bolton beat us 4–3? According to my dad, Barrass 'kicked the shit' out of Hickson that day and at the end of the match Dave walked off all bloodied and battered. *Ken Myers, California, USA*

We were 4–0 down. We came back to 4–3 and missed a penalty, so we should really have taken them to extra time. Something terrible happened there and they reckon it was Barrass. Whoever it was, he really belted me. He thumped me so hard that my eyes were filled with blood for weeks and weeks and my mum went mad because I was disfigured for ages. It was terrible, and he'd never have gotten away with it now, he'd be charged with assault.

I can't remember much about that game to tell you the truth. I do remember I was through on goal, I saw it on Pathé News later, and I still can't believe I missed it. If I hadn't had concussion I'm sure I would have put it away.

Does he remember playing against a complete yard-dog of a centre-half, Ronnie Noble of Rotherham United, when Everton were in the Second Division? *David Catton, Sheffield, England*

I certainly do. He was a hard player, but he wasn't the hardest. I never feared anybody, but the man who used to give me trouble was Danny Malloy from Cardiff, he was the one who gave me the toughest game. If he said he'd do something you believed him. Malcolm Allison used to try to threaten me and I would just say: 'Oh yeah?' Noble was hard, but nothing I couldn't handle.

Is it true that you hit a six clean over the poplar trees at the old Bowaters cricket ground? *John Roberts, Chester, England*

Oh, I could easily have done that. I come from round there and my Mum and dad worked at Bowaters. I probably did the same at Bootle Cricket Club too. Everton used to play them as part of the pre-season training and they'd always give us a good game there. I loved playing cricket and I played every Sunday for Port Sunlight until a few years ago when I got the job here at Goodison.

John Willie Parker was a goal-line hero. Did Dave mind having to work so much harder for his goals than John Willie? *David Catton, Sheffield, England*

Not really. I always believed there are players for players and they hunt in pairs. You've got to have that blend and I think John Willie was ideal; we used to read each other. I liked playing with Bobby Collins too. Roger Hunt and I played well together, we scored 20-odd each at Liverpool.

Do either of the following rate as his best goal for the club:
a) the winner against Aston Villa in the FA Cup in '53
b) the winner against Man United in the same year? *John Lloyd, Stirling, Scotland*

They're probably the best-remembered goals, but I always say one of my best goals was at West Brom when we beat them 3–2 and mine was the winner. I went from the halfway line with their big centre-half, Ray Barlow, chasing me. There were three or four of them closing in on me. I passed them all and scored, but I was absolutely shattered at the end of it. The rest of the team jumped on me in a mad celebration and, to tell you the truth, I nearly got crushed to death. I should have kept moving. That was my best goal, but the other two are well remembered because they were also good.

What was his biggest disappointment as an Everton player? *Mike Coville, New York, USA*

Other than leaving the club, getting beat in that FA Cup semi-final at Maine Road. We'd have won it too, because we'd have beaten Blackpool and Stan Matthews would never have got his medal, I'll tell you that much. They were a good side, but we had a great spirit at that time.

It was certainly the bitterest pill I ever had to swallow because we were Second Division and had already beaten all the good teams. Then we came up against Bolton.

As I never had the privilege of seeing Davie Hickson play in the

flesh, which current-day player would he say most resembled him (of any team)? *Rob Hamilton, Melbourne, Australia*

Maybe Dion Dublin when he's having a good day.

There were a number of games in which Dave got his name taken twice yet finished the game on the pitch. This was in the days before two bookings meant dismissal. Would he have stayed on the pitch for long with today's referees? *David Catton, Sheffield, England*

People always ask me if I would be off all the time, but I don't think I would. You would adapt to the conditions of today, and on the reverse side of that I probably would have got even more penalties because I was always getting walloped.

In those days, they used to let things go and it was bad at times. I was a big lad and it was deemed to be all right if they wanted to kick me a bit. If you knew the whistle was going to blow and you would be protected then that would be great, I'd get more penalties and free kicks, and probably more goals. It's all right them saying it's harder to score today, if you've got a winger who can put that ball where you want it, it doesn't matter what game you're playing or where it is.

There wasn't a lot of revenge and retaliation on my part, I just seemed to get booked all the time and usually for things I shouldn't have, like the time I got booked for giving the ref a dirty look.

In light of an article in The Guardian can you ask Dave Hickson about this one?: 'I was left out at Everton, I think for disciplinary reasons, but I was playing all right. Then Liverpool came in and it seemed as though Everton would let me go.' What was the full story? *Mike Royden, Ellesmere Port, South Wirral*

It wasn't anything I'd done wrong, it was just suspension from being booked so many times. A lot of people say I never got a chance to play for England because of my disciplinary record. Walter Winterbottom was the manger then, and he didn't like that kind of thing at all. He wouldn't let anybody who'd been booked in the team!

Of all the quotes from Evertonians I remember his famous 'I'd have broken bones for all the clubs I played for, but I'd have died for Everton' is the one that I recall most. What exactly was it about Everton that made him go weak at his knees? *Darryl Ng, Singapore*

Yes, those were my actual words, and I meant it too. I don't know what it is about this club, it's so homely and friendly and I took to them right away. A lot of people ask me why I went to Liverpool, but I didn't request a transfer. Phil Taylor had his eye on me and he saw that Everton had left me out. I felt as though I was playing well enough to stay in the team, but they left me out a couple of times and that was when Liverpool made their move. I didn't want to leave the city and I wanted to play top-flight football. I was about 28 then and I thought I might as well just do it. I never wanted to go because I love this place.

Ever since I can remember Dave was the icon in our house. I wasn't taken to the match until my eighth birthday in 1958, so although by then he had peaked I was still in awe of him. Any stoppages in the game I would look for Davey to see what he was doing. He never disappointed me. Like every player he had off days, but he never hid or looked disinterested like certain other modern-day icons (sorry Dunc, but as much as I love you there are times when you frustrate) I remember sitting in the Goodison Road stand when a fan ran on with a banner saying 'if Dave goes we all go'. This was my first Everton trauma and my dad assured me he would not go, but a couple of days later he sat me down to have a man-to-man chat. I was terrified as a couple of months earlier this was the way he started to tell me my mum had died, and when he told me he was going to Anfield I vowed never to go to a game again. This lasted until the next game. How did you feel when that fan ran on and every one applauded you? Roy Coyne, Wavertree, Liverpool

It was fantastic. There were quite a few who ran on that day, and I believe the day I made my debut at Liverpool, Everton played away at Newcastle and got beat 8–2. After that game there was a demonstration about me going, but that day (at Anfield) there were a few on the pitch.

How did the Liverpool players treat you when you went over the park? Stuart Roberts, Guildford, England

Oh, they were brilliant. Ronnie Moran and Billy Liddell were the first ones I met there and I can't speak highly enough of them, they made me feel very welcome. Liverpool did well really, they finished third in the Second Division the two years I was there and they could have gone up. Bill Shankly came halfway through my time and he wanted to change it all and bring his own five or six players in. They didn't go up the following year, but the year after that they did and the rest is history.

Dave Hickson

Please ask him if he thought Anfield was the lowest of the low as far as stadia were concerned in those days? (It was, believe me.) *Dave Kelly, Blackburn, England*

It was just on a par with Goodison, to be perfectly honest. Liverpool have built it up now, but in time I think they will have to move as well, even though they've spent a lot of money. I don't think we could share a stadium. I'm not biased, but I just don't think it could happen.

Did you feel betrayed when you were sold across the park? *Ray Finch, Havant, England*

Liverpool is a great club, but I didn't want to go really, so I did feel a teeny bit betrayed. I started here so young and played my way all the way through, the D team, the C team, B and A. I had to go into the army for a spell, but I signed for Everton and because I'd played for four years as a junior they gave me a bit of a retainer, I think it was £4 a week, just to hold me.

They say you should 'never go back'. Did he ever regret returning to Everton? *Tim Gunnion, Frankfurt, Germany*

No, not for a minute.

As young lads, my dad and his cousin saved their money and bought a wedding present and a card for Dave Hickson and his wife, Pat. They took it round to Dave's house in Mostyn Avenue, and were invited in for lunch plus a few autographs. I just wondered if there was any chance Dave remembers this. It's a long shot, I know, but my dad was made up to meet his hero. *Keith Giles, Perth, Australia*

A lot of people would visit me in those days but I didn't invite them all in so they must have been nice lads. That's lovely that they've remembered me and taken the time to write in.

He is famous for sporting his quiff hairstyle. Did he still have it during the feather-cut days of the mid-'80s? *Kenny Fogarty, Amsterdam, Holland*

I've always had the same '50s haircut and it's helped along with a mixture of Vaseline and soap, which I rub into my hands and onto my hair.

His hair. I should have such hair. Did it help with his heading? *Gary Hughes, Whiston, Merseyside*

I suppose it did, yes. The ball never bothered me.

I'd ask Dave who he thinks has the best hair in the modern game.
Mark Hoskins, Dublin, Republic of Ireland
There's David Ginola, he's got nice hair, but I won't be growing mine like that because I don't like it to be too long.

Are you sick to death answering all the 'hair' questions? *Steve Fairclough, Toronto, Canada*
No, not at all, it's my hallmark and everybody always makes some kind of reference to it.

Did the run-up to the Wimbledon game a few years ago bring back any unpleasant relegation memories? *Tim Gunnion, Frankfurt, Germany*
There have been a couple of times it was all brought back to me in the last few years. Coventry was the other. We've certainly had a couple of scares. It's not very nice at all, but they said back then that it would never happen again, and I honestly don't think it will. We've got too many good players to go down. All we need now is a bit of consistency, we need to pull together and gain a bit of confidence and we'll be fine.

Does he consider receiving the Millennium Giant of the 1950s award his greatest achievement? *David Chow, Manchester, England*
That was marvellous and a great honour. It was a terrific feeling, especially when you think of the great players in that era, Peter Farrell, Tommy Eglington, Wally Fielding, there were so many. To be voted the best was one of the greatest achievements of my life.

Who would he have voted for? *David Chow, Manchester, England*
I would say Tommy Eglington. He was a nice fella too, Tommy.

How has he stayed so fit over the years? Did he drink, smoke or have any other vices? *David Catton, Sheffield, England*
I don't drink a lot. I have one now and again, but I would never drink and drive, so that puts a stop to that. I still train a couple of times a week and I play for the 'Over the Hill Mob' every week, weather permitting.

Which players of the past does he think would be most capable of playing to today's style and which 'greats' would struggle (if any)? *San Presland, New Brighton, Merseyside*

Dave Hickson

I always think that good players can adapt. Tom Finney was my idol. I think Tom could have played in any era. Stanley Matthews? Of course he could, he'd have that much more room now, we didn't have any space then. I think all the great players of my time would adapt, there's no danger and suggesting that they couldn't is absolute rubbish.

I still think that the football played in those days was better than the present play. What does he think? *Mike Coville, New York, USA*
Well, we could say that about everything, but it was probably more exciting then because the referees let it flow. People would go hunting other players, it was end-to-end stuff and there was a lot of action in the goalmouth. Now it's all stop and start and a lot faster, but if you can get a run and nobody's allowed to tackle you then you're bound to be a lot faster.

In those days, the players were as fit as they are today without any doubt. If you talk about the Dixie Dean era, at that time the training wasn't so intense, but from the late '50s it got strict. I certainly couldn't have been any fitter. We used to take bangs and knocks, today they're finely tuned athletes and much more fragile. It's a different kind of fitness. We had strength and stamina, and now they have speed and they're not allowed to tackle too much. I like to think it was better then, and more technical now.

I remember my dad telling me some story about a game against Bolton, around 1958, where he ripped this other player's shorts off (or almost off). I think the name was Barrass. *Brian Sayle, Wallasey, Wirral*
I don't remember ripping anybody's shorts off, but I had a right old tussle with Barrass. In fact, I had many a rough game against him, but it probably stemmed from the semi-final. We played them a couple of times the following year, and there was always an element of revenge.

In about 1953–54 I was nine years old and idolised Dave Hickson. I met him in a filling station in Walmer Road, Waterloo. My dad had just stopped to fill up his car and noticed Dave when he went in to pay, so he called me in to meet him. The filling station doubled as a second-hand car showroom. Was he involved in the second-hand car business as a sideline during his playing days? *David Catton, Sheffield, England*
No, I wasn't, but I got a car from there and I was visited quite often because I knew the chap who owned the place.

In his time with Huddersfield did he recognise the qualities in one Bill Shankly that would make him world famous? *Tim Gunnion, Frankfurt, Germany*

Oh, yeah, I did, really. Bill lived for football and boxing, he was mad about boxing, he loved it. He came from Carlisle as Andy Beechy's second-in-command and you could see he was going to be a great man. And talking about Huddersfield, you could tell Denis Law was going to be great too. I played inside forward to Denis when he was about 16. When he arrived, he was a weedy lad with glasses, Shankly built him up and the rest is history. Denis is a smashing bloke too, I really like him.

If he could change any rule in football what would it be? *San Presland, New Brighton, Merseyside*

One thing I've never really got over is having a number 35 on the field, I'd go back to the 1–12 again and try and work something out from that. I suppose they have to have these squad systems with all the merchandising, but it's a shame. I don't like seeing a number 23 run out on the field and there's no number 9 or 10 playing. How could that have been allowed to happen? I don't know, but if they could work something out then I'd be a lot happier.

In view of the fact that Barmby has caused himself so much bother in moving across the park, did Dave try and give him some advice on how to handle it? *Jon Berman, West Derby, Liverpool*

I didn't really, no. Pat, my wife, was very friendly with his wife and used to sit with her every game in the Joe Mercer Suite. Nothing was said at all, it was kept quiet, and it was all done very quickly, which was why it was such a shock. He made a statement that he wanted to play for his boyhood team and he got his wish. It was probably the way he said it that the fans found difficult to swallow. It was a bit different with me, I went there for football and I found it was great, but my heart has always been at Everton and always will be. All I can say is good luck to him.

Which of the post-Hickson Everton centre-forwards did he find most exciting and why? *Tony Kennedy, Loughborough, England*

Joe Royle was good, but he never improved to his potential. I thought he was going to go on to be better, but he was always steady and reliable. Graeme Sharp was great, he was exciting to watch, and so was Bob Latchford, but Sharpie was more mobile than Bob. I like Kevin Campbell too.

Graeme Souness said that Everton had bigger potential as a club

than Liverpool. Is he right? *Steve Kirkwood, Crowthorne, Berkshire, England*

I won't argue with that. I always think that we have much bigger potential than Liverpool. We've been up there with them and I don't think we're far away now. Man United are outstanding, but to be perfectly honest, there's not much between any of the others.

If we name bits of Goodison/Bellefield appropriately (i.e. The David Unsworth Fast Food Bar, The Danny Williamson Treatment Room, The Terry Darracott Main Stand Roof, the Stuart Barlow Substitute's Bench) which bit would be his? *San Presland, New Brighton, Merseyside*

The Dave Hickson/Gwladys Street Upright!

What was it like playing for all three Merseyside clubs? Was it strange and what sort of reception did you get from each set of supporters, especially from the Blues after his (Barmbyesque) move to Liverpool? *Ste Daley, Speke, Liverpool*

Every one of them was great. On my debut for Liverpool they won 2–1, and I got the two goals against Villa, another old club; I'd spent four months there. Peter McParland scored the goal for them and he was a great player too. The Liverpool fans were made up, and I remember a chap running on the pitch and saying: 'You're one of ours now'. I thought: 'Hhhhm, yeah?' It was strange, but they made me welcome.

Tranmere was fantastic. I spent just over two years there, and that's a family club like Everton. Then I went to Ballymena, Northern Ireland, as manager, but the troubles started in 1969 and we had to think about things because it was quite bad then. I knew a couple of people who were threatened so it wasn't worth taking any chances.

If we had to move from Goodison what would he like to see happen to the current site? *Rob Hamilton, Melbourne, Australia*

It would be great if we could get it for an academy, then the youth teams and Everton Ladies could play here rather than the Halton Stadium in Widnes. I think we own the ground so we might have to sell it to help fund a new stadium. Maybe we could get some European funding, but we'd have to put some cash in ourselves.

Where does he want the new stadium to be? *Steve Kirkwood, Crowthorne, Berkshire, England*

It's too late now, but I always thought the old airport would have been perfect. It was my first choice since the idea of a ground move was mooted. The access was good, and looking to the future, the airport is nearby for when we get into Europe, and for London. There could be hotels, training facilities and the ground, all right there, but it's all been built on now. That would have been ideal. Aintree would have been a good one too. It could have been there in the middle with the racetrack around the outside. It had the stand, so you could still see over the top to the other side of the track when the racing was on.

Was there any decision he made about his career that he would have changed, given the chance? *San Presland, New Brighton, Merseyside*

Not really. I think I made the right choice by coming to Everton in the first place. To tell the truth, I did have a chance to go to Liverpool at the very beginning, I've still got the letters from way back, but I chose Everton and I know it was the right one.

Does he think that Everton will rise again? *Mike Coville, New York, USA*

Yes, definitely. They will rise again, whether it's at Goodison Park or the new stadium. The new stadium could be the catalyst, and that would be a good place to start.

Dave Hickson was my favourite and my idol as a teenager. I remember the FA Cup game versus Man United on Saturday, 14 February 1953, as though it was yesterday. I was four days shy of my 13th birthday and I was in the Gwladys Street End. The crowd was over 77,000 and I had a lot of trouble seeing the game, so we found a rubbish bin down in the bottom of the stands and took it up the passageway steps and stood on it to see the match. The only problem was that the crowd kept on swaying back, so we had to jump off the bin and carry it down the steps every few minutes. Obviously, the most memorable moment was seeing Dave scoring the winning goal with blood streaming down his face. Does he have as fond memories of that match as me? How bad was the injury above his eye? It looked terrible from my vantage point, but eye cuts bleed badly and as a 12-year-old I was easily impressed with blood. *Mike Coville, New York, USA*

I have a very vivid memory of that game, I can still see it as though it was this morning. They were third from the top and we were halfway in the Second Division. Jack Rowley scored for them and I scored the winner in the Gwladys Street End after Tommy Eglington had got the equaliser. I've been on the pitch since and seen the spot I scored from. It's unbelievable really, in the very corner of the 18-yard box, and it went into the other corner right along the floor. I had to go off and get a few stitches in my eye, but I came back on because there were no subs in those days.

I should have taken it easy, I suppose, but the ball came so invitingly that I just had to head it – if I could have made it 3–1 then it would have killed the game. I headed it against the post and my eye split open again. It was quite bad, but maybe not as bad as it looked.

What do you think of the wages of the modern player? Knowing that you have had to work for a living since you gave up football, I guess a few bob more during your playing days would have helped. *John Roberts, Chester, England*

I suppose so, but it never mattered to me. I just loved the game, and although money is nice, it isn't everything. I think health is everything in life. If you can hang on to that, then you're very wealthy indeed. I'm not rich, but Pat and I just get by and we're happy with that. It would have been nice to be born a bit later, but only because I'd still be able to play now. I'd play for nothing, and I always would have done, that's how I feel about football and how I feel about Everton. It's my life.

MARK HIGGINS

Born 29 September 1958
August 1976 – December 1985
Apprentice

Sometimes, destiny deals a cruel hand and we can only dream of what might have been. There can be no twist of fate quite so ironic as a career-ending injury diagnosed at the tender age of 26 and leaving us all wringing our hands in despair.

I hand you to the man who knew him better than anybody, his teammate, partner and ally, Kevin Ratcliffe.

> Mark was a man when he was 13 and on the verge of an England call-up when his bad-luck finally caught up with him. It was a hernia that floored him, which by today's standards is a very simple injury. He was young enough to get over it and would only have been out a couple of months with the medical advances we've made since.
>
> Even more tragic than the fact that he didn't collect a single medal in the Glory Days is that I have absolutely no doubt that Higgy would have been an integral part of the Everton team for years to come. He would have delayed Derek Mountfield's inclusion and I'm not sure that there would have even been a Dave Watson. He was the pinnacle of the good times and the cornerstone of our team.
>
> Whenever I think about it, it makes me sad. Mark was a fantastic player, a dear friend, a good professional and a great man.

Mark Higgins, step up to the microphone and tell it like it is.

I remember seeing him play for England schoolboys at Goodison. He was exceptional in that he played two seasons for them. Whenever they were in trouble he would be sent upfront to pop

in a goal or two. Did he ever fancy being a Duncan Ferguson type?
San Presland, New Brighton, Merseyside

I got 19 caps for England schoolboys, which was a record, and I would have loved to be a striker but I don't think I had the skill to play upfront. I'd been playing football since I was nine and I was always the centre-half so that was all I really knew. But everybody wanted to score goals and the centre-forwards earned more money, too.

Did he have offers from other teams before he signed for Everton? *Julian Jackson, Hong Kong, SAR of PRC*

Man City, Man United, Tottenham, Liverpool and Arsenal all offered terms. If you play for England schoolboys then you're meant to be the cream of the crop, so there was quite a lot of interest in me. From my side, there was never much to think about because I knew where I wanted to be. Everton was a massive club, the training facilities at Bellefield were magnificent and the fans had a great reputation.

Your father, the centre-half John Higgins, played for Bolton Wanderers and no doubt was a big influence on you. What were his views on your starting a career at Everton? *Stan Nuttall, Sunnyvale, California, USA*

As a young lad my father and I would often kick a ball around on the lawn. He gave me a love for football and a good grounding for the game. He won the FA Cup with Bolton in 1958 and played there for 13 years, but I chose Everton because they were my team and my father thought it was a great move. I did too. I love Scousers and the people at Everton were so friendly. I never regretted my decision for a minute.

He came up through the youth team. Was there any difference between players brought in and those who'd fought their way through? *Steve Kirkwood, Crowthorne, Berkshire, England*

When kids make their way through the ranks there seems to be a lot more loyalty than with players who are brought in. It's much closer-knit when you work your way up. You've grown up together and shared your dreams to make it to the first team. It's such a good feeling when you get there and you never take it for granted.

Do you remember your first wage? *Rob Burns, Chorley, England*

My very first wage as an apprentice was £8 a week and I was paying 50p stamp.

Mark Higgins

What was the general feeling among the squad when we got rid of Gordon Lee? *Osmo Tapio Räihälä, Helsinki, Finland*

It was a bit sad really, because the lads actually liked Gordon. He was a comedian and a genuinely funny guy. It seems that most of the fans didn't really rate him, but we thought he was great.

Were you always concentrating that hard or did it just look like that? *Steve Tynan, Aldershot, England*

I was always concentrating that hard. Once you put the shirt on you wear it with enormous pride and I always wanted to win every game.

Who gave him the biggest roasting of his career? *Michael O'Connell, Galway, Republic of Ireland*

Joe Jordan. We had a tussle when he was at Leeds. I was only 19 and after about five minutes I whacked him. I thought that was it and I was on top of my game. The next thing I knew I was on my back and he'd broken my nose. I didn't forget that for a long time.

What did you think of Mike Lyons and what did you learn from him? *Steve Tynan, Aldershot, England*

Lyonsy was a great player in my eyes. I played for years with him and he had such a big heart. To me he was Mr Everton. Mike taught me a lot because although he wasn't the most skilful player he always gave 110 per cent and his love for Everton rubbed off on me.

Did he think that the bunch of no-hopers that Howard signed could replace The Latch? *Osmo Tapio Räihälä, Helsinki, Finland*

The answer has to be no. When Howard first arrived he signed about six or seven new players very quickly and there were only two left after a year. He was very lucky he had a good keeper in Nev.

As a defender were you happy with your goal-scoring record and can you remember your best-ever goal? *Bernie Flood, Ellesmere Port, Wirral*

I didn't score many goals, I must admit, but I did score two in one game against Coventry. They were both headers and that game really sticks best in my memory. I only scored six in total, so that was a pretty productive day.

If you and Kevin Ratcliffe raced over 100 metres what would your times be? *Steve Tynan, Aldershot, England*

Kevin was far quicker than me. I don't know about times for certain, but I think mine would be about twelve seconds and Rat's would be ten. It would probably be the same now, only in minutes!

Who, in your opinion, is the greatest centre-half to have played for Everton? *Rob Marwood, Wigan, England*
Apart from myself? There's been too many greats to name just one: Labby, Roger Kenyon, who I had a lot of respect for, Ratters, Micky Lyons, Waggy – it's impossible to choose.

When he played his last game for Everton did he know it was going to be his last and, if so, how did he feel about that? *Michael O'Connell, Galway, Republic of Ireland*
My groins were giving me pain and I knew I would have to stop and rest. I definitely didn't think it was my last game in a blue shirt, but I knew it was going to be my last for a while. It was the quarter-final of the Milk Cup at home against West Ham.

I was driving to the match against QPR. I stopped at the traffic lights on Queens Drive and he pulled up beside me in his sponsored car. I gave him the thumbs up and he gave it back to me. We were both going to see Everton win the league. How badly did it hurt him attending as a spectator? *John Quinn, Tewkesbury, England*
When I think back, I sat watching Everton at Wembley seven times, going back to 1977 and the League Cup. It hurt, but I kind of got used to it.

I remember his introduction being heralded as the answer to our centre-half problems and he was touted as a future England player. Was his injury a direct result of the pressure from the club and the press to continue playing and was he playing on through the injuries? *Dominic McGough, Ellesmere Port, Wirral*
Yes, I was. It was hard because I'm a true Blue and I wanted to play, but at the time I was made captain the club was under pressure. Howard had nearly been sacked and he asked if I would play because he needed me. I'd been there for such a long time and I really wanted to be involved so I played, although I was being jabbed before each game. Now I think it's wrong and I wouldn't do it if I had my time again. I honestly believe it's the reason my career was cut short.

Mark Higgins

Who would be the last one standing in a team-drinking session?
Wayne Hughes, Northampton, England

Sadly, that would possibly be myself. It's something I'm not particularly proud of, but if we went out drinking I was always there at the death. If you asked the rest of the lads they'd probably confirm that.

How did he feel watching Ratcliffe collect all those trophies? I imagine it was mixed feelings for him. **Martin Smith, New Jersey, USA**

It was bittersweet. I was so pleased and happy for everyone, the supporters, the club and Rats, but on a personal level I was gutted. I knew that if it hadn't have been for my injury it would have been me.

I saw a photograph of you and Adrian Heath in the dressing-room after the Cup-Winners' Cup final. What was going through your mind at the time? **Bernie Flood, Ellesmere Port, Wirral**

The lads were all on an almighty high, but Inchy and myself were really quite depressed. I can still see that picture now: Inchy was wearing my sweatshirt and all the boots and the debris were scattered on the dressing-room floor.

Injury brought a premature end to your playing career at Everton, yet a year or two later you returned to the game with Man United. What were the circumstances behind this decision and, in retrospect, do you consider it the correct one? **Stan Nuttall, Sunnyvale, California, USA**

I was told I was finished in 1984 when I was still the club captain. I was 26. I went to Wembley when we won the FA Cup and I was sat on the bench when Rats went to lift it up. If it hadn't been for all the injuries I would have been up there collecting it. I was out for about 12 months and they told me I was finished. I had four operations on my groins and I came back and trained. It was going well and then I broke down. I went to London where a specialist told me I was finished. My groins had gone and I would have to hang my boots up. At that age it's one hell of a shock.

I went down to London again and underwent my fifth operation. I came back and trained by running alone around the golf course, and I felt better. I went to see Howard and I said: 'I'm only 28, I think there's a chance I can play again.' But Howard had a good squad then, they were doing well and they'd cashed in the insurance. He told me to go to Holland, but I didn't want to do that, I wanted to play in England.

I was really sick when I thought I'd given my time to Everton for all those years and now there was no place for me. That was when I went to Man United. I trained with them for three months and then I signed.

Thanks for your contribution to Everton FC. I loved watching you play and thought you would be club captain for years, but, unfortunately, it wasn't to be. The injury that effectively finished your Everton career, would it be curable today with modern methods? *Steve Tynan, Aldershot, England*

Yes, it would. With the technology available now I'd have been almost straight back. I'd have had the operation I had last of all and been back playing in seven or eight weeks, but we didn't recognise that at the time.

Did you feel guilty coming back after you were 'finished'? *Paul McIver, Culcheth, Cheshire*

Not at all, how could I feel guilty if I didn't want to finish in the first place? I've had people ask me that before because I had my insurance money, but I paid that all back. If anybody thinks that a player would want to retire at the age of 26 when you've a chance of winning the FA Cup and being picked for England then they would be absolutely insane.

Was he disappointed that Everton gave up on his injury prematurely when Big Ron gave him a chance out of nothing? *Dermot Nealon, Dublin, Republic of Ireland*

I was very disappointed, but not at Everton Football Club. It was down to Howard and myself. When I went back, Howard had built a good squad and I was happy about that, but it was a bit hard on me when I was there for ten and a half years and I actually played with a lot of pain and having jabs all the time. I think he should have given me a chance, but he wasn't prepared to take that gamble.

It was only after Howard had turned me down that I went elsewhere and Big Ron took me on. Man United paid back the money that Everton were due and I had to pay back mine, but the main thing was that I was back in the game and with another big club, although it's no secret that if I'd had the choice I'd have gone back to Everton.

How did Man United differ as a club when he went there? *Jim Lynch, Brentwood, England*

They're a very big club as well and it was nice to be in the 'big time' again. I would have much preferred to be wearing blue than red, but I was lucky to go into a good side with players I knew – Robson, Whiteside and Strachan were all good friends of mine. I was there for two and a half years, but I had been at Everton since I was a lad so that's where my true love really lies.

How does he rate the present Everton squad in comparison to the one that Walter Smith inherited when he became manager? *Michael O'Connell, Galway, Republic of Ireland*

It's been hard for Walter. He's had to buy and sell and there must still be problems from when Peter Johnson was around. I think he's done a good job and I'm pleased to see that we've managed to stay up again. Hopefully, we won't always be struggling, though, and can work our way back up to the top six – but Walter has got his work cut out.

Do you get to see Everton much? *Tony Kuss, Melbourne, Australia*

I do get to a few of the games. I was there seven times last season.

Has television helped or hindered football in the last ten years? *Michael O'Connell, Galway, Republic of Ireland*

I think it's hindered it, to be honest. With the direction Sky has taken you can't even watch the national side on the normal television any more and I think that's wrong.

What is he doing now? *Julian Jackson, Hong Kong, SAR of PRC*

I'm the sales director in the family business started by my grandparents 50 years ago and then taken over by my father and his brother. It's called Buxton Spa Bakery and I've been working there for the last five years. We make and sell confectionery and cakes for the supermarkets and employ about 120 people.

Was the money he was on enough to set him up for life? *Julian Jackson, Hong Kong, SAR of PRC*

I was lucky, really. I didn't earn enough to set me up for life, but I made a very good living and it set me up to get on with my life. So I'm pretty sound and I've got no complaints.

Apart from the money he could earn, would he prefer to be playing now than when he did? *Michael O'Connell, Galway, Republic of Ireland*

Aside from the money, no, because of the way the game has changed. I was playing in the'70s and '80s with a great bunch of lads. We had such fun; we would train, play golf and go out for a drink together. Things have changed now and there doesn't seem to be the same team spirit built up between the players.

I finally finished at Stoke in the 1990 season and I can remember losing a game at home 3–0. George Berry, Peter Fox and myself were in the bath and we were really sick, but the younger lads were just asking each other which club they were going to next. That hurt because they didn't play with the same pride and passion and I fear that the money's taken over. In my day, we had a really close relationship and that camaraderie is missing now.

The injury essentially prevented you from receiving a full England cap and also caused you to miss out on one of the most successful eras in Everton's history. Does it make you bitter? *Stan Nuttall, Sunnyvale, California, USA*

You can't be bitter in life, things happen and that's it, you've got to go forward. At the time, I was depressed and sad and missing everything that was going on, but I still had lots of friends there, most of whom I still love to this day. I don't feel hard done by, it's quite the opposite – I feel lucky to have played for the years that I did. I've spoken to players who think the world owes them something, but I'm afraid they're wrong.

Most people go to work straight from leaving school at 16 and spend the rest of their lives doing jobs they hate. Anybody who's played football for a living is lucky, even if it was only for one game. It isn't just a job; it's a game that you love.

BARRY HORNE

Born 18 May 1962
July 1992 – June 1996
£675,000

Sometimes, being a football manager gives you the opportunity to make a boy's dream come true. In this instance, Howard Kendall was the man holding the magic dust.

> I made a few enquiries and ended up asking Peter Shreeves, who was managing Tottenham and Wales. He told me Barry was 90 per cent a great player, although his passing wasn't the best. It was a risk I was willing to take because I knew he was brimming with passion and that counts for a lot with me. It didn't take me long to realise that his work rate was immense and his contribution to the team, vital.
>
> He didn't score many goals, but there's one in particular that Evertonians will never forget and it's etched his name deep into our history. I'll just say Wimbledon and leave it at that.

My Bluenosed friends, I leave you to ponder this question: who needs Cantona when we've got Barry Horne?

Reach for your shin pads, it's the Welsh Wizard himself.

As a boyhood Evertonian, did you get to the match much? Where did you stand and which players stick in your memory from that period? *Phil Redmond, Warrington, England*
It was the Bob Latchford era, I absolutely loved him and he was my favourite. I liked watching Roger Kenyon and Bruce Rioch, but it wasn't the greatest Everton team to follow, although Bob, my hero, always seemed to save the day.

I started off watching from the old Paddock and latterly I would go with my uncles and sit in the Main Stand. I'll never forget the first time I sat in the top deck of the Main Stand, I was absolutely petrified, I honestly thought that if I tripped I would roll off the edge and land on the pitch.

What does it really feel like to be the focus of the boo-boys? How do you cope after the game is over? *Mark Wilson, Warrington, England*

To say it's unpleasant is an understatement. That time was one of the toughest periods of my career and there didn't seem to be a particular reason for it. It was so incredibly difficult that my dad stopped going to the games at one point because it upset him so much and he found it all too tough.

It's quite easy to say that, looking back, it makes you a better person and a stronger player, but at the time it's difficult to know how you're going to get through it. You just have to keep going and trying your best and it's not easy. The problem is that when it happens, you get sucked into a downward spiral and the harder you try the more you become aware of it. The only way out is to get a break further along the line. For a short spell my good friend, John Ebbrell, had it too. There's no one who's given more for Everton Football Club than John and it seems particularly sad. It always seemed to be the Evertonians who got the most stick and they're the last people you would think deserved it.

Did he ever dream, while playing for Rhyl and doing his degree, that he would one day play top-flight footy, become an international and win the FA Cup? *Phil Williams, Chester, England*

It was my dream as a child, the same as it is for every kid, but at 15 I made the choice to go the academic route. Back then it wasn't so easy to combine an education with a football career, although it's all changed quite drastically since. Now, with the introduction of football scholarships young players are able to combine the best of coaching with a continued education, which will set them up for an alternative career if they don't make the grade.

I made a conscious decision to go to university, but football was always the most important thing in my life. I captained the university team and went to play semi-professionally at Rhyl, but I'd really given up on the dream of becoming a professional footballer.

Hans Segers: crap or bribed? *Lol Scragg, Arbroath, Scotland*

Neither.

Which player did you have in your head when you pulled off the

Barry Horne

wonder goal against Wimbledon? *Colin Berry, Wavertree, Liverpool*

You have nothing at all in your head when things like that happen. It was very much an instinctive thing, as most goals are. I genuinely believe that when you think too deeply about things they don't happen.

What was the mood like in the dressing-room at half-time at 2–1 down that day? *Lyndon Lloyd, San Francisco, California, USA*

I can remember everything I was thinking and feeling about that game, but I was obviously really wrapped up in it because I can't for the life of me remember what anybody else did or said. To be perfectly honest, I wouldn't know if anyone even spoke at half-time. Obviously they must have, but I can't remember any of it.

How does he feel about the fact that I cannot say 'Barry Horne' without going 'Barry HooooooOOOOOOORNE!' like the commentator on my video of that match? *Patrick Clancy, Halewood, Liverpool*

Believe it or not, a number of people have said that to me. I've had a few bizarre chants around the place and that was one of them, people comment on it quite often.

Did he know that shot was going in as soon as it left his boot or did he think it was bending wide? *Lyndon Lloyd, San Francisco, California, USA*

I knew the moment I touched it and I'd have been amazed if the keeper had stopped it. I've scored a few long-range goals that don't compare in importance, but when you hit a shot you know instantly if it's going to be a goal. Sometimes the keeper surprises you and pulls off a remarkable save, but I knew that one had a chance.

When you scored against Wimbledon why didn't you go hurtling off like a lunatic, not even a smile? *Damien McKay, Tuebrook, Liverpool*

I wasn't aware of results at other games, but whereas a lot of people thought a draw would be enough, I thought a win was absolutely necessary. I remember thinking just before the goal, which was about 20 minutes into the second half, that somebody needed to do something very soon because time was running out, so after I scored, I just wanted to get on with the game and get the winner, really. As it turned out, a draw wouldn't have been enough after all.

What does he think about the whispers that Wimbledon (or Hans Segers at least) was given an incentive to lose the famous 3–2 game? *Ian Bonnar, Plaistow, east London*

I take all that with a pinch of salt. Football just doesn't work like that and I don't believe it's ever been a real issue or a problem. Imagine the scenario that a team's taken a bribe and found themselves 2–0 up after half an hour. There's a penalty comeback which the keeper couldn't do anything about, then the equaliser, which I'd like to think he couldn't have stopped . . . nah, it's nonsense and I don't give any of those whispers any credence whatsoever.

How does he feel when so-called 'respected' journalists like Hugh McIlvanney constantly imply that the Wimbledon game was a fix? (Repeated in The *Sunday Times* recently). Did Everton ever discuss this? *Paul Tollet, Oxford, England*

There's not much you can do about rumour and innuendo, that's the nature of the beast, but it is a little surprising when somebody of Hugh's stature goes on about it.

Do you sometimes wonder how many hearts you touched back then? Don't worry, it was a real goal. *Ari Sigurgeisson, Hafnarfjordur, Iceland*

As an Evertonian, I'm fully aware of how far and wide it was felt and people keep reminding me just in case.

The next day (when my uncle had regained a reasonable hue as opposed to the violent scarlet he adopted for the entire match) how did you feel? When did it sink in what you'd done and did you walk around for the next week hugging yourself and grinning inanely like the rest of us? *Neil Mckeown, Woolwich, south-east London*

In the run-up to the game, all I was thinking was how the last thing I would ever want would be a part in an Everton team responsible for relegation. I don't think it sank in on the night, it was probably on the Sunday morning when I looked at the papers and saw the final league table in black and white. When I'd actually read the match report and the sequence of events, I remember thinking: 'Christ, that was a close shave!'

What was the best partnership he had in midfield at Everton or any club? *Ciaran McConville, Dublin, Republic of Ireland*

Barry Horne

I used to love playing with John Ebbrell, he was a great footballer and very considerate. Parkinson was similar, if you missed something, he was always there to back you up. Two people like that with you in midfield and you can have your Kanchelskis and Limpar outside because the strength in their game complements the strength in the midfield – it all goes back to teamwork. I loved playing with Jimmy Case, and that will rankle with a few Evertonians, but he was a fantastic player, he was incredibly talented and if you talk about hard men, he was right up there.

My daughter Lucy was about six at the time and, looking at a map of Wales, she saw St Asaph and said: 'That's where Barry Horne was born.' Does he feel proud about that sort of thing? *San Presland, New Brighton, Merseyside* Oh, I definitely do. I'm actually from Holywell and the only reason I was born in St Asaph is that it was the only place nearby with a maternity hospital. I think you'll find that Ian Rush was born in the same ward.

I'd ask Barry Horne why he looked so miserable on the celebration bus after the '95 FA Cup final. *Keith Wilson, Waterloo, Liverpool*
I was probably hungover. I certainly didn't feel miserable, you must just have glimpsed me at a bad moment.

Have you still got all your curls? Was it 'cos your mum made you eat the crusts off your toast when you were a kid? *Ray Finch, Havant, England*
I've still got some hair and it's still curly, although I don't know if it's directly related to eating my crusts.

Which manager did you admire the most? *Ciaran McConville, Dublin, Republic of Ireland*
I admire Howard for his success in the '80s. He was immense and certainly the best around at the time. He battled hard to make the club great again and he signed me and gave me my chance for which I'll be forever grateful. Chris Nichol at Southampton had some great qualities too. The men who brought out my best years of club football were Joe Royle and Willie Donachie – I always put them together because they were a great team. On a par with them, I have to say Terry Yorath and Peter Shreeves, who I worked with at both international and club level.

A few times I've been to see the Super Furry Animals live in concert and they've dedicated a song to him. What's the connection? *Jason Palmer, Merthyr Tydfil, Wales*

They know I'm a fan of theirs because I met them at the Millennium Stadium and they did the same there, which was fantastic. It's just because I'm Welsh, no more and no less that that.

How did he rate the Everton fans when he was playing and how does he rate them now? *James Goddard, Ipswich, England*

Well, look at them now, the gates we're getting with the position we've been in for a number of years. At the time I was there, the worse things got, the more people came. We were bottom of the league and we were getting full houses every week, it was quite phenomenal.

Their continued turn-out is tremendous, but that's how it should be. Everton is a massive club and we shouldn't be surprised, although it would be nice for us to get a taste of success at some point soon. So, apart from when things were not going well with me, I always liked the crowd, they were knowledgeable and passionate and you can't ask for more than that.

My eyesight ain't what it used to be – was it him who stomped on Vinny Jones' head at Selhurst Park some years back and then pretended to be examining his fingernails while the berserk idiot ran round trying to find out who had done him wrong? *Paul Longke, Ealing, west London*

It might have been.

Which newspaper do you read? I reckon you're more *Guardian* than *Daily Mirror*. *Ged Fox, Wickford, England*

The Guardian or *The Independent.*

What gave you more pleasure, the immediate minutes after the referee blew his whistle in the '95 FA Cup final or the end of the Wimbledon game on the final day of the season? *Neil Mulhern, Belfast, Northern Ireland*

It's impossible to compare moments like that. If somebody asked what it was like winning the FA Cup twice and which was the most pleasurable, it would be a more valid comparison because you're comparing like with like, but you can't compare an apple to an orange.

Barry Horne

Does he think the 'hard men' of football are being phased out?
James Goddard, Ipswich, England
The game's changing and people have less licence, so because of that, yes, they are. The days when there was a physical element and the roughhouse tactics days of yore are long gone, so the days of the hard men must be numbered, too. It's a natural progression.

What was the worst moment of his Everton career? *Colin Berry,*
Wavertree, Liverpool
That whole period when I wasn't the 'fans' favourite' was horrible, but aside from that I can't think of too many times so I don't think there were many particular moments. There were a few instances when I was left out of the team – Howard did it a couple of times and Mike Walker once – but beside that I look back with nothing but fondness, and it all ended far too quickly.

Captain of Everton and a captain of Wales, it can't get much better than that, can it? *Jason Palmer, Merthyr Tydfil, Wales*
You're right, it can't. Those years were fantastic because it was when two worlds coincided. Wales were doing so well then too, we'd just missed out on the World Cup finals in the USA. I captained Wales for that qualifying period then after that I got a run as captain at Everton, and even if you only did those things once you'd feel incredibly lucky. When Joe and Willie came to the club it all seemed to work out for me.

Do you really like the Cocteau Twins? *Mark Tallentire, Walworth,*
South East London
Absolutely. Of all the bands that have come and gone, they're my favourites. They officially ceased to exist a few years ago, but they're still right up there for me, always and at all times.

Did he have a personal dislike of any team or ground? *Steve*
Kirkwood, Crowthorne, Berkshire, England
It's not so much a personal dislike, but there are grounds where you always seem to play well and you relish going there, and grounds where the opposite is true and that becomes a self-fulfilling prophecy. When I was at Everton I used to hate going to Maine Road. I actually quite like Manchester City but I couldn't seem to get my act together there at all.

I have many grounds that I love and I looked forward to visiting, but they're not the obvious choices. Highbury is one, it was a fantastic place, I used to love playing there and I always seemed to do quite well. Another is Selhurst

Park, and whether it was against Palace or Wimbledon I always seemed to perform. Goodison Park now is a top choice, and even during the bad days it was always special. The most magical times away from Everton were the first two years when Wales played at the old National Stadium at Cardiff; fantastic venue, fantastic times.

Can you ask him what was his reaction when he first heard the 'who needs Cantona when we've got Barry Horne' song? I hope he laughed his nuts off, I know I did! *Jamie McDonald, Beckenham, England*

It was really funny in an ironic way. It was slightly embarrassing because I felt that some people might not see the irony and the sarcasm that was intended, but I did think it was great and it's popped up around the country a few times since.

How much of a part does Barry feel that the 'Dogs of War' years played in the premature demise of Messrs Ebbrell and Parkinson? *Neal Clague, Douglas, Isle of Man*

None, really. Part of my reason for leaving was that Joe told me he was going to sign Gary Speed. He also wanted to push Tony Grant and he had Joe and John fighting for places alongside me. He thought that if I stayed I wouldn't be an automatic and regular choice.

Although I was desperately upset to leave Everton I had to make a calm decision. I wouldn't have been happy at that stage in my career to only be playing twenty games a season, as Joe predicted. Birmingham seemed like a good opportunity because it was an ambitious club, so I made a decision with my head rather than with my heart. It's amazing how quickly things turn around because within a few months Joe, John and Tony were all injured and I almost undoubtedly would have played nearly every game. I don't think the way they played was a contributing factor to their injuries. John's was a combination of things that had come on over a number of years and the result of an operation. Joe's was just wear and tear and his operation didn't quite work. It was more down to genetics than anything else.

Game against Blackburn: Alan Shearer goes down in a heap as though in mortal pain. Trainer comes on and treats his elbow. Barry comes over and gives the big baby a mouthful. Alan jumps up and runs after Barry seemingly telling him that he was indeed really hurt. Can he remember what was said in that exchange? *Richard Marland, Waterloo, Liverpool*

Yes, I certainly remember, but I don't think it's suitable for printing.

Barry Horne

Being an excellent tackler, did he like his intimidating and tough-tackling image? *Jason Palmer, Merthyr Tydfil, Wales*

Joe used to say that to be a good midfield player you had to be able to do two of three things really well: tackling, passing or scoring.

High-profile players have since told me that they didn't look forward to playing against us. There was something of a reputation about the whole team, not just individuals. While it's always nice to know that people don't look forward to playing you, I felt that people focused too much on that aspect of my game and overlooked others.

Tackling is an art and to make a good tackle requires the same amount of skill as making a goal, a save or a great pass – it's all in the timing. I played in the top division and was an international for ten years and definitely played more good games than bad.

John Ebbrell: useless or just unfortunate? *Lol Scragg, Arbroath, Scotland*

Definitely unfortunate. He could have been excellent but he never reached his full potential.

I have, in my own kit bag, a blue Nike boot bag that I absolutely cherish. Super Barry Horne 'supposedly' gave it to my mate, who used to drive the coaches for the Wales national team, although it could have been an elaborate wind-up. Is this true and did he really sing 'who needs Cantona?' to him on the coach? *Jason Palmer, Merthyr Tydfil, Wales*

I really don't want to rain on anybody's parade here, but I can't remember owning a blue Nike boot bag. He may have sung 'who needs Cantona' on the coach, but the only boots I've worn in the last ten years have been Mizuno and Adidas.

Groans came when he signed, but he gave me the best moment of the '90s, even better than winning the FA Cup. If it had gone off in the tunnel after the FA Cup final in '95 who was harder, you and Parkinson or Keane and Ince? *Gary Hughes, Whiston, Merseyside*

I would bet on the Blues, but only because Joe would have been there. I couldn't fight my way out of a paper bag and I'd have been down the tunnel so fast I'd have been a blur! Joe could have fought and won for both of us.

Did his back ever recover from having David Unsworth leap on

him like a (big) salmon during the '95 Cup final goal celebrations?
Rob Rimmer, Aintree, Liverpool
There was him and a few others, I seem to remember. That was no problem at all.

Are there any football pros you know who would be interested in so-called 'fine arts'? *Osmo Tapio Räihälä, Helsinki, Finland*
Probably more than you can imagine. People have an image of footballers as being uncouth philistines, but I think you'd find that quite a few would appreciate fine arts.

Since he is one of the few professional footballers in the UK who completed a degree, ask him if he thought that put him at a disadvantage with him starting later? Did he play for the university team and did he win anything? *Michael Dudley, Long Island, New York, USA*
I used to think about this all the time, less so now as I get older, but certainly in the best years of my career, I would often wonder 'what if . . .' but I always seemed to arrive at the same conclusion, and that was that I had some of the best years of my life at Liverpool University.

I captained the team to the UAU Championship, which in the grand scheme of things doesn't compare to what came later, but it was fantastic. Apart from that, my three years as an undergraduate were amazing, so in that respect I was very fortunate. I got a second chance, and my career, given the circumstances, couldn't have been much better, but I did often wonder where I would have ended up if I'd started five years earlier.

I played for Everton, which was the one club I'd dreamed of. If I'd started sooner, I may have played for a more successful club and won more trophies, but, on the other hand, I may never have kicked a ball in the first team for anyone. So, I wouldn't really change much because both of my careers worked out really well.

Did he have to dumb down and act thick in order to get along with his teammates? *Colin Berry, Wavertree, Liverpool*
Sometimes you have to just keep yourself to yourself, and I think that applies in many environments, not just football.

Can he tell me how to work out the latent heat of naphthalene?
San Presland, New Brighton, Merseyside

I could, but it would depend under what conditions, and I don't think this is the time or the place to go into it.

Does he think his education will mean that he stands a better chance of being a good manager, or does he think that management isn't really about 'intellect' and more about empathising with 'the lads'? *Nick Williams, Warrington, England*
I don't think a good education, in terms of chemistry, history or politics, is at all relevant in management. Intelligence most definitely is, and so are empathy and management skills, that doesn't matter if you're a football manager, a supermarket manager or the manager of a factory in charge of ten thousand people. Your job is to get the best for your employer out of the assets you have at your disposal. Your biggest asset is people, so you need some intelligence. If you haven't got O levels and A levels to back you up, you need to have a different kind of cleverness and you need to be wise. In order to communicate and utilise your skills you probably need a football background as well.

Many people who didn't quite cut it as players have gone on to be top-class managers, that's because they've got other strengths, but the reverse is true, too. Just because you're a top-class footballer it doesn't mean you'll be a good manager in any way, shape or form. There are certain qualities you need to be a good manager, as there are to be a footballer, but they're not necessarily the same thing.

Ask Barry if he remembers when Savo spat in his face in a game sometime in the mid-'90s versus Villa. *Carl Sanderson, Neston, Wirral*
Yes, I remember vividly; it was on the edge of the box at the Park End. I think it was the last match of the '96 season and one of the best games I ever played for Everton.

Would he consider going into management? *Phil Williams, Chester, England*
Most definitely. I've heard rumours about me being asked back to Everton, but, unfortunately, not from the source I'd have liked.

Why does it seem to be so difficult to manage Everton compared with other teams? *San Presland, New Brighton, Merseyside*
It's tough for me to answer that because I'm like you – on the outside looking in. I imagine there must be some financial restrictions on the managers, although they seem to have had a certain amount available. It's possible to

have limited success with a smaller budget, but Everton are looking for major success and that's one of the incompatibilities – you look at the top clubs and they're all big spenders. It all depends on how you judge success, but I have to imagine the financial position at the club can't be helping.

Will he come and coach for Everton, be our moral officer? With eleven Barry Hornes on the pitch we certainly wouldn't be having our current problems! *Eddie Pepper, Brighton, England*

I don't know if eleven Barry Hornes would be better than eleven Neville Southalls. It takes a blend because football is the ultimate team game.

How did you feel when the £250,000 move back from Brum collapsed on transfer deadline day in 1997 and Joe Royle was sacked instead – the same day Claus Eftevaag and Flo were meant to sign? *Mark Tallentire, Walworth, south-east London*

I was absolutely devastated. The timing was incredible, I was away with Wales preparing for an international and actually sitting waiting for my contract to be faxed to the hotel, but instead I got a phone call to say Joe had 'resigned'. If it had been a day earlier, or even an hour, then I'd have been back home, and it took me quite a while to get over it. It was one of the biggest disappointments in my career.

When Wales played Romania why didn't he just take Hagi out in the first ten minutes? *Phil Williams, Chester, England*

If I could have done, I would have done but he was an exceptional player. That was without a shadow of a doubt my worst moment in football. What magnified it was the fact that the 18-month lead-up was the best time I'd ever had.

Barry was a member of the 'Dogs of War' midfield. How would he have liked to play alongside Howard Kendall, Alan Ball or Colin Harvey, with the accent on creativity? *Dave Kelly, Blackburn, England*

I've played against all three of those men in training, Colin and Howard at Everton and Bally when he was at Portsmouth. Colin had a problem with his hips, but Howard and Alan Ball in five-a-side and head tennis were phenomenal. Alan Ball could tackle, pass and score a few, but his main strength was his vision and Howard's one-touch football was second to none. You could imagine what it was like playing with them, it must have been quite something.

I've been lucky enough to work with a lot of good players at Everton,

Barry Horne

Southampton and Wales. The team I left at Southampton included Shearer, Le Tissier, and Wallace, so I know what it's like to work with very creative, talented people. Matt Le Tissier used to say that he really appreciated what I gave to the team. Although he was the star and always got the headlines, he was the first to acknowledge the efforts of the other lads around him. I think that happens in all good teams, they have respect for each other.

What do you think went wrong after '95? Andy McGrae, Illinois, USA

The truth is that I don't know, but I don't think it was one particular thing. We had a good run in the league and finished just outside the top six, which was pretty respectable considering what had gone before and what's happened since.

I thought we were unlucky in a few games the following season and could have finished higher. I left in June '96 and it was that year it started to slide. Shortly after I'd gone the whole midfield fell to injury. Joe resigned and there was a whole tapestry of things happening on and off the pitch, including trouble getting another manager, and the club seemed to get caught in a downward spiral.

Did he ever get fed up at getting half the credit than less committed players who largely didn't care about Everton? Tim Bentham, Hammersmith, west London

If I thought about it too much it really would rankle with me, but I've always said that you can get labelled, and when you do, it sticks and you're known for doing one thing. I've often been asked this question and my answer is always the same. The most important people to have happy with your performances or contribution are your teammates, manager and coaches. If they're happy then the rest doesn't matter as much, because as a professional, that's the be all and end all.

Does he still get to Goodison? Rob Rimmer, Aintree, Liverpool

If there's ever a Sunday game or a midweek match and I'm not working, then I'm there. I've started bringing my son along with me and he enjoys it too.

What did he think of the Gwladys Street Hall of Fame evening at the Adelphi – a momentous occasion or just another night out with the lads? Mike Royden, Ellesmere Port, South Wirral, England

It's not just another night out, by any means. I think it's a fantastic evening and it's a great chance for the senior players to get some kind of recognition from the fans. The Blueblood charity side of it is a brilliant idea, I'm a patron and that dovetails very nicely with my PFA work. It's a raucous evening and I love going, I know I'm not the only one either. You should hear the noise in there; it's like being back at Goodison Park.

I'd ask him if he still held that special place in his heart for the Blues and whether or not he realised how special he is to us?
Stuart Brandwood, Netherton, Liverpool
I always have been an Evertonian – they're my team. I think most footballers have a team, but I'm not sure how many of them get to play for it. I've been really lucky in that respect. I go and watch them whenever I can and watch out for them and their results at all times.

How does it feel to be an Everton legend? Did you ever think you would be so popular? *Andy McGrae, Illinois, USA*
There was a long time when I never imagined being popular at all. Sadly, those times tend to temper the good. It's fantastic to be greeted with praise by Evertonians, but that was one of the reasons I decided to leave when I did – at the top if you like. I wouldn't want to have done it any other way, and now I can always go back and be welcomed and that makes me very happy. I wouldn't think I was a legend, but to be well thought of makes me very happy indeed.

BOB LATCHFORD

Born 18 January 1951
February 1974 – July 1981
£350,000

As part of the complicated exchange deal that saw Archie Styles and Howard Kendall go the other way, bustling Bob Latchford's arrival from Birmingham City wasn't met entirely with a fanfare of trumpets from the fans. Even for a big man with a big reputation, it's never easy to step into the shoes of a legend.

Strong in the air and with two great feet, the Big Man had an astonishingly delicate touch and there simply wasn't a ball he couldn't strike home. So when the *Daily Express* threw down the gauntlet Bob got the bit between his teeth and in April 1978 plundered his unprecedented thirtieth goal of the season. In that instant an entire generation of Bluenoses was spawned.

'The Latch' was here to stay and gave the Blues something to look forward to in an era where silverware was scarce but the will to win was overwhelming.

Ladies and gentlemen: give me a clenched-fist salute and I'll give you the maestro himself, and always remember this one thing: Bobby Latchford walks on water.

I remember the day he signed for the Blues. My dad, a staunch believer in the 'Holy Trinity', was so incensed with Howard's exit he swore never to darken the Goodison doorstep again. How aware was Latch of the depth of feeling towards Howard's exit? Did it unsettle him from the off knowing he was seen to be replacing a legend, even if that wasn't exactly the case? *Colm Kavanagh, Co. Wicklow, Republic of Ireland*
Not only was I replacing a legend, but I was also the most expensive player in Britain at the time. It was all quite daunting and there was a lot of pressure on me. The 'Holy Trinity' had been the fans' favourite, and although that midfield trio had long since broken up Howard Kendall was still revered by the

Evertonians. But I knew what I was capable of, I knew I had to perform and it just made me more determined to achieve it.

I took my wife along with me to the press conference when I signed and Howard and Archie Styles were there, too, waiting to go the other way. It was like a revolving door and quite unorthodox.

The first game my dad took me to see was on 30 April 1978 – I was seven at the time. Our sixth and your thirtieth convinced me that blue was the colour to love. How do you feel now, 23 years on, to know that you were instrumental in giving me a life of false dawns, ritual humiliation in the cups and constant piss-poor football (four seasons excepted)? *Lol Scragg, Arbroath, Scotland*
Ah, there were a few good years in the '80s when Howard arrived as manager, but you're right, there haven't been many since. No, I don't feel guilty, I feel kind of proud that I'm indirectly responsible for a generation of Blues. It's not all bad, being an Evertonian, imagine if you supported Birmingham City, then you'd really have something to moan about.

I would like to ask Bob how early in his career did he decide on his 'goal celebration'? *Ray Mckay, Warrington, England*
I didn't consciously decide on a celebration, but I suppose it depended on a few things, like how I saw the goal and where I was. I don't even know that my celebration was ever the same twice, so I guess it was just a reaction to how I felt at the time.

Could Bob comment on how he was received by the players and fans? Would you also extend my sincere apologies for hating him for the first couple of months? *Steve Fairclough, Toronto, Canada*
I didn't think anybody really hated me, but I knew I had to prove myself. The players certainly welcomed me and I didn't get much flak from the fans that I can remember. I needed to let them know that I meant business and I tried my utmost to deliver every time I pulled on my shirt.

Did he mind being called 'Fat Latch'? *Steve Tynan, Aldershot, England*
My fighting weight was always around thirteen stone four to thirteen stone eight, but I had a period at Birmingham, and maybe for the first year at Goodison, when I tipped the scales at over fourteen stones. I actually took off weight at Everton and maintained a better weight later on in my career. I was never fat, I was probably at my fattest, or heaviest, as I would prefer to call it,

when I was younger, and I became slimmer with age.

Doesn't he think today's goal celebrations make so-called modern footballers look like a bunch of tarts compared to his classic bended-knee-clenched-fist salute? *Mark Wilson, Warrington, England*

They look as if they've been rehearsing those celebrations for months and sometimes the celebrations are more interesting than the actual goal. Nobody was quite as demonstrative in my day and I would say a clenched fist would be sufficient every time.

Going out for that final game against Chelsea, did any of their lads make it known about helping/spoiling your quest for 29 and 30? *Steve Fairclough, Toronto, Canada*

I'm wondering whether you mean Everton or Chelsea! All our lads knew about it, and the Chelsea lads probably did, too, because it had been well publicised. The lads were feeding me the ball all night because they knew how important it was – only Trevor Francis had managed it before me. When the *Daily Express* threw down that challenge, I decided I would go for it straight away and I never wavered. I used to keep track to make sure I stayed on target and the more I scored, the easier it got.

When he walked up to take the penalty to make it to the magical 30 goals for the season, did it cross his mind at all that he might miss? *Mike Kidd, Pietermaritzburg, South Africa*

No, I knew it was going in. There was no way I was going to miss that.

Was 'that penalty' the first one he ever took? *Paul Tollet, Oxford, England*

I took one other at Ipswich away and scored that, too. I had a great record with my penalties, I took two and scored two, so it was a 100 per cent success rate. I didn't bother to take them normally because I didn't consider them to be a real goal, not like one that you actually score from open play. If I had my time over again I'd take them all, and I could probably add another couple of dozen goals to my tally.

Did he see the billboard on a church in town, which said 'Jesus Saves' – to which someone had added 'but Latchford gets the rebounds'? *Andy Richardson, Hackney, north-east London*

I was certainly told about it but I never actually saw it. Typical Scousers. I think that's brilliant, maybe somebody has a photograph of it somewhere.

When he got his 30 goals, did it bother him that he helped send Chelsea down too, in that last game? *Tom Davis, Texas, USA*
No, not in the slightest.

Did the Chelsea keeper let that penalty in? *Ray Finch, Havant, England*
That's outrageous! No way.

Did he keep all his congratulations telegrams he received? I sent him one because my inconsiderate sister chose to get married that day. *Billy Williams, Cologne, Germany*
Did you? Thanks very much. I have them all somewhere. I'm moving house soon, so when I get all my stuff out to pack I'm sure I'll unearth an awful lot of memories. I'm rather looking forward to it.

Did he get on with Gordon Lee? *Stefan Pun, Singapore*
Gordon was a good bloke and there was nothing he didn't know about football. Things just didn't seem to work out for him at Everton, which was a shame, but we all liked and respected him, he was good at his job and he was a football fanatic.

Bob, the beard I understand, but for God's sake the perm? Why? *Mark Murphy, Horsham, England*
I know, it's one of those crazy things you do in life.

As an Everton legend rivalled only by Andy King in the '70s you scored many goals in the famous number nine Everton shirt. I would like to know how many different parts of your anatomy have you scored with (any hidden gems like Maradona's 'Hand of God')? *Tony Corcoran, Leopardstown, Dublin, Republic of Ireland*
That's a great question. I never scored any with my hand, but I must have scored with every other part of my body: my shoulder, thigh, bum, face, chest, knee, hip, but never with my hand.

Does Bob remember the fuss outside Hillsborough when he came out of the dressing-room, to an enormous roar? Was anything mentioned on the coach going back to Merseyside about Gordon Lee not signing my programme because there was

Bob Latchford

a picture of Duncan McKenzie on it? *Tom Davis, Texas, USA*

I do remember the reception I got that day, but I don't remember Gordon Lee refusing to sign a programme, I'm sure he didn't do it on purpose – in fact, Gordon and Duncan got on quite well with each other. I think this story of them hating each other's guts is just folklore which has been embellished over the years at Duncan's after-dinner speeches.

Ask him to clear up the 'orange ball fear'. Was it the ball, or the fact that it was used in snowy, icy weather and it was more an indication that he was entering a field in less than 'Latchesque' conditions? *Paul Rigby, Connecticut, USA*

It was just the whole concept of an orange ball, and it was so hideously bright it just wasn't right. It's like playing golf with a yellow ball or seeing cricketers in those bright colours, it was wrong and it played on my mind. I hated that orange ball and it made me anxious, so it got into my head that I couldn't play with it and became a self-fulfilling prophecy.

How did the players react to Terry Darracott not clearing the ball before the winning goal in the 1977 League Cup final second replay? Do players bear grudges against teammates for such mistakes? *Mike Wood, Zurich, Switzerland*

No, you can't bear a grudge because it's a team game. We all make mistakes and each one of us could be held culpable for anything, but that's all part of the game. You all take the blame and you all take the glory. It was a feeling of total dismay, but he made a mistake and it cost us. At times you can make an error and it doesn't cost. That one did, but that's life.

Who was the hardest player he'd ever come across? *Robin Ashford, Maidstone, England*

Charlie Hurley, a big bruising centre-half who played for Sunderland, and George Curtis at Coventry was another one. They gave me a dog's life.

Ask him if he is a little peeved that the prize he got for reaching 30 league goals is less than what some whingeing teenage prima donnas with unproven talent get each day for lifting their sorry arses out of bed to go to the physio each morning? *Lol Scragg, Arbroath, Scotland*

I got £10,000 for my 30 goals. Half of it was given to a charity; I kept a grand for myself and shared the rest amongst the squad and everybody ended up with £192. Then the Inland Revenue got on my case and wanted to tax me on the initial ten thousand. So I spent more money fighting the case than I won in the end, but it was never really about the money.

It has all gone mad now. I think about the money we were earning then and it's laughable, although it was proportionally huge in those days – we got paid more than your average man in the street. I say good luck to them, and it's still not as much as the American basketball or baseball players, they're on deals worth millions a year. But it is getting a bit out of hand now, it has to be said.

What was the worst injury you suffered? *Terry McWilliams, Ontario, Canada*
I never had a bad injury inflicted on me, but I tore my hamstring in the November and was out until the following April. It was a slow process to recover from that. It would take ages to heal, then I'd go back to training, break into a sprint and it would break down again. It was so frustrating, but there was nothing I could do about it.

How many games did you play alongside Joe Royle and what did you think of Big Joe? *Steve Tynan, Aldershot, England*
I only played with him about half a dozen times. He was a great player, he really was, and I loved playing alongside him. Who knows what might have happened if he had stayed. I don't know why he was sold, but I do know that there's always a reason. There might have been some friction with the manager or something like that, but there's always an underlying reason why a player gets put on the transfer list. The fans would never hear about it and sometimes the other players didn't even know.

Would he agree with me that during his time at Everton, although he scored many goals and had great service from Dave Thomas, Andy King and Martin Dobson, we never won anything because defensively we were not strong enough? *Keith Wilson, Waterloo, Liverpool*
Every team needs a good goalkeeper and that's why Everton started to have their successful run when Neville Southall arrived. Your goalie is the last line of defence and if he's not up to the job then you'll never have a good team. Football is the ultimate team game, though, and it's hard to point any fingers. The harsh truth is that we just weren't good enough to win the league.

Let me set the scene: it's the '77 FA Cup semi-final versus the

Bob Latchford

RedShite at Maine Road and Clive Thomas is the referee. I know Bob was injured for that match, but what was his view of the goal-that-never-was and what is his view now, with hindsight? *Billy Williams, Cologne, Germany*

That was a goal and to this day nobody can actually say why it was disallowed – especially Clive Thomas. I was in the crowd and I watched it. He said it was offside, but it wasn't. Then he said it was an infringement on the rules of the FA, but he didn't really elaborate on that. It wasn't the only goal he disallowed, either. I think the problem with Clive Thomas was that he was an attention-seeker and he wanted the glory all for himself. He disallowed that goal in the World Cup when there was a corner and he blew his whistle as it was about to go in the goal. He was an arse.

Did the players hate Clive Thomas as much as the fans did? *Mike Wood, Zurich, Switzerland*

We probably hated him even more than the fans. He blatantly stole results from us on more than one occasion.

Which player or person was the most influential in your career? *Simon George, Birmingham, England*

Freddie Goodwin at Birmingham. When he first came to the club I was 18 or 19, I had just broken in and was playing for the first team. He arrived and turned me into the player I became. He knew he didn't have the money to go and buy a big centre-forward and he knew there was no choice but to work on me. Freddie invested a lot of time and effort in my progress. He would have me back training in the afternoons, he coached me, encouraged me and shaped me into what I went on to become. I owe him a great deal.

Did he know that Lee Latchford Evans of 'Steps' is named after him? Does he feel proud or revolted? *Andy Richardson, Hackney, north-east London*

I didn't know this until about six months ago when Steve Hopcroft, our Academy Recruitment Officer at Birmingham, mentioned it to me. I have heard of 'Steps', but don't know what they look or sound like I'm sorry to say. I believe it was his dad who named him after me. It's actually very flattering to hear it.

He scored five against Wimbledon in the Mickey Mouse Cup and stole the limelight from Martin Dobson, who got his one and only hat trick. Was this his best game? *Andy Richardson, Hackney, north-east London*

It was just one of those games where everything went right and every time I touched the ball it went in. It happens like that sometimes. It was a bit mean of me to steal Dobbo's thunder, and I got the match ball too, but I'm sure he didn't mind. It was all for a good cause.

Is it true he opened a men's fashion shop in Formby? *Mark Tallentire, Walworth, south-east London*
Yes, and it bombed. It was up by the Grapes Hotel on that parade of shops. I think that was the big mistake and it should have been in the village. Location, location, location.

The 1980 FA Cup semi-final replay versus West Ham at Elland Road – Everton broke my heart that night. For the love of God, what the hell went wrong in such a short space of time and how did The Latch and the rest of the Everton players feel, especially the sidelined Brian Kidd whose dismissal at Villa Park undoubtedly cost us the tie first time around? *Billy Williams, Cologne, Germany*
I think Brian Kidd felt it really badly, but we were all devastated. We went through every emotion in the spectrum that night: anxiety, joy and, of course, sheer despair being the final one. We really thought we had got it and we were so close.

Can you ask Big Bob did he ever eat Hafnia pork luncheon meat as I'm worried sick? *Colin Smyth, Ormskirk, England*
What? No, no, definitely not. Don't worry about me, I'm fit and well but thanks anyway.

What does he recall from the UEFA Cup game against AC Milan at Goodison? I remember him scoring from a corner despite being mugged by at least two defenders, and yet the goal was disallowed. Then another player took an elbow to the head when play was at Everton's end. Were AC really as dirty as they seemed? I watched that game from the Park End with two lads behind me discussing how long a sentence they would get for running on and hitting the referee and how much of a tax rebate they'd get when they were released. *Mike Wood, Zurich, Switzerland*
AC Milan just played like any other passionate Italian team. They were a bit rough, but that was how they all were. I was expecting something like that and that was precisely what we got, there were no surprises there, I'm afraid.

Bob Latchford

I recall similar looping headers away to Derby County in a league match in 1975 and in the League Cup semi-final, second leg in 1977. Does Bob remember these as being identical? *Colin Jones, Mossley Hill, Liverpool*

I don't think any two goals are identical. They might look similar, but they couldn't be the same for loads of factors, the build-up and the angle and the timing.

Were there ever offers from any of the other big clubs for you when you were at Goodison and, if so, which and were you tempted? *Sean Rostron, Wallasey, Wirral*

I don't think so, and if anybody did come in for me then I certainly didn't hear about it. That's the sign of a good manager when none of the gossip or rumour makes its way through to the players because that immediately becomes unsettling.

What did he make of Duncan McKenzie? *Steve Jensen, Wamberal, NSW, Australia*

I loved Duncan, he was a showman and he would have the ball for longer in one go than some players would have it in a whole game. The crowd loved him and he was a clown and a really good laugh. He's a lovely man, he's very funny, very talented and a pleasure to be around.

Another Duncan plays at the moment. What do you think of him? *Steve Tynan, Aldershot, England*

He has all the attributes to be a great centre-forward, but he's not consistent enough and seems to be plagued by injury. I don't know what's happening there, but he just needs to get fit and he could be spectacular. He's got all the ingredients of being a top centre-forward. He's big and strong and good in the air. Maybe a run of luck will sort it out. I wouldn't worry about him being too old, though, he's probably got another two or three years left in him. I was good and as strong between 30 and 34 as I was between 20 and 24, and my overall game was better as I got older, looking from an experienced point of view.

Given your brother's chosen careers was their any chance of you becoming a goalie? *Steve Fairclough, Toronto, Canada*

No chance whatsoever. When you have a kick around as a kid nobody wants to go in goal, except my brothers. They loved it, which was great. It meant I didn't have to bother and I could just be the striker. I hated being in goal and I was rubbish at it.

Why didn't we quite make the breakthrough to being a championship-winning side during the time he was at the club? We came quite close on occasions and looked promising on others, but somehow never quite made it. *Neil McCann, Bangkok, Thailand*

The reason teams don't win is quite simply because they aren't good enough. We had the spirit and we had the will to win, but that's not always enough and you need to have the talent too. We were close a few times, but the best team wins on the day and I'm afraid it's as simple as that.

He had a lethal partnership with Bob Hatton at Brum. Did he have anyone close to that at Goodison? *Tom Davis, Texas, USA*

Funnily enough, it was probably Duncan.

What was it like playing on that pitch at the Baseball Ground in those days and is Sefton Park in mid-winter better? *Colin Jones, Mossley Hill, Liverpool*

The Baseball Ground was appalling it has to be said. Actually, I think you're right, Sefton Park was in much better nick.

Does he still have dreams of Davey Thomas knocking balls over to him? *Tom Davis, Texas, USA*

I do! Dave was magnificent, he was like a hard-working version of David Ginola. He had the talent but he wasn't lazy, he covered every blade of grass in every game. Dave used to wear rubber-soled boots with no studs and he was the only player I ever saw who never lost his balance. If he was playing today, clubs would be paying about £18m for his services. If it hadn't have been for Dave Thomas I wouldn't have scored half the goals I did. He was the best crosser of a ball I've ever had the pleasure to play with. There was no ball he couldn't cross, he was a phenomenon and years ahead of his time.

One hundred and thirty-eight goals in seven seasons from a man who was lazy and slow. Do you think your critics were tough on you? *Steve Fairclough, Toronto, Canada*

I don't think I was that slow, but I was lazy at times. As I grew older, I became less lazy and I think that was as I was learning the art of the game. I used to do the minimum I could get away with and only make a run when I had to, but as time went on I was up for everything. I definitely didn't think I was slow, though – I thought I could hold my own against the rest of them.

Bob Latchford

Where did Bob get the bubble perm done and how much did it cost? *Mark Tallentire, Walworth, south-east London*
I had it done at a hairdresser in Formby Village, but don't ask me how much it cost because it's so long ago.

How did he rate David Smallman? *Roy King Miaa, Kristiansand, Norway*
He was a good player, but he always seemed to be plagued with injury so he never really had the chance to make his mark. I don't know what he's up to these days, but I saw him at the Hall of Fame dinner and he looked the same as he ever did.

I remember towards the end of Latch's career he was involved in a Franny Jeffers-style refusal to sign a contract and he threatened to go on strike. If I may be so rude, how much were you asking for? *Dermot Nealon, Dublin, Republic of Ireland*
I was earning £200 a week then and I was asking to double it to £400. I got it in the end. It sounds almost comical now when you say it out loud.

How disappointed was he that he wasn't chosen more often at international level? *Ted Neeson, Manchester, England*
It was a major disappointment. I always felt that with England I didn't get recognised early enough. There were a number of players who kept me out of the team from the moment I signed in 1974 until 1977, but I always felt I was as good as any of them and I was scoring and playing as well as any of them. Don Revie was the manager and he invited about 80 of the top players to Manchester when he took over. I don't know what it was but he must have played 79 of them, although he never played me. It wasn't until he left and Ron Greenwood came in that I got my chance. I always felt that if I'd played three years earlier and got established then I would have won more caps.

Was playing for Ron Greenwood's England team the fun that everyone makes it out to be? What was the pre-match briefing like? *Mark Tallentire, Walworth, south-east London*
I can't remember much of the pre-match briefing, but it was fun. Ron was a good coach and tactically very sound so it was enjoyable. It was light-hearted but we worked hard and played hard.

In all your derby games for Everton you failed to score against Liverpool, yet your first game for Swansea at Anfield saw you put

two in? Do you think you were fated not to score against the Reds in an Everton shirt? *Ged Fox, Wickford, England*

I must have played for Everton against Liverpool a dozen times and I never scored. I just think I was destined not to get one against them and, of course, the harder you try, the harder it gets. Either the Liverpool defenders had me sussed or I just had some bad luck, and I'm not sure which, probably a bit of both.

What went wrong in 1979? How come we went from fourth one season to nineteenth the next? *Andy Richardson, Hackney, north-east London*

Our coach, Steve Burtenshaw, left and I think it had a profound effect on us. You get used to people and you get into a routine. When that suddenly changes it takes time to readjust. Everything was so different after he'd gone and it all seemed to fall apart on the park.

Bob Latchford has been quoted as saying that he left Everton too soon. Who or what forced him out? *Mark Tallentire, Walworth, south-east London*

Nobody forced me out, but it's only now, when I look back, that I realise I should have stayed a bit longer. At the time, I just felt as if I'd come to the end of the line and I needed to go elsewhere to continue my career. But we all know that everything is much clearer with hindsight.

You left Everton shortly after Howard became manager. Was this a coincidence or did you not fancy playing under him? *Ged Fox, Wickford, England*

It was nothing to do with Howard returning, but I never played under him at all. There was certainly no malice or hard feelings between us, I just felt that I should move on.

Clive Thomas: buy him a drink, yes or no? *Andy Howarth, Long Beach, California, USA*

No chance.

Was Penydarren Park the worst pitch he's ever played on? (Wait for him to answer to see if he remembers.) *Jason Palmer, Merthyr Tydfil, Wales*

Now there's a blast from the past, Penydarren Park. No, it certainly wasn't the worst pitch I've played on, but it was, err, different.

Bob Latchford

Just thank Latch for having been the hero he was to many of us. Does he think he and Mick Lyons must be the unluckiest idols ever to pull on the Blue of the chosen ones? *Darryl Ng, Singapore*
It's very possible, yes. We were so close and yet so far.

Was it great to have another bite of the cherry by playing in Europe in the Cup-Winners' cup for Merthyr at the end of his playing career? *Jason Palmer, Merthyr Tydfil, Wales*
That was fantastic, it was a lovely end to my career and one of the memories that I really cherish.

Who had the worst perm, Bob or Mick Lyons? *Stewart MacLaren, Torrevieja, Spain*
They were both really bad, and it was certainly a close call, but I think Mick had a home perm, so I'd say his was worse than mine.

What do you think of players' inflated prices and salaries of today? *John Walton, Dubai, United Arab Emirates*
I'm afraid it's just the norm and the way it's going to be for the next amount of years. Average players earn vast amounts of money because there's a lot of mediocrity out there. If you're a good athlete with a good attitude and you're consistent, then you'll earn an awful lot of money in the Premier League or the First Division because there's so much money splashing around that it's filtering down. It's unbelievably silly money now. You could buy a house outright every week.

Do you think football today is more about money than anything else? *Marko Poutiainen, Oulu, Finland*
Money plays a large part in football but it's the same in most sports now. It's something that you just have to live with because it's a fact of life. Commercial interests do run the game more so now than ever before and I think this is the tip of the iceberg because there's even more money coming into the game again.

Bob is looking as good now as when he was playing. Has he found the elixir of life? Will he please send me a bottle and I'll send him a cheque. Does he still have his League Cup runners-up tankard? *Jim Lynch, Brentwood, England*
I certainly do, yes. I've still got most things.

When you were working for Ladbrokes setting the fixed odds for football matches was there ever a time when you thought Everton would be relegated? *Bernie Flood, Ellesmere Port, Wirral*

Hmm, they came very close one year and have been close on a number of occasions since. I never thought it would really happen, but there's always that danger. When you're down in that bottom half dozen it becomes more and more difficult to get out of it. It's just been fortunate for Everton that there's been worse clubs than them in the Premiership.

Why did you shave your beard off? *Stephen Hardy, Skelmersdale, England*

I was in hospital after I'd had a cartilage operation in 1976 and I was bored and looking for something to do, so I decided to shave my beard off. My wife saw my face with it off and said it was much better and she preferred it that way, so I've never grown one since.

First, I'd like to thank him for my first truly ecstatic Everton experience as the sixth goal went in and then I'd like to ask him if his feet got wet when he walked on water. *Andy Richardson, Hackney, north-east London*

If only!

I'd like to ask Latch what he thinks of all the money swilling around the game these days, given that he supposedly divvied up his prize for scoring 30 goals in one season. Does he think that that sort of generosity (of spirit, not just wealth) could ever exist again now that teenagers are becoming millionaires and players move on just to get an even fatter pay cheque? *Adam Yates, Dollis Hill, north-west London*

It's just indicative of the times we're in. The game has changed so radically over the last ten years, and even more so over the last two or three years, and hold on to your hats because it's going to change again. I can foresee not only a bigger European involvement in terms of a league, but I can see a world league happening one day. FIFA are trying to harmonise all the leagues, and once they do that, with travel and communication getting easier, I can see a global league being set up. It's probably already been talked about and it wouldn't surprise me if plans were already being made for another 20 years time.

Why has he never gone into management? *Simon Martindale, Bristol, England*

Bob Latchford

I never really had the opportunity towards the end of my career. I drifted out of football and once you do that it's very difficult to get back in. I had a period of about seven years out of the game, so management was something that's not really attainable any more, especially given my age. I'm at Birmingham City now where my full posh title is Assistant Academy Director, and I work with the 16- to 19-year-olds.

How come he manages to look so good now? Good diet? Does he work out? *Colin Jones, Mossley Hill, Liverpool*
I don't particularly work out, but I do try and watch my diet. I've only started working out this past season for the first time in about 15 years. There was no particular reason for it; I just felt I should be a bit fitter than I was and so I started doing a bit – but nothing too strenuous.

Along with many hundreds of other youngsters I played out your great moments in the street or the schoolyard. Yes, I am rotund and, yes, I was always Bob Latchford, although, unlike you, I could never quite manage the walking-on-water bit, dead important equalisers, 30 goals . . . If you could relive one moment from your 'so near, yet so far' Everton career what would it be? *Frank Hargreaves, Bootle, Liverpool*
There are a couple, actually. I would like to have been fit for the '77 semi-final against Liverpool to see whether I would have made a difference on the day. And while I'm having my wishes granted, my other choice would be the '80 semi-final at Villa Park. I came on and I almost scored from a corner. I was 'that' much from touching the ball in, but I couldn't quite stretch my leg far enough. It was bouncing in the six-yard box and I tried to get my toe to it and it was gone. It would have been 2–1, so I was inches from putting us into an FA Cup final.

MIKE LYONS

Born 8 December 1951
July 1969 – August 1982
Apprentice

It was the day Harry Catterick got assaulted at Blackpool for dropping Alex Young. Joe Royle made his debut and I went with my three mates from school – we were all mad Evertonians. Before the match we were walking down the beach and coming towards us was Alan Ball. We couldn't believe our luck when he stopped to talk and we tried our utmost to persuade him to come to Everton. I remember it as if it was last week, and I still like to think that in some tiny way we might have influenced his decision because Alan Ball changed the course of Everton's history.

If ever there was a man who wore his blue heart on his sleeve it was Mike Lyons. A local lad who worked his way up the ranks, he played every game as if it were to be his last. Formidable, dedicated and totally fearless, his commitment was epitomised by his 'never-say-die' attitude:

I always thought I was a fan and a footballer. I had the privilege to play football for a living and I couldn't believe how lucky I was to be wearing the royal blue of Everton. I never thought I was very popular with the fans because I was always getting barracked, but the ultimate compliment I received is that I never shirked anything and I'm very proud of that accolade.

Kiss your badge; it's Big Mick Lyons!

When you were in the first team did you notice the crowd had a different attitude to you than to other players? *David Cairns, Newtonards, Northern Ireland*

You really get slagged off if you're a local lad, it was always like that and probably always will be. If you go through the years, there's Terry Darracott, Sammy Lee, Phil Boersma, Steve Seargeant – we were always the worst paid, we always put our heart and soul into it and we were the first to get berated. Some players who came along didn't give a damn about Everton, but we loved the club. Tony Cottee was a great player, but his heart was never in it. Duncan McKenzie was an entertainer; he always had a different philosophy than me. We'd always go to try and win but they'd go to entertain and it was a different attitude altogether.

Who were your footballing role models? *Tony Kennedy, Loughborough, England*

I only had heroes and my first one was Jimmy Gabriel. I chose James as my confirmation name in his honour, and my brother Joseph named his son Alex after the Golden Vision. They were very different players, as we were. Joseph was more skilful and I was more of a battler. Later on, I went and coached with Jimmy at Everton, so it all worked out perfectly.

Who had the biggest influence on him in his playing days at Goodison? *Jon Berman, West Derby, Liverpool*

I played for the team of the Holy Cross and we kept winning matches all the time, so I went to Everton as a striker. The coach was Tom Casey and he had an enormous influence on me.

When I was in the B team I was playing for my school on the Saturday morning and my dad would whisk me straight to the game afterwards and nobody would know. Sometimes I'd turn up with dirty legs, they must have thought I didn't wash very often.

Did you really wear a blue-and-white scarf in the Kop for a particularly awful defeat? *Tony Lloyd, Brockley, south-east London*

It was 5–0. I was only a young kid then, about 13, and the Kopites were all laughing at me.

What was the average wage you enjoyed in your era? *Paul Holmes, Hoylake, Wirral*

I started off on £6 and I got a rise to £8 a week. The first time I got in the first team I was on £20 and the most I ever earned in my whole career was £500.

Mike Lyons

The players they bought in were always on more than the locals, and I remember when Billy Bingham got sacked he called me into his office. He told me I'd done really well for him as captain and to give him a ring in a few days' time and he would tell me how much I should really be on.

I remember a derby match at Goodison when Alan Waddle scored the crabbiest winner you will ever see. Minutes before this, Mike scored at the Park End with a fantastic header, but laughing boy Emlyn and the Anfield Iron frog-marched the referee over to the linesman and after lots of pleading (I can see Hughes' crying face to this day) the ref changed his mind and the goal was disallowed. *Dave Kelly, Blackburn, England*

That was my 22nd birthday. Joe Harper had pulled the ball back from the line and I'd got up and headed it over Alec Lindsay – I didn't touch him. They gave Joe Harper offside, but he had actually pulled the ball back. It was a crazy decision but typical of the decisions that always seemed to go against us whenever we played Liverpool.

The ref was wrong, I never fouled Alec Lindsay, he didn't appeal and I don't know how they judged it to be offside for the life of me. After the match, we went out and got rotten drunk for my birthday. I share my birthday with Terry McDermott, we discovered that when we went away to Portugal with the England B team and I pinched his passport on the way back. We were both born in Mill Road Hospital too.

You played a number of positions for the Blues. Which one did you enjoy the most? *Steve Fairclough, Toronto, Canada*

I was probably most effective at centre-half. My skills were more suited to defending because I was better at destroying than creating, but I used to quite enjoy the challenge of playing somewhere else. I was OK upfront for one or two games, but then everybody expected me to be a centre-forward and I never really had it in me. I always thought that when I played upfront I had more of a nuisance value – for both teams! I even played in goal for Everton a couple of times, once against West Brom when we got beat 4–1 and my last ever game at Goodison when Nev got injured. We drew 3–3. I scored a goal, made a goal and ended up in goal that day.

I used to have a scrapbook about schools football and I seem to remember him scoring the winning goal for De La Salle. Does he still cherish that memory? *San Presland, New Brighton, Merseyside*

We beat David Johnson's school, Speke, 3–0 in the Echo Cup final, and then we won the Martindale Cup final. I remember when we won the Echo Cup it was a bit damaged because the year before a lad had pinched it and tried to melt it down in a frying pan.

Our school has produced a few players over the years; Paul Jewell and Francis Jeffers were there. There's a teenager there now called Rooney, keep an eye on him, he shows potential.

Was Paul Croft the best footballer the world had ever seen for his age? *Frank Hargreaves, Anfield, Liverpool*

He was in my kids' team and he was a good player. I thought part of my responsibility was to help build them as men as well as players, and whenever I hear of one who's done well I always feel delighted and proud.

Clive Thomas, Maine Road, 1977. Honest opinions of this fella, please. *Colm Kavanagh, Co. Wicklow, Republic of Ireland*

We all know the story of that game. He disallowed the goal, and when he came in the dressing-room Ken McNaught asked him why. He said it was obviously knocked in with a hand. At the end of the game he came back in the dressing-room and this time he said he'd disallowed it because 'it was an infringement of the rules of the Football Association' and we should watch it on the television and he'd be proved right. On the Monday he said he'd disallowed it because it was offside, but the linesman didn't flag. Knowing that, I went to a sports forum in St Helens and the linesman on duty that day was there, too. He said Clive Thomas had come to them and said: 'Listen, lads, we'd better get our story straight here.' All I know is that we were robbed.

Was it him I remember with his leg in plaster, jumping up and down in front of the dugout after Andy King scored that goal against the Reds? *Ray Finch, Havant, England*

I don't know if I was in plaster, but I'd had a bad cut and had a load of stitches in my knee the week before when we'd played QPR. I remember that game for one particular reason. I was in the dugout and I wanted to be right there because it was Liverpool. My mum had bought me a watch for my 18th birthday and I lost it during the game. To this day, I don't know where it went. I might have jumped up and it flew off somewhere, but I never found it again.

I met Mike in hospital when he was convalescing in Lourdes following a bad leg injury. Can he recall some cheeky kid getting past the security of the nuns and mother superior to get in to see

his hero? Does he remember a Neil Young tape that was given to him by me? *Jon Berman, West Derby, Liverpool*

Was it 'After the Gold Rush' or 'Harvest'? It must have been. I do vaguely remember that now that you mention it. Thank you.

When Manchester United battered us 6–2 on Boxing Day '77, were the players recovering from a hangover? I remember him and Gordon Lee on the cover of the match programme for two consecutive home games toasting the fans. *Kenny Fogarty, Amsterdam, Holland*

That game should never have been 6–2. We attacked and they attacked, but Gordon Hill scored four volleys from outside the box. Everything they hit that day went in, and I think we'd gone about two dozen games undefeated. It was a freakish game.

Does he ever look back at some of the old videos and think: 'What was I thinking about getting a haircut like that?' You remember, the curly one!! *Andy Howarth, Long Beach, California, USA*

To be honest, the worst part about that perm was that it was Roger Kenyon's wife who did it. She was chatting away and having a drink with Trish, my wife, and forgot that it was on my hair, so that's why it went funny. Never mix perms and drinking, it's a recipe for disaster.

It obviously meant so much to you being the captain of EFC, so what do you think of the attitude of players today when asked to play more than their complement of 30 games a season? *Paul Holmes, Hoylake, Wirral*

One of the things wrong with today's game is agents and their influence on the players. For us, we just got through games. I remember once at Sheffield Wednesday I had three broken ribs and I found out from Reidy that if you have an epidural in your spine, it numbs the pain enough for you to play. So I had that done at Walton Hospital and played against Newcastle. We beat them 4–2, but it was a big secret that I had those broken ribs. I think the problem is that players don't play if there's a little bit wrong with them because they fear they might get injured.

He had a wonderful reputation for bringing us back into matches from the dead by inspiring comebacks. Which was his most memorable? *San Presland, New Brighton, Merseyside*

They used to throw me upfront for the last ten minutes in the hope I could do something. I suppose my most memorable occasion was when I was in the reserve team. We were playing at Blackburn and were 1–0 down at full-time. I got myself up to the front and scored two goals in injury time and we won 2–1. I'll never forget that.

During the '70s I felt that some of our players went into derby matches with an inferiority complex, or at least a lack of confidence. Is there any truth in that? *Mike Owen, Childwall, Liverpool*

No, I would never say that, but we often got set up and cut-up. One time, Chris James, the *Mirror* journalist, asked in the pre-match interview whether I thought we had a chance. I said of course we did. The next day the headline read: 'Lyons says it's our game tomorrow'. I was misquoted, but we always went on the park believing that we would win.

I was going to ask him his opinion of Emlyn Hughes. Should be worth a laugh. *Pete Rowlands, Enfield, north London*

We all know what Emlyn's like; he was just full of himself. I used to do radio with Ray Clemence and I heard loads of stories about Emlyn. What Tommy Smith says is fair comment.

Is there still a place for a 'traditional' centre-half, or can Everton relax and watch a skinny ball-playing lad like Michael Ball develop into a central defender of note? *Mark Wilson, Warrington, England*

Dave Watson was a great centre-half, and I thought Materazzi was crap. He got injured every game, he never won a header and was always rolling around on the floor. I'm not a great lover of Rio Ferdinand, either. I think he comes out and looks the part and he can pass nicely enough, but he doesn't head or pick-up. He's a one-trick pony. Everton always did well when Dave Watson was playing.

You got to captain the team of your boyhood dreams, but didn't win a major trophy in your career. Would you swap one for the other? *Steve Fairclough, Toronto, Canada*

No, not really. There are players who've won trophies but not done particularly well in their careers. Look at somebody like David Fairclough, he played a total of about 85 league games in his whole career. His success was because of the team he was with. I've always been proud of what I did. I can tell the kids I played nearly 450 games for Everton, and I think I did OK.

Mike Lyons

Why did you selfishly score the fifth goal against Chelsea in 1978 instead of heading it back for Fat Latch to score his 30th of the season? *Ged Fox, Wickford, England*

Everyone bollocked me for that! I'd gone up to head it, knocked it into the other corner and the whole crowd just went 'Hhhhhhhhuh'. But I went down against Mickey Droy for the penalty so Latch could get the last one but I think the ref was kind that day. Of the £10,000 Bob won as a prize we all got a share of £192 and then he got stung for the tax.

As a kid I wanted to be the new Bob Latchford. Should I be ashamed? *Osmo Tapio Räihälä, Helsinki, Finland*

No, that would be a great person to be. The only thing you should be ashamed of is if you had a perm like Bob.

When they threw you up front for the last few minutes (a feature of my first two visits to Goodison, both v Norwich) did you go up sensing glory or did you trudge up like an errant child forced from in front of the telly to bring some coal in? *Neil Mckeown, Woolwich, south London*

I went up for every set piece, anyway. I would knock the centre-half and say: 'Come on, let's go', and I would get into his head. I scored a few, but they seemed to come in batches. I was always a decent runner, I wasn't very quick but I could get up and down. The strange thing was that in 1973–4 I was the leading goalscorer at Everton with nine but I used to get more from centre-half than centre-forward. I scored against Plymouth in the FA Cup, we won 3–1 away and I got two of them. I tried to lob the keeper from long distance, miskicked it and bent it right round him. Nobody could believe it, especially me.

Do you think that any players today would get a bus to the game like Terry Darracott? *Paul Holmes, Hoylake, Wirral*

A few of us used to get the bus to the game. I shouldn't think it would happen now, I don't think the players even know what a bus is any more.

He once put a diving header into the Leeds net while Norman Hunter tried to powerfully clear the ball with a thumping kick (that missed the ball). Did it ever cross his mind that had 'Bites Yer Legs' kicked him in the head he would have been in his grave now for 25 years? *Osmo Tapio Räihälä, Helsinki, Finland*

I think it was just instinctive. I saw the ball and went for it, but everyone does that. The photo of that was always up at Bellefield. Graham Smith, the youth team coach and director, used to have it. Now I think about it, I'd like to get a copy of it for the Southampton youth academy.

How much did it hurt never to win anything with Everton as a player (and Team Superstars doesn't count!)? *Neil Wolstenholme, Muswell Hill, north London*

We got robbed in Superstars, anyway! When we played against the athletes they had Geoff Capes, Paul Dickinson, Keith Connor and Daley Thompson. We had Andy King and Gordon Hill. We were winning 4–3 and they offered double points for the last game because everyone was involved and it was the tug of war – Geoff Capes beat us by himself!

Gordon Lee said that he was really impressed by the bike-riding event and would investigate the team riding to training every day (honest, I'm not kidding). Did this ever happen, or was Gordon employing a hitherto unsuspected sense of humour? *George Lee Stuart, Lismore, Australia*

I think he was. He never made us do any bike-riding. Where would we have all got bikes from, anyway?

Surely his own goal v Liverpool at the Anfield Road End would have totally eclipsed Sandy Brown's effort if it had been televised. Can he describe it for those who haven't seen it and how on earth did it happen? *San Presland, New Brighton, Merseyside*

Mark Higgins knocked the ball down to me and I knocked it back to George Wood with a half-volley. My touch was never the best and it sailed over George's head. The only thing I've got going for me was that George said he couldn't see the ball in the sun. As we know, George wore contact lenses and he didn't see much at times. Everyone knows the story of me winning a Blue money that day. The last time I was in Liverpool, I met the guy and he reminded me I'd won him 40 quid. Then a Liverpool fan told me I'd won him £100 and I was gutted.

Why could Dave Lawson never get more than six inches off the ground when he jumped? Is it infectious and, if so, does Mick have any theories as to how Dave passed the disease on to Paul Gerrard? *Neil Wolstenholme, Muswell Hill, north London*

I haven't seen enough of Paul Gerrard to comment. I know one thing, though, Paul Gerrard has got better shoulders than Dave Lawson. Dave never even had shoulders – he was like a triangle!

Mike Lyons

There is a notion amongst some supporters that the Everton team of Mike Lyons' day slipped into a habit of not training as hard as they might have. Does that idea have any credence whatsoever? *David Cairns, Newtonards, Northern Ireland*

No, that's crap; we really trained hard. There's a different school of thought about training these days. Then, we would go for a pint after the game, but I'd never been in a pub in my life after Tuesday, not even for a half. But all the players who had a drink with the local lads would always go training and nobody could accuse any of us of not working hard. Howard Wilkinson was manager at Leeds when I was in charge of the Everton reserves, and he came into the dressing-room and said: 'You see this lad here? He's the best professional I've ever played with.' So I'm not having anyone saying otherwise.

Why didn't he seem to be afraid of anything? Was it a question of timing or stupidity? *Osmo Tapio Räihälä, Helsinki, Finland*

Probably a mixture of both. When I was at Wednesday I played against Liverpool and the game had been going about four seconds. I knocked the ball back and Michael Robinson had gone right over the top and I kicked the ball right down the line. I never wore shin pads and I ended up with a great big gash in my leg. Our physio ripped my sock open, stitched it up right there and I went straight back on. I never felt the pain, there's lots of adrenalin coursing around and something else takes over.

Does it still amaze him that people from all corners of the globe come up to him and ask him to sign their 1977 League Cup final programme (as happened when he was commentating for ESPN STAR Sports and I was showing him a video of that great 6–0 result v Coventry from 1977 in my office)? *Julian Jackson, Hong Kong, SAR of PRC*

I remember this guy. I really enjoyed doing the commentaries there. My friend does them now, a lad called Scott O'Donnagh. He played for me in Singapore. Yeah, no matter where I go there's an Evertonian asking me to sign a programme or something.

Winger Gary Jones had brilliant skill so why did he not make the grade? *George Mason, Clearwater, Florida, USA*

He did have brilliant skill; he thought he was Peter Thompson, didn't he? I don't know why he didn't make it. You see a few players who have lots of talent but they don't quite make the grade. Gaz was a bit scatty at times, but he was a real nice kid and a good Evertonian, too.

How hard was it for him as an Evertonian to be the only one trying during the dark days of Gordon Lee? Why didn't he just hit him on our behalf? *Jim Lynch, Brentwood, England*

I liked Gordon Lee, he was a good guy. He was honest, he was straight, he worked very hard and was completely football-orientated. When we went down to Norwich the drive home was the coach journey from hell – about five or six hours. We were all dying for a pint and stopped at a pub. I was sitting next to Gordon and before I'd even had a taste of my drink he was doing all the formations using our pint glasses as defenders. Every time I tried to take a sip he was off again, moving us about all over the table. He only ever thought about football.

One of my big things against Gordon Lee was his preference for Jim Pearson over Duncan McKenzie, but I'd be interested to know how good Mike thought Pearson was. *Colin Smith, Princeton, New Jersey, USA*

I'd have Jim every time. He worked hard, was a great player and altogether more of a team player. Duncan was an entertainer and he was great when we were winning. Danny Blanchflower once said that Duncan was the icing on the cake – but you needed the cake first.

Does he wish that he had a chance at managing at the top level in England as opposed to perennial strugglers Marine Castle in Singapore? Does he think he will ever get the chance? *Julian Jackson, Hong Kong, SAR of PRC*

I managed at Grimsby and that was a terrible place. If you won four games in a row they would all say: 'Huh, we'll definitely get beat next game.' I arrived there in bad circumstances and it unwittingly involved Everton Football Club. The chairman had no interest in football whatsoever, and he put his son on the board. Then Grimsby came to Everton and Paul Wilkinson scored. It finished 1–0 and knocked Everton out of the League Cup.

All the Grimsby team were staying in the Adelphi and had a good few drinks in celebration. The son of the chairman copped off with the barmaid and ended up leaving his wife. His dad got him thrown off the board and I arrived at Grimsby as player–manager that same week.

The chairman had no interest in football and all he wanted to do was sell players. We sold any decent player we had. We had a lad called Andy Peake, who was pretty good. We played at Brighton and after the match one of the lads asked me what Jimmy Hill was doing interviewing Peaky about going to Charlton. I went to the directors' box and discovered that the chairman and the managing director had arranged to sell him without even consulting me.

My former neighbour in Halewood reckons she went out on a date with you and (as proof) she got me your autograph. She mentioned that you carried a notepad around with you so you could give it to people if they didn't have any paper on them. True or false? *Ged Fox, Wickford, England*
That never happened. That's definitely not true. I might have had a pen. I could have been somewhere and had something in my pocket, but I didn't carry a notepad with me on the off chance I'd get asked – honestly.

What was it like playing in the same team as Duncan McKenzie? *John Walton, Dubai, United Arab Emirates*
Infuriating at times. I remember one day in training when Dave Thomas was there. He was a good pro and never used to lose his temper or anything like that. One day he completely lost his rag and screamed: 'Duncan, you are the worst professional I have ever played with in my entire life!' Duncan just shrugged his shoulders and walked off, but we were all gobsmacked, we'd never heard Dave Thomas even raise his voice before, never mind say something so harsh.

Did he ever get a kick of the ball when he trained against Duncan McKenzie? *Kenny Fogarty, Amsterdam, Holland*
Yes. Duncan wasn't really a team player, he did his own thing.

How did he get on with Gordon Lee and did he have any say on the way Duncan McKenzie was treated by the manager? *Andy Howarth, Long Beach, California, USA*
I got on very well with Gordon Lee and I had no say in anything. We all worked hard, we had a good rapport and, to be honest, the crazy thing about football is this: ask any old Evertonian, they'll tell you they really liked watching that team because there was always something happening.

Where did the Harvey era go wrong? I think we had the players, the quality, but not the know-how. Instead of moving forwards the three years he was in charge, we appeared to take a step backwards. *Alex Langley, Leeds, England*
I don't agree with that. When Colin Harvey got sacked we were about seventh in the league. Colin was always top class. I think he was such a perfectionist that he took too much on himself. He was so intense about

Everton Football Club, and to this day he is the best trainer I've ever met in my life. Some of the players didn't like Howard, but when Colin arrived they really loved and respected him.

How did he feel when Howard Kendall ended his time as an Everton player, with the likes of Mark Higgins coming through the ranks? Did he feel things were on the up for the club? *Colm Kavanagh, Co. Wicklow, Republic of Ireland*

I just felt sad. I thought Higgy and Billy Wright were good players, but one of the reasons I became pretty good was because I played alongside Roger Kenyon, and he helped me to become what I did. I'd like to think I helped Mark Higgins and Billy Wright. There's nothing you can do to hold back time, it was just a natural progression.

Why did he leave Everton? Did he jump or was he pushed? *Julian Jackson, Hong Kong, SAR of PRC*

I don't think Howard really fancied me any more and there were younger lads coming through. You seem to become part of the furniture and you get taken for granted. I would say that I was so much more appreciated at Wednesday than I ever was at Everton. They spent money on me and seemed to really back me. That's one of the disadvantages of being a local lad. I didn't want to stay in the reserves, I still got paid, but it wasn't the same as playing, and it didn't seem right.

What were his thoughts when he ran onto the Goodison pitch in '84 in Sheffield Wednesday's colours? *Osmo Tapio Räihälä, Helsinki, Finland*

I remember the first time I came back I got a great reception and it was a real battle of a game. We had a right good go and drew 1–1. Brian Marwood went over the top and Adrian Heath was really badly injured. When I was going off the pitch I got booed and slaughtered. So I was clapped on and jeered off.

I don't know if you remember, but when Neville played at Wembley he had a T-shirt with 'I love my wife' written on it. My mate at Wednesday was Martin Hodge, the keeper. So we went to John Quinn's sports shop in Sheffield and had T-shirts made with 'We love Nev's wife, too'. Before the game at Hillsborough, Hodge showed his T-shirt to Nev. We got stuffed 5–1, I marked Lineker, who scored two, so that was our retribution.

Who had the worst haircut at the club during his time? Trevor Ross? *Colm Kavanagh, Co. Wicklow, Republic of Ireland*

Mike Lyons

Trevor's was natural. I think it had to be between Latch and me. Gary Jones used to eat his hair. Even in the middle of a match you could look over and he would be eating his hair.

What was the atmosphere like when Jimmy Case assaulted Geoff Nulty and ended his career? Did the off-field bonhomie have a bit of a tinge that evening? *George Lee Stuart, Lismore, Australia*
That tackle was bad, but that's the way football was in those days, especially derbies. I remember one time whacking their keeper, and Graeme Souness kicked me so hard in the backside that I had to go off.

As a life-long Evertonian did you say anything to Marwood after the Goodison game about his assault on Adrian Heath? *Ian Roberts, Wallasey, Wirral*
Brian Marwood was never the bravest player, anyway. He once scored 30 goals in a season and every one of them was at home. He disappeared when we were away. I think that incident happened out of fear. I don't think he would have done it out of badness, it was just poor timing on his part.

I saw Mick at Southampton after he'd moved to Sheffield Wednesday and I think he was suspended. We won, as we often did in the '80s, and, wearing his blue and white Everton scally hat, he had no bother relating to us travelling supporters. Many of the players these days wouldn't understand what we do to watch Everton. What was his most memorable away day watching the Blues? *Steve Kirkwood, Crowthorne, England*
That would be the FA Cup final when we got beat 3–1 by Liverpool – remember when Gary Stevens made the mistake and we got done? I was commentating for Radio Merseyside and was manager of Grimsby at the time. I'd driven there with Lawrence Darracott, Terry's brother, and my mate, John Cooney, who was a Red. We had a red scarf out of one window and a blue one out of the other.

We all know how the game went, and it was awful. I still had to do the radio stuff after the game had finished, and I felt sick with disappointment. When we were leaving there was this guy standing in the middle of Wembley wearing top hat and tails with two arm puppets and a paper bag. It was Liverpool's own Doctor Fun. I could have died on the spot for him! Lawrence said: 'Oh, there's Jimmy, he lives round our way, give him a lift, Lyonsy.' So, like a big mug, I gave Doctor Fun a lift all the way home.

As soon as he got in the car he was trying to give me beer, although I was actually driving. He was sitting behind me when he cracked a can open and it shot all over the back of my head. He was telling us how he used to mime to Beatles records at Butlins, and it was like a waking nightmare. Then he took his shoes off and his feet stank but that was only the tip of the iceberg. All the way home, whenever we passed a coach, he wound the window down and was shouting: 'Look who's in the car, Mickey Lyons, and we stuffed them 3–1!'

We got to Knutsford services and my mate said he would drive to give me a rest. Doctor Fun was going on about how he was going to ring Billy Butler and tell him I'd given him a lift.

We finally got him home and were trying to get rid of him as quickly as possible. We bundled him out, John put his foot down and sped off. We looked again and Doctor Fun was running alongside the car. We were waving at him and saying 'Yeah, see ya!', and trying to get away, but he was going mental, waving and pointing frantically. We realised we had his coat-tails in the car door and we'd ripped his coat right up to his neck. He was livid and stalked off to the pub, and instead of phoning Billy Butler he slagged me off all night. He's probably still slagging me to this day.

When Billy Wright made it to the first team did he not think that the lad hadn't aged since his days at Wolves and England? *Colm Kavanagh, Co. Wicklow, Republic of Ireland*

I was the best man at Billy's wedding. I was Andy King's best man, too. Billy was a good player who was prone to putting on too much weight. I don't think Howard did him any favours when he said he had to lose weight and told all the press. He said Billy had pissed the fatness test, being sarcastic, which didn't do him any good at all.

When Howard came back to Everton, Colin had been manager and he had gone. There was Terry, Paul Power, Graham Smith and myself on the coaching staff. Howard wanted Colin to come back as coach, so he got rid of us all. Then he told us that it was a directors' decision, but that was a load of bollocks, it was his own.

What was managing–coaching an Arab team like? Could he compare their performances with some of Everton's during the '70s? *Jon Berman, West Derby, Liverpool*

Well, this person doesn't know any geography, does he? Brunei is in Borneo!

I really enjoyed it. We just had to get on to them and really make them work hard. It was the same as coaching anywhere else, really.

Mike Lyons

What was the Sultan of Brunei like? *John Walton, Dubai, United Arab Emirates*

I used to take his son, His Royal Highness Prince Billah, for training three times a week. He was a really nice, quiet lad. As a goalkeeper he wasn't that good, and when we had matches I used to tell the opposition that they mustn't shoot too hard.

He was a big fan of Schmeichel and I couldn't have that, so I got in touch with Nev and he gave me his shirt. I gave it to Prince Billah, the next Sultan of Brunei, and told him to remember that Neville Southall was the best goalkeeper in the world.

There was a story a few years ago that the Sultan was going to buy Everton, and I think my mate started that. Jim Pearson and I were over there working, and it all seemed to fit.

It's a yellow and red world in the Premiership these days, not to mention 'video review panels' and trials by tabloid that make the scandals of the '60s seem rather tame. How many times would an in-his-prime Mike Lyons have been sent off or yellow-carded in an average season of ground-level heading and knee-high, must-win-the-ball or stop-that-big-bastard tackles? *Mark Wilson, Warrington, England*

I don't think I was ever a dirty player. I never did anything bad. I never even went over the top – well, maybe once, at Wednesday.

Is it true you wore an Everton shirt under your Sheffield Wednesday shirt? *Ged Fox, Wickford, England*

No, that's not true.

Does he believe that there has been another Everton player since himself who has worn the Blue of Everton with more pride? I say this as I remember watching on numerous occasions as he threw himself in front of blasts at goal, something that you don't see a lot of nowadays. *John Walton, Dubai, United Arab Emirates*

I think Dave Watson was a great player. I always say that as a centre-back you should keep it simple and give it to the players who can play. Waggy never makes a mistake because he doesn't try anything too complicated. He was a good player and great to coach because he always wanted to do extra and improve himself. Waggy is right up there in my estimation. To be honest, when I last came home I saw Hutchison and thought he was great. I was never a lover of Dacourt, he was a showboat, and when they did all the stats at the end of the season I think Hutch made 17 goals and Dacourt made one. He seems to be doing better at Leeds, but he was no good for us. Hutchison was our best player because he made things happen. You tell me why the manager would get rid of his best player. It sounds crazy to me.

Anyone you played with that you thought was really in a different class? *Paul Holmes, Hoylake, Wirral*

Of the people I played with that would have to be Bob Latchford, he was just brilliant. I went to see him at Birmingham last week, where he trains the kids. I spoke to his lads and told them that Bob had been my hero. I invited him over to Perth, so maybe he can wangle that. I'd love to spend some time with him again.

Would you like to take the opportunity of this book to give a definitive and public ruling on the vexed question of wearing red hats at the match? *Tony Lloyd, Brockley south-east London*

It's quite strange that when you're in the City of Liverpool it's Everton or Liverpool. But when you live abroad you support them both to the death – well, I don't let anyone have a go at them. But you really shouldn't be wearing a red cap to go and watch Everton. I know I wouldn't.

What's he up to nowadays? *Andy Howarth, Long Beach, California, USA*

I'm Director of Football at the Southampton Academy in Perth, Australia.

How's it going over in Oz? Does he plan to stay there for good now? *Colin Jones, Mossley Hill, Liverpool*

I don't know, I seem to have been over this side of the world for ages now. I'm really happy where I am and it's full of Scousers and Jocks, so it's just like being at home, but with the sun shining every day.

Does he despair at the thought of what Everton is going through at the moment? *John Walton, Dubai, United Arab Emirates*

I can't understand a lot of what's gone on at the club. Selling Hutchison still mystifies me – why would we sell our best player? I can't understand it for the life of me. I think football has become shady these days, and I'll leave it at that.

Mike Lyons

If offered the chance to come back and work for Everton in some capacity would he take it? *Neil Wolstenholme, Muswell Hill, north London*

There's a story there, but I really can't repeat it. It still makes me sad.

Move from Goodison Park, yes or no? *Paul Holmes, Hoylake, Wirral*

I think to go forward as a club we have to move. Goodison is a great place, but it's got obscured views and it's quite dated, so we need to move for the good of the club. A lad told me he'd offered Everton a 60,000-all-seater stadium somewhere up the motorway, outside Liverpool, because he owned all the land. He even said he would build it for them, it's farming land and worth so much an acre, but if there was a stadium there it would be worth a fortune – I don't think the club got back to him.

What happened to the team he used to run in the West Derby Sunday League (circa 1978–80). They used to be called MALPAS and because of Lyons's 'celebrity' status in Liverpool they got quite a bit of local media coverage. Did any of the lads go on to greater football heights? *Ian Ainsworth, Chiswick, west London*

George Wood was the assistant and Davie Jones was the coach. Paul Jewell was one of my lads, so was Sammy Lee.

What do you say to people who, although admirers of yours, imply that you were lacking in skills but made up for it with commitment and competitiveness? Do you regard that as a compliment or an insult? *David Cairns, Newtonards, Northern Ireland*

It was a bit of a backhanded compliment and it made me feel a bit resentful. I played at the highest level and for England Under-23s, so you have to be of a certain standard. To be a centre-half you have to be good in the air and able to tackle, and that's what I did.

How close do you think that Everton was to having potentially a championship-winning team in the '70s? *Paul Holmes, Hoylake, Wirral*

We were really close. We got robbed in the Clive Thomas incident, and everybody knows that. We were robbed in a few other matches too, but we had a good side. There was Latch, Dobbo, and Dave Thomas. We scored some good goals and had great players. I thought our main problem was we didn't have a top-class keeper. Go back to how many times Clemence saved Liverpool, while we went between Lawson and Dai Davies. While no one could turn around and blame them, top keepers win you the game and that's why, when Neville arrived, things took a turn for the better.

What was his proudest moment for Everton? *John Walton, Dubai, United Arab Emirates*

There are lots of different moments I'm proud of. We got to the final of the League Cup and that was great. Even when we got a result I was happy, but, overall, I was most proud when I was made Everton captain because that had always been my ambition over and above playing for England.

Did he ever feel like giving up due to all the bad luck he had as a player in a Blue shirt? *Jon Berman, West Derby, Liverpool*

No, I didn't have any bad luck. I played for Everton for nine years and I went on to have good years at Sheffield Wednesday. I never had bad luck. I had a few decisions that went against me, but they say you're given a big shoulder so you can carry the burden.

I remember the day I went to Sheffield Wednesday and that record by Jon and Vangelis, 'I'll Find My Way Home', came on the radio and I started to cry because I'd left my beloved Everton. I went to a pub in Maghull called The Meadows on the way home and was sitting at the bar remembering all the good times with tears in my eyes. This fella came in and said: 'Hey, you, Lyons, you were always shite, I'm glad you've gone', so it brought me back to earth with a bump.

Mick Lyons is up there with the dyed-in-the-wool Blues who supported the team and then went on to fulfil the dream we all have to wear the royal Blue. I would like to ask him, at a time when so many young players who grew up supporting Everton have slipped through the net and ended up playing for Liverpool, could he ever have been tempted to pull on the red shirt? *Tony Kennedy, Loughborough, England*

I always admired other players, and I think Shankly once said that of all the Evertonians he wouldn't mind me. I think I was similar to their mindset. But I'm a Blue, and you're an Evertonian all your life. Nothing will change that.

KEVIN RATCLIFFE

Born 12 November 1960
November 1978 – August 1992
Apprentice

Football was never the same for me after I left Everton, how could it have been? I was the captain at the club I'd loved all my life in its finest hour. I went on to play for other clubs, and although I always wanted to win losing never really seemed to hurt any more.

Howard Kendall had spotted the talented young Ratters from over at Ewood Park:

I had my eye on him for a while because I liked his style. I enquired about his availability as part of a swap deal with Kevin Stonehouse. Everton told me I had no chance. It's funny how it all works out in the end, because, of course, I inherited him not long after.

Kevin was special and you could see that straightaway. The 'original' Roy Keane, he was disciplined, a natural leader and epitomised everything I wanted in a captain. He made my job a lot easier and he wore his shirt with enormous pride, and as a manager you can't ask for more than that.

Tenacious, impulsive, committed and, without doubt, 'Blue' to the bone, Kevin Ratcliffe is made of stern stuff, make no mistake.

I'd always get a good tackle in on the centre-forward early on, it would enhance my performance and he'd be nervous the next time he got the ball, knowing that I'd definitely be coming in from behind. It was a case of dictating who was the boss, and that's the way I played it.

Get the picture? Kevin Ratcliffe, spill the beans.

What do you remember about your debut against Man United in front of 45,000? *John Walton, Dubai, United Arab Emirates*

Was it only 45,000? It seemed like a hell of a lot more. I was told the day before at about four o'clock that John Gidman was ill so I'd be playing centre-back with Mick Lyons and that Billy Wright would move to right-back. It was amazing, my chance had come at last and it was to be against Man United. There's only Liverpool that would have been a bigger game.

We had Bob Latch and Brian Kidd, so we had a good side ourselves. Lou Macari and Joe Jordan were upfront for them and I just loved it. The biggest cheer of the night was when Jimmy Greenhoff came on. He'd been out injured and it was one of his comeback games.

Funnily enough, about 16 years later I'd gone to Mauritius with the over-35s and I was rooming with Jimmy Greenhoff. This fella arrived, he was limping and looked like he was getting on a bit. I explained that it was a private function for footballers only, and he told me he was Jimmy Greenhoff! I remembered him as this blond-haired lad and a fantastic player, but time hadn't been kind to him.

Was it power or clinical precision that took his 40-yarder into the Kop end in '86, and does he have a picture of his fist-clenched reaction to that goal that we could post on the Internet? *Paul Christopherson, Nottingham, England*

It certainly wasn't precision, was it? I never scored many goals, so I tried to make the most of them, but I was thinking: 'How the hell's that gone in?' and I still can't believe I've never been called up in the court case!

It was a 40-yard screamer that bobbled six or seven times before it took a wicked movement on the last bounce. It was just a badly hit shot, which found its way under Bruce. I'm not really one for photos and I've not seen that one for years.

Ask him if Gary Lineker tried to claim that goal, as I swear to this day it deflected in off him. *Dave Richman, Johannesburg, South Africa*

He did say it grazed his bottom stud, just the faintest of touches, but I think Gary had already scored about 30 goals that year, so he wasn't getting that one, it was definitely mine.

After Ratters scored against Grobbelaar, he clearly didn't know how to celebrate properly! Did he practise in front of a mirror

afterwards, just in case it happened again? *David Tickner, Bowring Park, Liverpool*

Not really, I scored once every two hundred games so it would have been an awful waste of time. You don't know how you'll react when you score a goal, although the lads these days look as if they rehearse their celebrations. It's a thing I never really thought about; well, I wouldn't need to, would I? But when you score against that lot it's the best feeling in the world and anything goes.

You had a very similar heart to Mick Lyons. Was it him who inspired you as a youngster? *John Walton, Dubai, United Arab Emirates*

No, absolutely not. Mick was an out-and-out battler and his game was all about winning. Whatever he competed in, he wanted to win, he needed to win and he would win. He thought he was playing for England in every game, even in training.

I had an argument with Mick about a long-distance run, which I was hopeless at. He told me to imagine I was running for my country. I told him it was useless and I just couldn't do long distances. He said: 'Well, I can!' and I said: 'Yeah, but you can't run a short distance, but I can, and I win every one of them!' Mick could do the 12-minute run with ease, but he thought everybody should be the same as him and if they weren't, it used to get to him at times.

He was a full-on Evertonian, whereas I was a bit more conscious about what people thought. A lot of the team weren't playing with enough dedication for Mick because they weren't dyed-in-the-wool Blues who would die for the cause. Mick thought everybody should feel the same passion as him. It was a crying shame he didn't win anything with Everton because there's never been a bigger Evertonian than Mick Lyons. To win something would have been an absolute dream. I'm a mad Evertonian, but I keep a lot of it to myself. He can't keep it quiet and he wears his heart on his sleeve. Just speak to him and you'll realise he still dreams about the club to this day.

Ratters ended up at left-back in a back line containing four centre-halves. Would he have left Everton if he had continued playing there? Sorry, Kev, I thought you were crap at left-back, but a god in the centre. *Clive Blackmore, Washington DC, USA*

That's a fair comment. I actually played left-back coming towards the end of my time at Everton and I quite enjoyed it when I was more experienced. Early on it was a little bit nerve-racking, I was very close to the fans and I could hear the abuse they were giving to me.

Yes, I would have moved on, but then again, would I have made an impact on the game if I had? It's quite possible I'd have only ended up a left-back somewhere else. Deep down, I knew that my position was as a centre-back and I made my debut as a centre-back. I didn't enjoy it on the left at all until I was older and wiser. I think my distribution got better with age, but I was never the greatest left-back in the world.

During your youth years at Everton did you ever think that you would make the grade with all the boo-boys on your back? *John Walton, Dubai, United Arab Emirates*
I set a target that I wanted to play for Everton at 19 and I achieved that. I wanted to be an international by the time I was 21 and I actually made it at 20. I couldn't understand the boo-boys' mentality, because I was a Blue and all I ever wanted to do was play for Everton. But then you realise there's more to it than that and you do need a little bit extra. I was young, and most probably playing in the wrong position, but I don't think I got too many boos when I played at centre-back.

I've got this idea in my head that he never warmed up on the pitch for home games, but he did away from Goodison Park. If this is the case, I'm sure it can easily be explained away as a footballer's superstition, but something must have triggered this ritual. What? *Gary Hughes, Whiston, Merseyside*
Early on in my career, I never warmed up at all – home or away. In fact, I never even used to go out when we were at home. I would have a bath at two o'clock, do some stretches and just get ready for the match. When I went out, I'd have a couple of sprints on the pitch and that was me, sorted. After a while, I did warm up at away games because I'd been stuck in a hotel all day and I needed to get a bit of fresh air. I never warmed up too hard though, and I certainly never broke into a sweat.

When I came back after my groin injury, I realised the importance of it and I think the older you get, the more care you take of yourself. There was no deliberate superstition about it, although if you thought something worked, you would do it all the time.

Howard was superstitious. He would always play our lucky Bruce Springsteen tape. Another tape we had was The Christians. We played it on the coach in every cup game in '85 and when we got to the final the tape wasn't on the bus and we got beat. Martin Keown used to play 'Simply the Best' by Tina Turner. I used to absolutely hate it, and to subject us all to that was unforgivable.

Kevin Ratcliffe

Some say the Oxford match, others, like me, the Coventry match in the Milk Cup where Reidy came on as sub. What did he think was the turning point? *San Presland, New Brighton, Merseyside*

I certainly think of the Coventry match as the turning point, but I suppose people have got different recollections of what happened at different times. I remember that match clearly because Adrian Heath was playing, so it was well publicised, and the TV cameras were there. We actually played that game in front of 9,000 – you could almost count the crowd and you knew exactly who was heckling you.

We were getting slaughtered and Reidy came on as substitute. Sharpie had gone over on his ankle and we'd used all the subs, but we got back into the game and were drawing 1–1. A cross came over in the last minute and Graeme – even with his bad ankle – rose above Brian Kilcline. The ball hit the side of Graeme's head and went in to the back of the net. I'll never know how he got there or how it went in to this day. It wasn't the best of games, but we were applauded off. That's massive pressure for a young team that's just getting together and if you can come through a game like that, you can do anything. It was certainly the turning point for me, it all seemed to fall into place after that, and I think Reidy is of the same opinion.

Of the people you played with, who would be your starting eleven? *Keith Wilson, Waterloo, Liverpool*

I don't think you can sway too far from the Championship-winning sides, but I'd put Paul Power at left back – he was a good signing. Dave Watson, Steve McMahon and Bob Latchford would most probably have got in those sides too, but I can't decide who I would drop. It's a tough call.

Who was the person he didn't get along with most during his tenure as our most successful captain ever? *Kenny Fogarty, Amsterdam, Holland*

It was very rare that I didn't get on with people, but Pat Van den Hauwe was one that I didn't particularly like. I didn't enjoy his company and I thought he was on a different planet from me, but I respected him as a footballer. I didn't blank him, we did speak if there was something to be said, but we never saw eye to eye.

Thinking back over his Everton career, how relieved was he that he didn't sign for Ipswich when things were not going right? *Rob Bland, Morecambe, England*

I never got to hear about Ipswich until about six months after they'd come in. Howard was very cute in that way. Eventually, he pulled me to one side and said he'd had different offers for me – the other was Stoke City. But he blatantly turned them down and said he wanted to see me to sign a new contract. That was great news to me, because there was only ever one club I wanted to play for and that was Everton. It gave me a great sense of belonging too. I knew I was wanted and a part of the master plan, so it spurred me on.

Les Ferdinand claimed Everton Football Club was the most racist in the league. Was it? *Mark Kenyon, Minnesota, USA*
It was a fact that there were no black players at Everton, so maybe it seemed like that at the time. But you have to remember that until John Barnes arrived, there were no black players at Liverpool either, so Ferdinand might have had a point in that respect. I don't know how it worked out that way but there certainly wasn't any racist element involved.

Who was his bestest pal at Everton? And who was the funniest? I have a sneaky feeling it's Big Nev, but I may be wrong. *David Chow, Manchester, England*
No, he wasn't the funniest! My best mate was Sheeds, we changed next to each other and we roomed together, although I'm fortunate to be able to say that I had a few good mates. Graeme Sharp is still a very good friend and so is Big Nev, who I shared lifts with down to the Wales games before he could drive. I was lucky that I got on with everybody, but Sheeds was my true friend and he probably knows more about me than anyone else. He wasn't very funny though.

There were a few characters about in those days, but I'd say John Bailey was the funniest. He was good company and he always had a joke to tell. We had quite a squad who were renowned for playing tricks on people and you always had to be on your toes, you couldn't relax for a minute in and around Bellefield. Nev was very sharp witted because he was so cynical. He came out with some great one-liners, I'll give him that.

How knackered were you in the FA Cup final against Man United? How much did the team's tiredness really affect the outcome against ten men? *David Cairns, Newtonards, Northern Ireland*
There's a lot of emphasis on the amount of games you have to play, and there's no doubt it played a big part. But the turning point was the sending-off because that gave Man United that bit extra to fight for. If you look at the

tape, we absolutely battered them, they never got out of their own half and when they did, they scored. It was just one of those games because up to the sending-off we were absolutely murdering them. We created all the chances, but they put Frank Stapleton at the back and things just went from there.

Which striker did he fear the most? *Ciaran McConville, Dublin, Republic of Ireland*
That has to be Ian Rush. I did well against him for the first five years of my career and after that he took over. I'm convinced he owes his success to me because I made him a great player. I got him the move to Juventus and back to Liverpool, and if it wasn't for him playing against me he might never have made it as big as he did.

Rush was different, he worked on pace and space and was a very clinical finisher. He caused us a good few problems, to say the least, and now he's my best mate in football, which just makes it worse. John Fashanu wasn't the greatest player in the world, but he was robust and what he didn't have in skill he made up for in willingness. He was aggressive and a bit of a bully on the pitch. Dave Watson and I still have the scars to prove it. Mark Hughes was good to play against and I didn't want to be meeting people like Ian Wright either as I was coming towards the end of my time at Everton.

I remember him getting sent off for smacking Tommy Hutchison by the corner flag. What happened there? *Clive Blackmore, Washington DC, USA*
It was just naivety, allowing myself to get wound up by an old pro and trying to take the law into my own hands. It's something I bitterly regret and something I learned from. I still believe it cost us a Wembley appearance because City went on and played Tottenham in the Cup final.

How and why did the Double slip out of our grip and into the greasy RedShite hands? Surely there had to be something more scientific than Lineker's 'lucky' boots going AWOL at Oxford! *Colm Kavanagh, Co. Wicklow, Republic of Ireland*
If you think about it, we lost the Double on two games. We lost it against Liverpool in the Cup at Wembley and the Oxford game in the league. The year before we were one game off the Treble against Man United at Wembley and then the Double the year after that. There were a couple of times when the Double was up there and we never did it, it was bitterly disappointing.

Precisely how much contact did Vinnie Jones make with you when he nutted you and you dropped like a sack of spuds? *Richard Marland, Waterloo, Liverpool*

Contact was made and that was enough. I was lucky he didn't catch my nose, although now as I think about it, he might have straightened it for me. But he caught me on the forehead and what do you do in that situation? I never actually fell to the floor – I dropped down on one knee. There was a big campaign to try and get Vinnie off with it, but he had made contact and the intent was there. It was part of his tough-guy image, but it didn't wash with me, I've certainly met much harder men than Vinnie Jones – Steve McMahon, for instance.

What did Vinnie Jones say to you after he got sent off for butting you? *Ian Roberts, Wallasey, Wirral*

We've never really spoken since then, although we've crossed paths and played against each other. When he went to Sheffield United and I was at Chester they brought a team up, but we never communicated, not even in a tackle.

Did he ever wear the white trousers and floral shirt he bought at the shop I worked at in 1979? They looked good when he tried them on. *John Walton, Dubai, United Arab Emirates*

Sometimes people would mix me up with one or two other players, but if this guy is an Evertonian and he says I've gone in his shop then I must have bought them. But that doesn't mean I wore them, I might have just wanted to do some shopping. I'll admit, I've owned white trousers in my time, but I definitely can't remember a flowery shirt.

Did he really batter Steve McMahon on the training pitch at Bellefield? And if he did, tell him thanks! *Kenny Fogarty, Amsterdam, Holland*

No, Stevie and I were big mates. We came through the ranks together as Evertonians, so I grew up with him from 16, and I used to go to his mum and dad's house in the afternoon for sandwiches if we were playing a game at night.

When he left Everton, he was one of those we sorely missed and all for the sake of Howard not backing down to his wage demands. Having said that, you can't knock Howard's decision because we went on, produced a number of midfield players and won things, but he was missed. We kept in contact while he was at Aston Villa but as soon as he signed for Liverpool that was the end of our friendship. The hardest thing for me is to accept is that he's now a Liverpudlian, and always will be. He comes from an Everton background and went from being a fanatical Blue to becoming a Red. I still find it hard to believe or understand.

I remember you booting Ian Wright up in the air in 1990 when he played for Crystal Palace and that there was a bit of a ruck going on. Did you get on with him away from the park, because there was always a bit of friction when you played? *Kenny Fogarty, Amsterdam, Holland*

There was always friction with Crystal Palace because there was always something nasty going on when we played against them – not to me, but to other players in my side, and I felt as if I had to protect them sometimes. I was always a bit of a hothead, even later on, and I didn't like anyone in my team being bullied.

I've met Ian once or twice since I finished playing, and I've got on great with him. I wasn't a great socialiser with other players, in fact there's no way I would socialise with anyone from another team unless it was Ian Rush, or they were Welsh.

Who finally managed to get through to you that your early '80s moustache looked quite ridiculous? *Ian Roberts, Wallasey, Wirral*

It was the 'in thing' then, along with flares and those really thick-heeled shoes. If you put that muzzie in relation to the gear we used to wear, it was almost acceptable.

I was watching the Everton video not so long ago and there was this player on the bench. He was wearing a brown suit with a waistcoat and I was wondering who the bloody hell he could be. I rewound it about three or four times and it was me! I didn't even recognise myself, that's how embarrassing I looked, but it was just one of those things – I looked 32 at 16. There are youth team pictures of me and I can imagine people saying: 'Who the hell is he? He's never 17, I'm not having that, I want to see his birth certificate!' With the likes of Stevie Mac, Mark Ward, Paul Lodge and Joe McBride beside me, I looked like I could pass as their dad.

But, I hold my hands up, it definitely was a bit ridiculous, but something I'd had for a few years. One thing I've got going for me is that I never went for the curly hair, I wasn't that stupid. I'd have looked like a proper Scouser then, wouldn't I?

Higgins, Waggy or Mountfield – who was better? *John Walton,*
Dubai, United Arab Emirates

If you look at stats, then it's probably Dave Watson, but I would like to have
seen what would have happened if Mark Higgins and me had carried on
playing together. I don't think Dave Watson would have even been at the
club if Higgy had not been injured, and that's with the greatest respect to
Dave.

You talk about bravery and Mick Lyons; well, Higgy was even braver. As a
player, he was quicker and more skilful with the ball than any of those players.
As a captain, he was a great leader and he taught me everything I knew,
leading by example. It was nothing short of tragic that he had to retire so early
from the game. A lot of people don't realise that it should have been him
going up the steps for the FA Cup instead of me. The biggest regret I have is
not asking him to come up with us. If I could turn the clock back now, I would
do just that. I suppose I was just being selfish, because I was so young, but I
deeply regret it now.

What was it like playing with Derek Mountfield? Was he just a
stopper beside your class or was he underrated despite his
achievements? *David Cairns, Newtonards, Northern Ireland*

Derek played really well and he scored about a dozen goals in one season
from centre-half. He was most certainly an asset and the partnership seemed
to work. He was strong in the air, got a good few tackles in and at that stage
he was quite unbeatable. I sometimes wonder how it ever worked, but it did.
I don't actually think I played too long with him. I played more with Dave
Watson than with Derek.

Can you still run really, really fast? *Keith Wilson, Waterloo,*
Liverpool

I can't even run really, really slowly any more. I played for years with injuries
and had a couple of knee injuries when I finished at Everton. They slowed me
down a hell of a lot. I never really got the straightness back in my knee and
that's put pressure on my back. I get a few pins and needles down my leg now
and I really can't do too much any more. I don't even play in charity games, so
I've put on a bit of weight too. Those pictures of me in the *Echo* are old –
don't be fooled by them.

I saw you make a number of, shall we say, 'strong' challenges –
Gary Shaw in the '84 League Cup semi-final comes to mind,
where you managed to make him spin 180 degrees through the

air. But an abiding memory I have is of a number of games in the late '80s against Wimbledon and Chelsea where you seemed to start each game by kicking Dennis Wise up the arse in the guise of a tackle. Was that coincidental, or did he just annoy you the way he annoys everyone else? *Ian Roberts, Wallasey, Wirral*

Ah, you've just picked out a couple of games there where I might have come across as a bit rough. It wasn't intimidation, or anything, but that was the way we played against Wimbledon. I always felt that if you didn't give it, you were gonna get it, so you might as well get in there first.

I always enjoyed playing against Dennis. He didn't really need to beat you to put a cross in and he's turned out to be a good player. He's a passionate lad and he's a dyed-in-the-wool Chelsea Blue now, but I'm sure if he had played for us he'd have been exactly the same. It's those sorts of people you admire because they always want to win. I thought he was a nice enough guy, but he was small enough to have a go at.

Does he think David Unsworth looks a bit like him? *David Chow, Manchester, England*

No, I don't. I think he does now because we're about the same weight! Sorry Unsie. I was a bit slimmer than him, but I definitely didn't score as many goals as him. I probably wasn't as adaptable as him either. I was an out-and-out centre-back and that was it. I can see where the resemblance comes from, but he's bigger built and about two stone heavier than me at my peak. I think that goes for most of the Premier League these days. They seem to be heavier and bigger now, although our height and stature are similar, I suppose.

What was it like having Neville behind him moaning all the time? *Pete Rowlands, Enfield, north London*

The Big Man was awesome and probably the best goalkeeper in the world between '83 and '89. I always believe that it was between him and Bruce Grobbelaar. If you had played with Nev you'd say it was him and vice versa, but it was the people you played against that mattered and Nev would have won it hands down. He didn't do stupid things on the football pitch and he didn't want to be the centre of attention because it wasn't in his make-up. The strangest thing about Nev was that he used to make even better saves in training, and that's quite true.

Be honest, do you envy Reidy at Sunderland now? *Darryl Ng, Singapore*

I don't envy anybody, I've got a nice life, a lovely wife and kids and I enjoy my job. I'm pleased that he's a friend of mine doing well in the game and I hope he goes on and on. He's very unique in the way that he manages, but he's got my utmost respect. We got close towards the end of my time at Everton, he was a good, strong-willed character and he's carried that on into management. I wish him all the success in the world.

At what point did you feel the injuries had taken their toll? *Mark Kenyon, Minnesota, USA*

I was out the game for ten months and they didn't diagnose my injury as a hernia for about eight months. Maybe I came back too quickly, but the club weren't doing too well and needed me to play. In my absence, the pace of the game had changed so much that even the lads I'd trained with and played against were suddenly faster than me. I was physically and mentally drained. For the first time in my life I was going home from training and sleeping for two hours – I found it very tough. I was absolutely knackered for about a year and then I picked up one or two other injuries and lost my pace. Perhaps I should have had a couple more weeks off and played a few reserve games to get me used to it before I went back.

It was very convenient of Everton to give £250,000 for Matt McKay just when Chester was going to go to the wall. Is he worth it? *San Presland, New Brighton, Merseyside*

Mattie was the yardstick I would use for any young player. He's got great talent, but hasn't had a chance to shine yet. When I watch youngsters now I still compare them to Matt. He was money well spent, wait and see.

Ask Kevin if he remembers a big guy coming up to him in The Alt (pub) one Sunday night with a large piece of silverware (the Lol Hunt Memorial Trophy) in his hands and saying: 'I bet you would love to know what this feels like, you carthorse.' It was just before we started winning things. If he does, tell him I was pissed and I'm sorry. *Kevin Hazard, Maghull, Liverpool*

It doesn't matter if he was 6 ft 6, he would have only been 5 ft 6 if I had caught him. I can't remember that because I don't remember the pub, but I accept your apology.

What was your most memorable experience in a Wales top? *John Walton, Dubai, United Arab Emirates*

My last cap when we played against Belgium. I'd been missing from the squad for about two years through injury, and I was playing for Cardiff. There was a lot of pressure on Terry Yorath to pick me even though Cardiff were playing in the Third Division. Terry turned to me one day at a game and said he was getting stick for not picking me and I said: 'Well, you know how to stop that then, don't you? Pick me.' He did, and I played. We won and it was the biggest delight I've had playing for Wales because there was a lot of pressure with me coming from such a low division to play in the national side. It was Ryan Giggs's first full international from the start and he scored from a free kick, but it was important that I played well, and I had a brilliant game. It gave us a good chance to get to the World Cup finals too, but we went on to lose against Romania. I didn't play in that game because I was injured again and we never made it to the World Cup in the end.

I would select the last minute of the '84 FA Cup semi-final as my finest moment as an Everton supporter. What was his finest match in an Everton shirt? *Billy Williams, Cologne, Germany*
It's got to be Bayern Munich at Goodison. That was some night, and the atmosphere was electric, it made my hair stand on end. It wasn't just the game either, the whole build-up was awesome. To begin with we couldn't even get near the ground because there were people everywhere! 50,000 fans, 49,500 of them Evertonians, we knew we couldn't possibly get beaten, we couldn't let those fans down. It was something very, very special. They went 1–0 up before half-time and we came out for the second half and battered them. I'll never forget it and I've never experienced anything remotely like it since.

The Bayern Munich game at Goodison – is there one particular bit that sticks in your mind? *Ian Roberts, Wallasey, Wirral*
There are a few, like when Reidy had to go off and put a sponge down his sock, and the resulting free kick where he held his head. It was a real battle and not the prettiest of matches, it certainly wasn't one for the squeamish or the faint-hearted.

I can still picture their faces when we scored, too. Bayern thought they could win and then they went 1–0 up. They had a pretty good winger and we were quite worried about him. There wasn't one other person in the side who bothered us. Rummenigge's brother was playing and Hoeness, a big centre-forward, but we were more concerned about this midfield winger fella. It wasn't long before he felt the wrath of a few tackles from Reidy and myself, and that was the end of him.

What was going through your mind, coming out for the second half against Bayern and hearing the noise? *Steve Fairclough, Toronto, Canada*

I just knew that we couldn't get beat. We'd had the half-time team talk and Howard said it was all going to plan except that we hadn't scored, we weren't to change anything, just carry on and the Gwladys Street would suck the ball into the net for us. We knew if we put them under pressure they'd break eventually. I was always told that I didn't win games – I saved them. I was the security at the back and I had to keep it tight and leave it to the other lads to score. I was there to tidy up and keep the ball out. That was what we did. All we knew was that we couldn't possibly lose that game.

Does he still get the chance to watch the Blues? If not, is it our result that he looks for first? *Tommy Davis, Texas, USA*

Unfortunately, with the position Shrewsbury Town finds itself in at the moment and over the last couple of years, I'm afraid it hasn't been because I'm looking down below at who's won there and to make sure we're out of the relegation fight, a bit similar to you, I should imagine. But after that it's straight to Everton's result. I don't get to see them often enough either, because in this job you're very tied down and when I do get a day off on a Sunday or a Monday night then I usually want to stay at home with my wife and kids. I've got a problem though, and that is that two of my kids are Evertonians, but unfortunately the other's a Man United fan. I blame Posh Spice because she loves David Beckham, lets face it, you wouldn't mind him on our side, would you?

Was he allowed to take the FA Cup home with him after he collected it? *Andy Clarke, Billericay, England*

I think Adrian Heath slept with it that night. We couldn't get him off it, or out of it!

I've never really said this before, but winning the FA Cup wasn't as big as I thought it would be. When I look back now, of course, it was brilliant, but at the time I felt a little bit flat. I was the oldest of the young ones at 23, and we were so full of confidence that we all knew we were going to win. The most disappointing thing to me was losing against Liverpool. To win that match would have meant a lot more to me than beating Watford. No disrespect to Watford, but we were such favourites on the day that there wasn't a lot of pressure on us. It shouldn't have been that way, but it felt like that at the time. Losing to Liverpool seemed to take the shine off it.

Kevin Ratcliffe

Does he remember when we would sing 'When "The Rat" goes up to lift the FA Cup, we'll be there, we'll be there'? *Tom Davis, Texas, USA*

You've just reminded me of that and it's sent a tingle down my spine. You're the first one who's really said that to me. I can remember a couple of the songs: 'Tell me ma, me ma, to put the champagne on ice, we're going to Wembley twice, tell me ma, me ma.' They sang that at Arsenal and it was unbelievable. I was on holiday in Portugal and Kenny Sansom was staying in the same hotel as me. He came up and said: 'What brilliant fans you've got.' He told me that when the Evertonians sung that, even *his* hair stood on end. Our fans always seemed to start a new cult with a song. I loved 'When The Rat goes up', it made me so proud and I feel really nostalgic now just remembering it.

Is he aware that he was the last captain to climb 39 steps to collect the FA Cup? That part of Wembley was remodelled before the next final. *Andy Clarke, Billericay, England*

I realised that it was changed, but I didn't know when it was done. Wow, that's brilliant – thanks for letting me know.

What effect do you think the Heysel disaster had on your career? *Phil Pellow, Waterloo, Liverpool*

It had an enormous effect. We were the best team in Europe by far and we missed out on a European Cup medal. It was the biggest factor in the break-up of the team causing us to lose our players and management. We all missed out financially, but more importantly on career recognition. Looking at the bigger picture, it had a massive effect on Everton Football Club and even now the club isn't as big in Europe or worldwide as it would have been if we hadn't been banned.

When the team started to break up after the Euro ban did you consider a move to be able to play European football? *Steve Fairclough, Toronto, Canada*

Yes, but, unfortunately, every time I thought about it seriously I seemed to pick up some kind of injury and I was more concerned about getting fit and winning my place back in the side than moving on. We weren't doing very well and needed to get back into winning ways.

Colin Harvey brought a few new players in. I never played against Leeds with Nev's sit-down protest because I was on the bench and I think that was my time. There had been one or two enquiries from French clubs and I should have gone. A change of scene might have given me a new lease of life, but I couldn't bear to leave. I wanted to stay and do as well as I could for as long as I could. When I sit back now, I realise that nothing lasts forever, but you can't put an old head on young shoulders. They say that once an Evertonian, always an Evertonian, and there was never a truer word spoken.

TREVOR STEVEN

Born 27 September 1963
July 1983 – July 1989
£300,000

A shrewd mission was accomplished when the ink had dried securing the sublime talents of Trevor Steven. Hours of scrutiny from the Turf Moor stands had finally acquired Howard Kendall the paradigm of his midfield master plan.

> I went to watch him play and tried to keep a low profile because whenever I was in a crowd the press would report it. I couldn't believe he hadn't been spotted and, although I didn't want to alert anybody to my potential secret weapon, I couldn't stay away. I was like a moth to the flame because he mesmerised me with his skill and reminded me so much of Alex Young. I would have paid whatever Burnley had asked, but I got away with £300,000. It was a steal and I still smile about it now.

Thus, bursting with ambition, 19-year-old Trevor Steven arrived on Merseyside and it wouldn't be too long before everyone knew about it.

> One day, Bob Paisley was in the boardroom at Everton. He said he'd also had his eye on Trevor but had never seen him finish a game. How he must have cursed when he went on to become a permanent fixture in the England side for years to come.

Look everybody, it's Tricky Trev.

> I'd had my teeth bashed out in one of my previous games and if you care to look at any photographs taken on the day I signed for Everton, you'll see I've got two big bright gleamers which obviously don't match the rest of my teeth. I'm pleased to say I've since had that rectified.

What made him sign for Everton since we were not doing very well at the time? *Mike Coville, New York, USA*

Everton was a huge step up for me. I was playing at the bottom of the old Second Division, waiting to be relegated, and the First Division was where I wanted to go. John Bond had arrived at Burnley and told me I was definitely going to have to move anyway, so it was the right time and everything was geared up for it. But Howard Kendall was the catalyst, he showed the interest, he talked a very good game and he quickly convinced me that Everton was the place to go.

In 1983, £300,000 for a young player was a lot of money. Did his price tag affect him in any way? *Ciaran McConville, Dublin, Republic of Ireland*

Not the price tag, but I was probably a little bit overawed by going to the First Division. I was only 19 and the expectancy level was high. I'd been at Burnley a long time, I knew the club inside out and it wasn't such a leap for me to get in that first team and do well. To get into the Everton first team wasn't guaranteed by any stretch of the imagination. It was hard going and I was a little bit nervous, so I didn't fulfil my potential early on.

I imagine that Howard did me a favour pulling me out of the first team squad for the mid-part of the season. It allowed me to get used to my surroundings and out of the firing line. It was a pretty hot time for everyone at that point. He brought me back in towards the end of the season again, and by that time I'd adjusted. It was nothing to do with the transfer fee, it was probably the expectancy level that I had of myself and the difficulties Everton found themselves in. But we all came through it, thankfully.

I'd ask Trevor how he felt after the infamous 0–0 with Coventry at Goodison on New Year's Eve 1983 and what he thought the future had in store for him as an individual and for Everton as a team. *Mark Hoskins, Dublin, Republic of Ireland*

It was bleak for everybody. You know how it is when you can't see light at the end of the tunnel and every day is gloomy. Howard tried really hard to keep the motivation going, but football management is a fickle thing – if it doesn't go well everybody wants your head. We knew we were in truly desperate straits when he started to grow a beard and a moustache. But time passed, and some old heads were brought into the team – back to basics if you like. I was brought out of the limelight and learnt a lot very quickly, but you're right, they were desperate times. We didn't think we were going to go anywhere and we certainly didn't think we would be lifting the FA Cup by the end of the season.

Trevor Steven

I first saw him play against LFC at Anfield in a League Cup (or whatever it was called at the time) semi-final. Was his transfer already sorted by then or still in the offing? *San Presland, New Brighton, Merseyside*

At that point I had no idea that I would leave Burnley at all. I think it was the winter when the Liverpool game took place. Liverpool beat Burnley 3–0 at Anfield and Burnley beat them 1–0 at Turf Moor, but that was well away from the end of the season and Burnley still had visions of staying in the Second Division. It didn't turn out that way, but if we'd survived I may have stayed another year. There was no indication that I was going to be moving anywhere, although those games did help me to get myself onto another stage because they were televised and people started to notice that I wasn't a bad player.

During the pre-match warm up, a group of four or five players would congregate near the centre circle and play a game of two-touch 'keepy-uppy' in a circle. This group included Steven, Ratters, Sheedy, Bracewell and possibly Reid. Their ritual fascinated me. I would like to know who was the best at this game, who was the worst and who was the player that the rest of the group used to stitch up so he would lose? *Gary Hughes, Whiston, Merseyside*

The situation with the keepy-uppies at the start of the game was this: it didn't matter whether you had good technical ability, if Kevin Ratcliffe was playing he would win. You're meant to deliver the ball nicely to your teammate, but the way Kevin played was cut-throat and he probably had more wins under his belt than anybody else. He had the ability to knock the ball at you at hip level and he pulled rank because he was captain. I would never stitch anyone up for anything, but Kevin Ratcliffe would, especially at keepy-uppy.

What was his plan for penalties and did he ever miss one for us? *Steve Kirkwood, Crowthorne, Berkshire, England*

I did miss, but thankfully not that many. I think the record books will tell you that I'm the most successful penalty-taker for Everton. When I struck a penalty my plan was to put the ball in the corner I was running towards – normally the goalkeepers' bottom left – because you got a good strike on the ball. But with all the TV coverage you have to have some versatility and it didn't cause me too much of a problem to do it the other way. Of all the missed penalties there are three that I really remember. One against Ray Clemence at home, and another against Nottingham Forest which was on television. However, the worst was in the semi-final of the Milk Cup against Arsenal at home. We went out at the semi-final stage and I have to say I choked on it then and I still do to this day.

My best penalty moment was against Watford at home and it ended up on 'What happened next?' on *Question of Sport*. I scored, but just then, a white plastic bag blew across the goalmouth. It was like a scene from a cowboy film, with the tumbleweed. The referee decided I would have to retake it, but I'd already placed it in my usual spot. I took it again, but put it in the top corner that time, which was completely out of character for me! So I scored twice but it only counted once.

Has he ever been mistaken for Gary Numan? I'd pay good money to see him sing 'Are Friends Electric' on the karaoke. *Dave Kelly, Blackburn, England*

Kevin Costner, yes, Gary Numan, no.

I've seen him play centre-midfield, right-wing, wing-back (oh yes he did) and as a striker for us. Was his favourite position right-wing? I always thought he was better in centre-midfield. *Steve Kirkwood, Crowthorne, Berkshire, England*

No, it was definitely not right-wing, but that was the only way I could get a game every week for Everton. Howard always saw me in that position, but I didn't at all. I saw myself as a central-midfield player as I had been in Burnley's first team. I was often frustrated at not being involved in the game enough, but it was done to suit the team.

Was the midfield of himself, Reid, Sheedy and Bracewell the best he played with? And if not, what was? *Ciaran McConville, Dublin, Republic of Ireland*

The whole team was exceptional, not just the midfield. We were all on the same wavelength. We got away with using about 14 players in one season, which is just unheard of these days. The demands were heavy then too, and how Peter Reid survived a whole season I'll never know, but he and Andy Gray both managed it.

We were very close off the field and very in tune on it. I played within that four for the whole season, although Kev Richardson came on in various places and played exceptionally well too, and we mustn't forget him. But when that four were together we just knew exactly how to operate. We would rotate across the pitch, close down and attack together. Sheeds was always great for me because of his ability to knock a ball 40 or 50 yards and keep me involved.

Trevor Steven

Sometimes, I would come in from the game and be frustrated that the ball never came my way, but over the period of time Sheeds and Ratters kept me interested. We were a rock-solid unit, there's no doubt about it, and certainly the best unit that I've ever played in.

Did the chant of 'Champions, Champions, Champions' rolling around White Hart Lane after he'd scored the second in '85 have the same effect on him as it did on me? I was in amongst Spurs fans and couldn't outwardly celebrate, but the hairs on the back of my neck were standing to strict attention. *Mike Burke, Highbury, north London*

I remember the fans travelled in their masses to see that game and it was a wonderful feeling to score. We had a routine for every game, arriving at the ground at the same time and playing our lucky Bruce Springsteen tape. There was a lot of superstition and familiarity about our situation, but that was an extra-special game and the dressing-room was tense and quite electric. That goal is another one that stands out clearly in my memory because it's always particularly nice to round Ray Clemence and score. Not only was he ex-Liverpool, but also one of the great English goalkeepers of his time. We believed we could win at White Hart Lane, but it was a different thing to actually go and do it. They were vying for the championship too, and they weren't that far behind us.

Is it true that when he first got picked for England, he had his courtesy club car painted with 'Trevor Steven of Everton and England' but he wouldn't wait for it to be done professionally and so either did it himself or got someone else to do it? It looked shite, and subsequently, after driving round for a week or so with it like that, he had it resprayed? *Colin Berry, Wavertree, Liverpool*

I was looking through a *Match* magazine the other day, you know when they used to go round to your house and have a look at your lifestyle and habits. There, in the drive, was my car. The stars of today would not be seen dead in a white Escort 1.6L, not even with alloy wheels, but instead with, quite literally, a handwritten name in block capital letters. I didn't write it on there, it arrived like that. It was so pathetic, yet it was my pride and joy in those days! It was a bad job, it wasn't a great car, but whoever supplied it I thank them wholeheartedly – it was a joy.

Why was he crap when he first came to Everton and what made him improve so much? Did it have anything to do with Peter Reid? *Andy Richardson, Hackney, north-east London*

No, it had everything to do with me being happy and comfortable in my surroundings, being encouraged and working really, really hard. I proved to myself that I was as good as, if not better than, the people who were there. I had to prove that to myself on a daily basis because all those players already had high esteem when I arrived. Sometimes I gave too much respect to other people for their abilities and didn't appreciate my own. It took me a while to understand that I did have a place there and I just had to grasp the opportunity.

I'd ask him if he had a good view of the 'Hand of God' incident in Mexico. *Mark Hoskins, Dublin, Republic of Ireland*

When I think back now I was convinced that Peter Shilton was about to thump the ball back up the field and I sort of half glanced away. I looked back in astonishment when the ball was trundling into the net and Maradona was running away with his arms aloft. Now, it was blatantly obvious, because he was so far under the ball and Shilton was so far above him, that he had to punch it, but as the television evidence proved later it was Maradona's hand. The thing that we couldn't believe at the time was that nobody else had seen it. The linesman and the referee were quite determined to give the goal. Our protest didn't matter, there was no indecision at all from them and we had to accept it.

You were the leading scorer in 1986–87, surprised? *Steve Fairclough, Toronto, Canada*

I was the penalty taker and I scored eight of them, but I'm very proud to have walked away with the Dixie Dean award for top scorer – and in the Championship-winning season too! It was a very nice reward for a year's work. But we were nowhere near as good as we had been in the 1984–85 season, we stumbled towards the title and it was hard graft. The team was changed around a lot through injury – it was probably a typical season really, but it felt unusual for us. We got there in the end though. It was nice to score so many goals, albeit from the penalty spot, and I'm happy and proud to have that accolade.

As probably one of the most talented players of his era, he also seemed to be one of the most passionless (you could say 'composed'). Did he ever 'lose it' either with pleasure or pain? *San Presland, New Brighton, Merseyside*

Not really, I just had this mentality of getting on with things. I had a very high tolerance level and was acutely aware of what people were trying to do by kicking me and fouling me. I felt that I already had 'one up' on them if they had to foul me to prevent me doing something positive on the football field. I had a philosophy that I should get on with it and not get distracted by other things going on around me. I was there to concentrate on the game and contribute towards the team.

How come your shorts looked much smaller than everyone else's? Did you ask for the smallest ones? *Ray Mckay, Warrington, England*

No, I actually asked for the biggest ones, but it was what was inside them!

The strip wasn't the best, it was tight, it was uncomfortable and it was a bit of a mismatch. The good thing is that, looking back at the photographs, none of us looked good in it. Happy times, but not a happy strip, it has to be said.

How good was it to know that every time he put another quality cross into the box there would be at least one Scottish lunatic throwing themselves on the end of it? *Rob Rimmer, Aintree, Liverpool*

It was very comforting, very comforting indeed. My remit was to get down the right-hand side and get crosses in. If I couldn't manage it, it was up to Gary Stevens to knock them in. We actually had three very good centre-forwards then – I have to include Adrian Heath. He was excellent at getting half a yard in front of defenders for the bad crosses, the ones that didn't pick out Graeme Sharp and Andy Gray. Together we were fantastic: Andy Gray was totally rejuvenated and had a new lease of life when he came to Everton; Graeme Sharp was an excellent all-round footballer; he had that same aggression as Andy had in abundance, although he kept it covered up sometimes. When he got into the flow of things we knew whenever we put a ball into the box we would get some kind of result out of it.

Despite the good link up on-field did you really get on with Gary Stevens off it? *Andy Morris, Widnes, England*

Yes, definitely, we played, we socialised and we roomed together, particularly with England. We played together at Rangers too, and knew each other's game inside out. Gary was tremendous and he'd be the first to admit that he didn't have every trick in the book up his sleeve, but what he did have made him a great defender and a great athlete. He could get forward up and down that line all day long. We've known each other a long time and we're still in touch now. He was magnificent and much better than anybody else I've ever played with.

Brace said that pass to him against Sunderland was intentional. Is that true or was it just lucky? *Jonathan Gard, Woolton, Liverpool*
I think Paul was one of the unsung heroes in the team, he more than held the midfield together with Peter Reid and he had great ability when he was given a chance to show it. But that pass was unquestionably lucky. Nah, it wasn't, I'm only kidding.

In that particular game we'd fallen behind and started to pick up the pace. We scored some excellent goals, but I would say that that pass was inch perfect. There was a huge gap and I was wide on the right. I was begging him to put it where he did and when he volleyed it over Pickering's head it was just where I wanted it to be. I had the momentum and Pickering was left floundering by my unbelievable burst of pace. No, to be honest, when I got into the penalty box I was overstretched, under pressure, and I just flung my leg at it and the ball ended up in the roof of the net. It was a goal I really enjoyed, but I'll give every bit of credit to Brace.

As he currently speaks with a distinctly Scottish twang did he speak with a Scouse accent when he left the Blues and which accent does he expect to finish up with? *Mike Benson, West Derby, Liverpool*
Good question. I've got nothing specific as far as accents are concerned, I used to have a North–East accent coming from Berwick-upon-Tweed, but that's very near to Scotland. Scots surround me now and I seem to find it quite easy to blend in with whomever I'm with. The Merseyside accent is so strong, relative to where I'd come from, and it was easy for me to pick it up. I have no idea what kind of accent I might end up with, but I think it will depend on where I live.

What was it like going with fellow Evertonians to Mexico in '86 purely as covers, but knowing England only started to produce the goods when they were brought on? *David Chow, Manchester, England*
That was quite satisfying. We arrived under a bit of a cloud because Man United had beaten us in the FA Cup. We travelled together and I think there was only Bryan Robson from the Man United team, so we outnumbered him nicely enough and had him surrounded on the plane on the way over. It was brilliant to know we had the bulk of players vying for a position, albeit

we were only used when things got into dire straits for the England party.

I want to know which kit he preferred to play in. Was it the all-blue one with the white lines around the shoulders, the half blue/half white thing made famous by the Lineker pictures, or something else? *Keith Wilson, Waterloo, Liverpool*

You can't say that anybody would have enjoyed the Coq Sportif strip because it was just awful. There was a battle every week in the dressing-room just getting into that gear. I'd look around to see Neville Southall trying to pull those shorts on and it was not a funny sight. I think my favourite was the Umbro one towards the end, which had a better shape and was a bit more 'with it'.

How many titles did he win in total? *David Chow, Manchester, England*

I think it was eleven. One at Burnley, 1981–82, then two with Everton, seven with Rangers in all and one in France with Marseille.

Did you really know that guy that owned the clothes shop 'Pelle' in Southport? I worked for him for a while and he kept going on how much of a good friend you were of his. *Julian Jackson, Hong Kong, SAR of PRC*

I thought the shop was actually called 'Pele' and I wondered what the hell he was doing opening a shop in Southport. I went in expecting Pelé to be serving behind the counter, and I have to say I was slightly disappointed, but I made friends with him anyway. He's still a friend of mine, I won't deny that, but to be honest I was disappointed it wasn't the real Pelé.

After Tricky came back from his squad sessions and games with England he never seemed to be the same player. Did Don Howe coach the adventurous attacking style out of him? Did he tell him never to go for the goal-line behind the defender ever again as it was only for men in long shorts in Harry Enfield sketches? *Mike Royden, Ellesmere Port, South Wirral*

It was always difficult coming back from international games. By the time you travelled back you only really ever had one proper training session, then you were on the bus to an away game or you'd be preparing for a home game and there wasn't a great deal of time to get your breath back. As a consequence, your game on a Saturday would sometimes be dulled. I wouldn't blame Don Howe for anything, it's just the nature of the beast, and sometimes, too much football dampens your performance.

I want to get him to dish the dirt on Lineker. Did Gary fit in with the team and how much of a surprise was it when he went to Barca? *Steve Kirkwood, Crowthorne, Berkshire, England*

Gary and I were room-mates for the year he was at Everton, and it has to be said a nicer guy you couldn't wish to meet. I was surprised he left so soon, but who would turn that down? He had a super season with us, scoring goals for fun. He was unquestionably one of the fastest I've ever played with, a very direct player, and he deserved what he ended up with, which was a superb move to Barcelona. But you can't really dig dirt on Gary because there ain't any.

I am sure he was on the pitch in the penalty shoot-out against Germany, so why didn't he take a penalty instead of that Waddle plonker? If he wasn't on the pitch, then don't ask that question. *John Quinn, Tewkesbury, England*

I was on the pitch and if Chris Waddle had scored then I was to take the next one. To be quite honest, I wasn't looking forward to it, I was basically filling my trousers at that time. But I was definitely down to take the sixth penalty and, of course, it never got to that, but the penalty-takers were picked well in advance. I didn't start the game, so that was the way it developed.

I remember Tricky Trev being played upfront at some stage in the late '80s against Boro and he scored a superb goal. Does he look at strikers today and think that even on their best days he could have 'em? *Darryl Ng, Singapore*

I was a stop-gap centre-forward for Everton. I played a little bit up there for Rangers as well, but mainly for Everton when other people were injured. I enjoyed it because when I was young I used to play upfront. It's not quite as easy as the good centre-forwards make out though, because it's all about timing your runs and being expected to finish. We midfielders score the odd goal, but when you're actually upfront you're expected to be cool, calm and collected in front of goal. That takes a certain kind of mentality and a great deal of ability.

Was he impressed with Howard Kendall and what did he think about Harvey as coach? *Mike Coville, New York, USA*

It was a great relationship they had. Colin was driven by football to the point of crippling himself in training every day, just to compete. Howard was very good at man-management and tactically he was excellent. He had the respect of all the players and, although he could be hard at times, was very good at getting his message over. He was a great communicator and that, combined with Colin's enthusiasm, made every training session competitive. There was nobody more competitive than me, except perhaps Colin Harvey.

It still hurts to this day how the brilliant mid-'80s team and manager were allowed to split up. Was the ban on English clubs in Europe the main reason why you and others left the club? *Karl Williams, Kinmel Bay, North Wales*

Everton were slow in offering me something new. They did eventually, but it was far too late for me to consider it very seriously. The ban made things difficult. I didn't go to another English club, I could have gone to Man United but didn't. I went to Scotland with Graeme Souness to try something new, but also to try and continue European football. That was the main reason for going, but a close second was that Howard had left and it was difficult to maintain the drive and the momentum. Colin did as well as he possibly could under the circumstances, but the players had lost a little bit of something and maybe it would have taken Howard to maintain it. The fact that he had been allowed to leave made it easier for me to go, too.

What make of boots did he wear and was he on a contract to wear them? *Steve Kirkwood, Crowthorne, Berkshire, England*

I initially wore Nike boots and that came from the Burnley days. Ian St John used to work for Nike, and when I was about 17 he approached me to wear their boots. I accepted, not because of Ian St John I should add, but I wore them all the way up to the Mexico World Cup. Then I decided to jump ship and go with Adidas. I regret that now – not because I don't like Adidas, but I ignored good advice and it still haunts me. I was still at Burnley at the time, we were in the shower and Willie Donachie said to me: 'Now as you're in the first team and earning a few bob, do two things: invest your money in property and stick with Nike.' I put my money into property, but I didn't stay with Nike and I regret that because it's a huge company and now I don't really have a close relationship with a sportswear manufacturer.

In the '89 FA Cup final he had an absolute stinker and he played like it was his last game (it was). A guy ran on the pitch, grabbed his own Everton shirt, pointed to the badge and then gobbed off at Trevor. Does he remember what he said? *Kenny Fogarty, Amsterdam, Holland*

I do, and to be honest I wouldn't give that guy the time of day to even discuss it. What I would say is that I didn't think I played badly in that game, I really don't, and if anybody would care to look at it I think I actually played quite well. I'm not even going to go into the incident, but there were things happening at Everton at that time which should have been sorted out. My position at the club should have been clarified a lot earlier, but they left it until the last three months of the season. As somebody who'd won several things with the club I found this particularly hurtful. I felt it was negligent on their part. I have no bad feelings towards the club whatsoever, but I do have bad feelings towards that individual and hope he regrets his action on that day as much as I regret having to have experienced it.

Did the players get up to any mischief on the '87 tour of Australia? *Rob Hamilton, Melbourne, Australia*

I don't really remember that trip, so I guess it was pretty uneventful. I think Hawaii might have been a different thing though, because we went there on holiday on the way back.

Did Everton try really, really hard to persuade him to stay? *Neil McCann, Bangkok, Thailand*

Colin Harvey tried as much as he possibly could, but in the end I'd made up my mind because of Howard leaving and the lateness in which they dealt with my position. Once I got to that stage I decided I was going to leave anyway. I just wanted to get somewhere else and see what I could do. Colin did try hard, but it was too little, too late.

How does the Merseyside derby compare to the Old Firm game? *George Mason, Florida, USA*

In Glasgow, when the fans get their colours on, it's pretty horrendous stuff. The families on Merseyside can be split down the middle and support one or the other, sometimes just out of spite, but that doesn't happen at all up there and there's a more severe situation between the sets of fans. A lot of hatred and sectarianism comes to the surface, which was an eye-opener to me. If you look at the Merseyside Cup-finals that went on in the '80s, that could never have happened in Glasgow. Even now, if you win a competition with Rangers or Celtic, there's no open-top bus ride around the city because they wouldn't make it out alive. So it's one of those things I was unaware of when I came to Scotland and I don't have any time for it.

As far as playing in those matches is concerned, you just get that extra sense of hatred coming through where it's not at all relevant. On Merseyside, there was intense rivalry but not this vitriolic anger. It tends to only be on the match day and not in day-to-day life though, I'm pleased to say.

Trevor Steven

Are you balding yet? Big Nev said he saw you not so long ago and you looked like you had more hair! *Darryl Ng, Singapore*

When I first arrived at Everton Andy King called me Herbie after Terry Darracott. I was 19 years old and that was quite a confidence shaker for me. In fact, I blame Andy King for the lack of form I had in the early days! I'd just arrived at Rangers and Neville sent me something in the post that was basically a wig. He said it had been found under my place in the dressing-room after I'd left. He thought it definitely had to be mine so he was just returning it. I've still got it and I'm still wearing it, so thanks very much Neville!

Does he think more British and Irish players should be playing and experiencing life abroad in the light of the Euro 2000 performances? *Sean Corr, Dublin, Republic of Ireland*

Definitely. There's a particular way of playing football in the English Premiership, it's too narrow and not that tactical or technical. I think the knowledge and information that can be absorbed by playing abroad is phenomenal. I was away for just over a year, but I learned a hell of a lot. It's a vital part of every footballer's education, especially if you're playing at the highest level. I know we want to keep all our stars, but there are not that many players who stay long nowadays, it tends to be a bit of a revolving door at most clubs. I think it's great for the player as an individual to experience other walks of life – it can only do them good. But they should only go if it's the right place, there's no point going abroad to struggle at the bottom of a division somewhere.

Does Gary Stevens still follow him round everywhere? *Pete Rowlands, Enfield, north London*

We're no longer joined at the hip, but I never get tired of him.

What did he think of Pat Nevin as a player? I always thought of him as 85 per cent of a Tricky Trev, which, of course, made Pat a great player. *George Lee Stuart, Lismore, Australia*

Pat was different to what we'd been used to in the Everton team. He was gifted and very skilful, but very much an old-fashioned player with great ability on the ball, but limited as far as defensive situations were concerned. At that time, I don't think he was the right buy for Everton, although he did do pretty well and he even took us to Wembley on one occasion.

England: who was it keeping him out of the side? Waddle? Hodge? Why? *Steve Kirkwood, Crowthorne, Berkshire, England*

It was probably Chris Waddle. Chris is an extremely talented footballer, but he had more of a wanderlust thing and he would never fulfil a position. When I played in the England team I always seemed to be filling a slot, whereas Chris had more of a free role. We were two separate entities and it tended to be that when things started to go wrong they would resort to me coming on and trying to steady the ship.

Who was the best player he had the privilege to play with? *Darryl Ng, Singapore*

It would be difficult to name one, but Neville Southall was a fabulous goalkeeper, probably the best in the world at that time. His frame was big, but he was light on his feet, and very aggressive. He was most certainly the best goalie I've ever worked with. All the players in the team had their own particular strengths, but if I had to pick out one it would have to be Kevin Sheedy. He had ability and a technique not many others could claim, and his left foot was absolutely magnificent. He could pinpoint passes, he could hit the ball like a thunderbolt and overall he had something that was very special indeed.

Did he ever have the chance to come back? Wasn't he supposed to come with Durrant and Dunc? *Colin Berry, Wavertree, Liverpool*

I did talk to Peter Johnson when he was discussing Durrant and Ferguson. The problem I had was that I was injured so much. I'd played so much in my early career and managed to fend off injuries for a long time, but when I got back to Rangers they all surfaced at once. Peter Johnson was enquiring whether I would go back and I said I would when I was fit and if the conditions were right. But the moment passed, I took longer than I thought to regain my fitness and I'd missed my chance. I don't think it would have been wise for me to go back as, indeed, it wasn't wise for me to go back to Rangers. They say you should never do it.

Do you feel your performances for England got the recognition they deserved by either the managers, the press or the fans? *Tim Gunnion, Frankfurt, Germany*

It's difficult to say. The fact that you get a number of caps shows that you were appreciated. I fulfilled my potential on several occasions with the England team, but not as often as I would have liked. I look back on my time with Bobby Robson with particular fondness. He gave me my first cap and I went to two World Cups with him. The fact that he picked me meant I was at two of the major footballing tournaments of the time, and that's one of the highlights of my career.

Trevor Steven

What's he up to now and does he have a website as we might be able to do one for him? *Julian Jackson, Hong Kong, SAR of PRC*

I don't need a website as an individual, but I have one for my children's shoe shop, which is www. famousfeet.co.uk, so check it out. I really don't see that I need one because I'm a FIFA agent by profession, but if you've got any bright ideas let me know.

What does he think of the ground move? Can he see us sharing a stadium with the Shite? *Patrick Clancy, Halewood, Liverpool*

I'm laughing because of the way this question is worded! I don't see a ground-sharing possibility. It will be very sad for the club to move away from Goodison Park, but I don't think it's the be all and end all of Everton Football Club. I'm not up to speed with where the new stadium would be, but as long as it's not too far away from Goodison then I could cope with that. For me, it would be ideal to be able to see the old stadium from the new one.

Does he get to many games nowadays? *Darryl Ng, Singapore*

I see plenty of football in Scotland, England and on the continent. I also do a bit of TV work, match commentaries and analysis and that kind of thing. I represent players so I'm always on the look-out for talented youngsters who I think will make it to the top.

Does he think he should've got more England caps? *Jonathan Gard, Woolton, Liverpool*

I can only blame myself for that because you have to prove that you're good enough. I was probably doing a job on the right-hand side of midfield that I never fully enjoyed and I don't know whether that began to tell in my performances. I stuck at it for as long as I possibly could and when I went to Rangers I played central-midfield, which I did enjoy more, but by that stage I was already out of the England squad. I did get back in the reckoning when I went to France, but I was always playing in central-midfield then. As far as team achievements were concerned, because I didn't really enjoy the role as much as I should, it probably took its toll on me.

From '86 onwards did he get frustrated by not playing regularly for England? He always seemed to be a back-up, but whenever he came on (if I remember right, as full-back in one World Cup game) the team immediately appeared to have balance. *Paul Tollet, Oxford, England*

Yeah, I'm disappointed. I think a lot of footballers will look back on their careers and just wish they'd had a little bit more self-belief at times. I've been guilty of that at some stages. When you play in the England squad you need to believe that you're as good as the next guy. Maybe once or twice I didn't play as well as I should have done because I didn't have much self-confidence. Nobody really lasted long in that position so I think I did miss out on caps. Thirty-six was a nice number but I'd have liked to have just got fifty.

How did he enjoy his brief spell at Marseille? What were the circumstances around that move and why did it all fall apart so quickly? *Kenny Fogarty, Amsterdam, Holland*

Initially I enjoyed it immensely. I went there as a big-money buy and there was considerable pressure on me. In the first 12 or 15 games I'd scored four goals and things were going very well. What happened at Marseille was a financial problem. They had trouble paying the transfer fee and paying my wages, and because of that, the whole thing fell apart. They owed me money right up to the very day I left, so it became an unhappy stay because they couldn't deliver what they'd promised. What they'd done was budget to go to the European Cup final and they were knocked out in the second round by Sparta Prague, which meant that the plug was pulled out of the bath somewhat.

Is he glad he chose a career in the media rather than continue in coaching or managing? *Colin Jones, Mossley Hill, Liverpool*

I don't really have a career in the media; I only fill in the spaces in my life with a bit of TV work, really. My general job is looking after the players I represent and working within football at a different level. I love the business of football. As for coaching, I toyed with the idea but the opportunity never arose for me. I didn't take my coaching badges, which indicates that I never really had the aspirations to go on and really prove myself in that way and I don't have any regrets about that. I enjoy what I'm doing now.

Any regrets from your Marseille experience? *Steve Fairclough, Toronto, Canada*

No, none at all, other than that if they'd been able to pay up then things would have been a bit merrier.

He never had a bad game for England, much like Steve Coppell. Any advice for aspiring England youths? *George Lee Stuart, Lismore, Australia*

That's very nice of you to say I never had a bad game. I had a few mediocre games, but it was always a pleasure to pull on the England shirt. It was a boyhood dream and going back to the self-confidence thing, every time I pulled the strip on I thought it might be my last chance and every game was the 'last-chance saloon' for me. I had that chance 36 times and I'm thankful for that. I knew my job and I knew what I could get away with. It's difficult to give advice, all I can say is try and do whatever it is you're doing to the best of your ability at all times.

Does Trevor consider the time when he had a perm at the back and straight and short at the sides a deliberate act of self-mutilation? *Julian Jackson, Hong Kong, SAR of PRC*
When I said I had no regrets I'd forgotten about that hairstyle and it has come back to haunt me on several occasions. To be honest, I'm surprised I could grow that much hair because I'm pretty sparse in that department, so it was a major achievement for me to be able to even get a perm. But Chris Waddle did it better than me and, like in my England days, I was a poor substitute.

What kind of music does Tricky like? *Patrick Clancy, Halewood, Liverpool*
That's changed many times, too – a bit like my hair.

Is he aware of a one-man campaign that some guy waged in the footy magazines towards the end of his career? This guy constantly wrote to *FourFourTwo, Total Football,* **etc., demanding that Tricky be played as sweeper by England.** *Jonathan Gard, Woolton, Liverpool*
I was aware of that because I got some mail from him. I think his name was Mr Morgan and he was constantly extolling my virtues as a sweeper. It didn't get me anywhere, but it's always nice to have someone battling your corner – albeit for a position I never played.

Did he have any other offers in, or before, 1983? *Mike Coville, New York, USA*
So it was reported. Liverpool seemed to raise their heads when they knew I was going to Everton, but I was already committed to going with Howard at that point. Howard was fabulous for me, he obviously had faith to pay good money and take me to Everton in the first place. He looked after me well in that first year to set me on my way, and that was crucial for my career. Then he plucked me out of the first team before I lost too much confidence. I think I would have made it, eventually, but he was my guiding light.

You made it look so easy. Was it? *Steve Fairclough, Toronto, Canada*

Anything that looks easy has got an enormous amount of hard work behind it. I put a lot of work in when I was younger, and not just playing matches. At schoolboy level I used to practise a lot and not play so many games and I think that stood me in good stead. Technically, I was pretty decent and as long as you've got that ability with the ball you've got a chance. After that, it's a case of hard graft.

Where did he most enjoy playing: Burnley, Everton, Rangers or Marseille? *Andy Richardson, Hackney, north-east London*

The best enjoyment for me was unquestionably at Everton because it was the start of a lot of things for me, the international side in particular. I'd already won something at Burnley, so I knew what winning was about, but to do it at Everton after the period of famine and drought they'd had was brilliant. To play in the team was something else, and it never even realised its full potential because of the European ban, which was a bitter disappointment to all of us. At Everton, I really enjoyed my football, it was all fresh and new and the challenge of the English First Division was a great one.

Where does his goal against Bayern (or Rapid) rate as career highlights? *Rob Rimmer, Aintree, Liverpool*

When I look back I didn't have a great deal of success in Europe because we were banned for such a long time, so the Bayern goal is a huge moment in my career. Winning that game had taken us to a European Cup final, albeit the Cup Winners' cup final, and that was a new experience for everybody. That night was probably the most memorable I've ever had and I think that if you asked the same question to all the players who were involved they'd agree. From the build-up to the moment we went one—nil down, and then it was all a case of rolling the sleeves up and knocking over one of the giants in European football. To score in that manner was brilliant and the atmosphere in the stadium was unbelievable. To get a goal in the final was great too, but we thoroughly deserved to win the final because we were by far the better team. So Bayern Munich I would single out as my best occasion and best goal.

Which of his many medals and trophies is his most precious? *San Presland, New Brighton, Merseyside*

I've got some great medals. It's especially nice that I've got a World Cup medal, it's not a winner's medal, I suppose it's equal to a bronze, but it's always good to know you've done something on the world stage and gained some recognition for it. But for me, the turning point was the FA Cup win with Everton. To win there and take Everton on to a new level was brilliant, and that medal is the one I cherish the most.

DAVE WATSON

Born 20 November 1961
August 1986 – May 2001
£900, 000

Howard Kendall sneaked in on a summer deadline day to sign Dave Watson from Norwich, where manager, Ken Brown had said that losing him would be like cutting off his right arm. Before he reached for something sharp, Kendall and Waggy were out the door and heading for Merseyside. With the transfer deadline looming, time wasn't on their side, but Howard had a cunning plan.

> We'd already verbally agreed terms but couldn't make it back in time to Goodison Park to meet the deadline. Aston Villa kindly said we could use their office and facilities so we sent the fax off to the FA confirming the deal before it was all finalised. We thrashed out the terms and when the photographers arrived to capture the moment we had to turn the clocks back in the office.
>
> Dave was a tremendous professional and he had a job on his hands to win the crowd over – after all, he was stepping in to Derek Mountfield's shoes and he was a hard act to follow. I had to make sure I was replacing Derek with a top-class centre-half. But Dave Watson's record speaks for itself.

Ladies and gentlemen, doff your cap, it's Waggy Watson – the blue-eyed boy. It's enough to make your heart go wooo ooo oooh!

As a boy who did he want to be? *Frank Hargreaves, Anfield, Liverpool*
I was a Red when I was a lad and, believe it or not, my hero was Tommy Smith.

You started playing for the Reds before you went to Norwich. Did you have any doubts about signing for Everton when our interest

was first mooted or were you tempted to 'hang on' for Liverpool?
Nick Williams, Warrington, England

There was no doubt at all. It was a case of getting back home and playing for a big club and, at the time, Everton was the biggest club in the land. That was what appealed to me most of all.

How difficult was it for him to come to terms with playing for 'the enemy'? *Colin Berry, Wavertree, Liverpool*

It was really difficult, and not least because I was also taking over from an Everton legend in Derek Mountfield. So I knew it would be hard at first, but I had every confidence that I would win them over.

I have heard you were a bit of a 'scally' in your youth (robbing cars, for example). Is this true and what would have happened to you if you hadn't made it as a professional footballer? *Bernie Flood, Ellesmere Port, Wirral*

I don't know about robbing cars, but I suppose I was a little bit of a scally. It sure gave me a good grounding for life and made me a bit more streetwise, although I don't know what would have become of me if I hadn't become a footballer.

Was there any personal animosity/jealousy between you and Mountfield soon after you arrived? *Nick Williams, Warrington, England*

None at all. I knew what it was all about at the time and the best player was going to get a game. After that, your destiny lies in your own hands and I knew it was up to me.

Do you think being an ex-fan of the opposition gave players like yourself, Reid, Rush, Fowler, etc. an extra edge in derby matches? *Bernie Flood, Ellesmere Port, Wirral*

I think so, yes. It certainly added something because I wanted to prove a point. They'd said that I wasn't good enough to play for Liverpool and I wanted to show them what they'd missed.

How pissed off was he that when he first arrived the fans weren't 100 per cent behind him because he was replacing a hero in Mountfield? Did he see it as more of a challenge to show them what he could do, or did it disappoint him that he was maybe prejudged? *Colin Berry, Wavertree, Liverpool*

Dave Watson

Both really. It was more of a challenge because I was never one to sit back and let something like that get the better of me. It was a challenge to put it right, but it's never nice to have the fans on your case.

How many seasons did it take playing for us for Dave to become a whole-hearted Evertonian after being a Kopite in his youth? *David Chow, Manchester, England*

After about half a season people were beginning to realise that things were going to work out well for me. That was underlined when we won the Championship in our first season, by which time I was totally committed to the cause.

What was it like clinching the title with Everton at Carrow Road, of all places? *Bernie Flood, Ellesmere Port, Wirral*

It was fantastic because it took about seven hours to get back and we just partied all the way. No, it was really nice and, not to rub Norwich's nose in it because I had a great time there, but it was the journey home that was so special. There were so many supporters there and they were passing the coach on their way home. Great memories.

What did it feel like to have Steve Bruce call you 'the hardest man in football'? *Jeremy Wyke, Wigan, England*

It's nice when people say things like that, but at the same time it winds people up. All of a sudden everybody you're playing against wants to have a go at the 'hardest man in football'.

When he first joined Everton did he find it difficult to get in to the team? *Ciaran McConville, Dublin, Republic of Ireland*

It wasn't difficult to get in the team, but it took a bit of time for me to settle in, getting used to players around me and adjusting to a different way of play. But the lads were different class. Kevin Ratcliffe, in particular, was tremendous with me and when I was getting a lot of flak he was always there to cheer me up. I owe him a great deal.

Did the players realise how bad Mike Walker was before we did? *Nick Williams, Warrington, England*

He was put in the job because he'd done a good job elsewhere. Things didn't work out for him and there were maybe one or two questionable signings, but I don't like to criticise managers.

How did he feel about the hefty price tag he carried? At the time,

this was a fair bit, particularly for a defender. Was it an issue when he went out on the pitch at all? *Colin Berry, Wavertree, Liverpool*

It wasn't an issue at first, but maybe once or twice during a game I thought I had to justify it by doing something I wasn't good at. Everton bought me as a defender, but because of the price tag I did try to do things I wouldn't normally do, like hit a 40- or 50-yard pass or have a dribble. I did try it once or twice, but I soon learned not to gamble and just to defend.

What was the 4–4 at Goodison like to play in? The match when Dalglish resigned. *Andy Richardson, Hackney, north-east London*

For the memories and the fans it was end-to-end entertainment and I'm sure it was great to watch, but it was a horrible game as a defender because we gave four goals away.

Why did he celebrate his goals just by waving his right hand above his head when all the theatrical celebrations had been the order of the day, especially in the '90s? *Osmo Tapio Räihälä, Helsinki, Finland*

I scored my first goal at Norwich and I did a daft 50-yard dash round the ground waving to the crowd and everybody was laughing so much that I've done it ever since.

Ask him what it was like playing in front of Big Nev, especially when Neville was suffering from PMT. *Pete Warner, Chippenham, Wiltshire, England*

It was an experience. Neville had so many warnings from policemen behind the goal to watch his language. At some grounds, when there was a big crowd it was nothing short of embarrassing. The things he used to say are unrepeatable, but I doubt we'll ever see anyone as good as him again.

Did Dave ever have the chance to move abroad? *Charlie Brewer, Seoul, South Korea*

No, I never had any offers.

He scored a lot of goals for Everton, 38 in league and cups altogether. Did he set himself goal-scoring targets at the start of the season? *Osmo Tapio Räihälä, Helsinki, Finland*

I always aimed to get four or five a season, although it doesn't necessarily work out like that.

Dave Watson

Who was the best wind-up merchant at the club past or present?
Colin Berry, Wavertree, Liverpool
Without a doubt, that would be Neville.

What was Pat Van den Hauwe like? *Bernie Flood, Ellesmere Port, Wirral*
He was a very quiet lad on and off the pitch, but he could certainly look after himself. I think he was deeply misunderstood.

Which player has been Everton's heaviest boozer during his time? *Dan Keats, Ealing, west London*
It was the time of the drinking culture and I don't know if there was just one heavy drinker. Everton were one of the better teams for drinking, but at the same time they were one of the better teams for winning, so it's only when things go wrong that people knock players about having a drink.

He's scored quite a few over the years. Which was his favourite? *David Shepherd, Shipley, West Yorkshire, England*
My best goal, rather than most important, was a left-foot shot from outside the box past David Seaman at Highbury. It went right into the top left-hand corner. I can still see it now.

Was he tempted to go when Reidy came in for him? What stopped him? *Andy Richardson, Hackney, north-east London*
Apparently, Peter Reid made an enquiry. When I spoke to Howard about it he told me not to read too much into my horoscope.

How come he was so strong in the air even if he isn't tall as a tower like Duncan? *Osmo Tapio Räihälä, Helsinki, Finland*
Just sheer determination, practice over the years and not being scared of getting injured.

Does he have 'Z-Cars' on his mobile phone? *San Presland, New Brighton, Merseyside*
I haven't, but my son has.

How did Norwich winning the League Cup compare with Everton winning the FA Cup? *Bernie Flood, Ellesmere Port, Wirral*
The League Cup at Norwich was fantastic and a great achievement. At the time, it was absolutely brilliant and I didn't think I'd have a better moment than

that in my career. But the FA Cup is the big one and to win it was something else. It's funny how things change, hey?

Who is the nastiest opponent he's faced? *Gagandeep Sethi, Minnesota, USA*
I wouldn't like to accuse anybody of that.

I don't expect Dave to have feared any particular opponent, but surely there were strikers that he thought about more than usual before a game. Who were they? *Osmo Tapio Räihälä, Helsinki, Finland*
You always get one or two. Big John Fashanu in his day was pretty daunting and Mick Harford at Birmingham and Luton. We always had a bit of a tussle. That's about all though, for sheer physical presence.

Does it hurt him as much as the fans to see the club fall from being League Champions to annual relegation candidates? *David Chow, Manchester, England*
It does hurt, and although it's bad for the fans sometimes it's even worse for the players. It's very disappointing the way the club has gone, but I want to assure you that the players really do feel it as much as the fans.

Who was the hardest: Parkie, Horne or Kaiser Ebbrell? *Osmo Tapio Räihälä, Helsinki, Finland*
That would have been a hell of a fight! Possibly Barry Horne, he was a nasty little sod.

Was he more relieved after Wimbledon '94 or Coventry '98? *Gary Davis, Saskatchewan, Canada*
The Wimbledon relegation battle, without a doubt, for the simple reason that we were 2–0 down and it really did feel as if we were going out of the Premiership. The atmosphere wasn't the best and I thought this could possibly be it. But we dragged ourselves out of it in the end and it was an enormous relief, I can tell you. There was a lot more character needed to fight at the wrong end of the table and we proved we could do it.

What's it like going up against Big Dunc? *Clive Blackmore, Washington DC, USA*
I've never played against him competitively, but in training he's a handful.

What went on between Kendall and Speed? I don't accept any answer like 'it was a personality clash', etc. Speed said that there were things that he wouldn't say about Everton, so it was more than personal. Dave and Speed were the team captains at that time, so I expect Dave to have been the first to know from both Speed and Kendall. *Osmo Tapio Räihälä, Helsinki, Finland*

I think it was something to do with the club needing money and he was a valuable asset.

Who was the best pairing of the centre-backs at Everton? *Gary Lambert, Netherton, Merseyside*

Kevin Ratcliffe and myself, of course.

Throughout the '90s he was the one consistently good thing about Everton. How annoying was it for him to watch the team steadily get worse as a series of players came and went with neither his ability or, more importantly, his commitment to the cause? *Tony Brown, Wigan, England*

It was frustrating, but if every player had concentrated on his job and done it to the best of his ability then those problems would never have arisen.

How good is Michael Ball going to be? *Dominic Lawson, Leamington Spa, England*

He could go all the way. Well, he already has gone to the top as far as England goes, but he could become a regular if he puts his mind to it.

When we won the FA Cup in '95 did he genuinely feel it was the start of better times for us, or did he feel it was an enjoyable blip in an otherwise torrid time for the club? *Tony Brown, Wigan, England*

I really did think that would be a taste of things to come, but as the records show it wasn't to be.

How does it feel to be immortalised in song? 'Everton's gonna win the Cup! Big Dave's gonna lift it up! Let's go, let's go!' 'Altogether Now' sends chills down the spine of Evertonians the world over. What does that song do to you? *Ken Myers, Long Beach, California, USA*

It brings back great memories and it always will do. That was sheer magic and the best day of my life.

Ask Waggy what he thought of Big Nev missing the after-match celebrations after the FA Cup final in '95. *Steve Tynan, Aldershot, England*

It was totally understandable because I know the lad's character. It's just a booze-up and there can't be anything more boring if you don't drink.

Did your wife object to you sleeping with the FA Cup after the '95 final? *Keith Wilson, Waterloo, Liverpool*

No, she didn't object at all. In fact, I think she quite enjoyed it.

What is his brother Alex doing now? *Julian Jackson, Hong Kong, SAR of PRC*

Alex is player–coach for Torquay, so he's still in the game, too.

When he became the caretaker manager he had no choice but to throw in youth players like Ball and Dunne and even gave Cadamarteri his debut. Was he ever afraid the youngsters would be scared in front of 40,000 fans? *Osmo Tapio Räihälä, Helsinki, Finland*

I never thought about them being scared because they're at the club to make their debut and it has to happen sooner or later. The sooner you make it the quicker you get started off in football, so I just told them to go and enjoy it.

Who was his best friend at the club? Did that change when he took over as caretaker manager? *Andy Richardson, Hackney, north-east London*

Big Duncan is a very good friend, Our relationship did change, but only because I had to keep a bit of a distance from the players.

How happy was Dave when he heard that Howard would come back in 1997? *Jim Conboy, Hesketh Bank, Merseyside*

I was delighted to see Howard back in the game. He was someone who knew about the club and players had worked with him before so at the time I thought the appointment was going to be right.

At his testimonial the Rangers fans were completely mental. Has he ever witnessed supporters as fanatical as that before or since? *Colin Berry, Wavertree, Liverpool*

Not really, but the year before Neville had Celtic and they certainly came close.

Dave Watson

Does he still support Liverpool on the sly and look out for their results? *Julian Jackson, Hong Kong, SAR of PRC*

No, I honestly don't. I have no association with Liverpool whatsoever.

Pre-season: should this be played at home or abroad? *Frank Hargreaves, Anfield, Liverpool*

I think it's good to go abroad to let the players bond and get to know one another a bit better because there are normally one or two new faces. Besides that, it's also good to get away from the pressures of being at home.

Do you feel that if you had left Everton for a more successful club (as Keown did, for example) you'd have played more for England? *Nick Williams, Warrington, England*

You never know, but I don't think so. I got 12 caps and I think I had a right good go at the England team, but at the time there were better players than me coming up and it's as simple as that.

Why, in your opinion, do most of the current team not have your 'do-or-die-for-the-club' philosophy? Too much cash? *Alistair Laignel, Jersey, Channel Islands*

Money certainly plays a big part in it. Years ago, you would play for your bonus money, but I don't think people even know how much their bonus money is any more.

Football violence: as players, were you ever aware when it was 'going off'? Did it ever get discussed? *Frank Hargreaves, Anfield, Liverpool*

In the early days, around '81, there was a bit of violence going on, but over the years the authorities have done a great job of stamping it out. I don't think there's much going on now, and if there is then the players are certainly unaware of it.

If it wasn't for his dodgy knees would he have done a Nev and carried on playing for as long as possible, even dropping down divisions, or would he still have called it a day? *Colin Berry, Wavertree, Liverpool*

I think I would have called it a day because it's not just my dodgy knees, it's my entire body which tells me I can't do it any more.

Since Michael Ball, Richard Dunne, Peter Clarke, Sean O'Hanlon etc. seem to progress under his tutelage, doesn't he think that the strikers would benefit from a specialist 'striking coach' (e.g. Ian Rush) and midfielders from a specialist 'midfield coach' (perhaps Kevin Richardson)? *San Presland, New Brighton, Merseyside*

It's a good point, but remember when Mark Lawrenson went to Newcastle as a defensive coach? It doesn't always work out the way you would like.

We all remember the mid '80s as our glory period and most of us pick out the Bayern game and/or the final at Rotterdam as our favourites. You didn't play in either of those and arrived mid-way through that period of success. What was the most memorable game you played in? *Nick Williams, Warrington, England*

It keeps coming back: the 4–4 against Liverpool and the Wimbledon game for sheer importance.

What sticks in your mind from the 3–2 Wimbledon game? *Joe Hannah, Sydney, Australia*

Work was being done to rebuild the Park End, so it was completely empty. I was defending a corner and for a split second I looked behind the goal line and there was a man sitting upstairs on a bus reading a newspaper. He was completely oblivious and I just couldn't believe he didn't know what was going on.

Who was the best player he played with and against? *Ciaran McConville, Dublin, Republic of Ireland*

We've had lots of good players at Everton, but they were good for different reasons. Peter Reid, not necessarily for his skill but certainly for his determination, Trevor Steven and Pat Nevin for their trickery, Limpar, the list is endless. I hate to say this but the best player I have ever been up against has to be Ian Rush, and Kenny Dalglish would certainly be up there, too.

Was his utterly magnificent, commanding performance for Golden of Hong Kong against Venables' pre-Euro '96 team motivated by a sense of injustice at not having received his due number of international caps? *Andy Cheyne, Hampstead Norreys, England*

No, it was purely because we were on so much money to get a result against England.

Does it bother him that someone like Tony Adams and Martin

Dave Watson

Keown received many more caps when essentially the two were very similar? *Colin Berry, Wavertree, Liverpool*

I don't begrudge them anything. I think Tony has been great over the years. You get what you deserve in football and I think he thoroughly deserved it.

How do you rate Mark Higgins and would you have liked to have him beside you at the heart of the defence? *Ari Sigurgeirsson, Hafnarfjordur, Iceland*

I can only vaguely remember Mark as a player, but by speaking to people like Ratters he was obviously great to play alongside. It was tragic that his career was cut short and I'm not sure if I'd have got a game if he'd still been around.

To me and the rest of the fans it's pretty clear that without Dave, Everton would have been relegated at some point over the last few years. Does he ever stop and think that he is the reason we are still in the Premier League and that every fan loves him for it? Did he realise the responsibility he had when he was playing? *Eddie Pepper, Brighton, England*

I certainly realised the responsibility, especially when it came down to the last game of the season, but I'm sure everybody else on the pitch did too. The pressure and burden of it was enormous, but that's what we were there for and we had a sheer determination to stay in the top flight.

How good will Peter Clarke become? *Joe O' Reilly, Dublin, Republic of Ireland*

He's got every chance of becoming a very good player but it's up to him to apply himself.

Did he think he would get the manager's job after Joe Royle/Kendall left? *Ciaran McConville, Dublin, Republic of Ireland*

No, and it wasn't something I was planning for. I was still there as a player and I wouldn't have thought I was experienced enough at that level.

Did he ever think Andy Gray was going to take over? *Frank Hargreaves, Anfield, Liverpool*

At one stage, I did, yes.

When he was caretaker manager how aware was he of the scale of the risks that Joe Parkinson was taking by playing despite being injured? *Andy Cheyne, Hampstead Norreys, England*

Not being medically minded, I really didn't understand the full extent of it, but with Joe being the player he was, nobody would have been able to stop him. Other players have carried on through injuries throughout their careers and it seems like a good idea at the time, but in the long term it's something you could live to regret.

How did he enjoy his caretaker manager spell and, if appointed again, having experienced coaching now, what would he do differently? *Jonathan Gard, Woolton, Liverpool*
I did enjoy it and I don't think I could have done anything much different.

Which players in the last two seasons have Everton missed the most? *John Walton, Dubai, United Arab Emirates*
Joe Parkinson certainly springs to mind, and John Ebbrell. They were the workhorses in the team and never got the credit they deserved.

What did he think about Billy Kenny? *Keith Giles, Perth, Australia*
Billy was a tremendous prospect, he could have been the best footballer around. He had everything, skill, nastiness and passion, but he obviously fell in with the wrong crowd.

How important is peripheral vision? *San Presland, New Brighton, Merseyside*
It's very important because you never know what's behind you.

Who was his favourite manager to work under? *Kate Mottram, Birmingham, England*
Howard Kendall, he was absolutely magnificent. His man-management was different class. But Joe Royle's a big mate of mine and I played with him at Norwich, and Walter has looked after me well.

Why didn't Tony Grant really set the world alight? *Osmo Tapio Räihälä, Helsinki, Finland*
I think his injuries kept him out of games. He got one decent run in the side and was doing well and then he had another setback. He just never seemed to play at the highest level for any length of time without picking up some kind of injury.

Who was the most misunderstood/underrated player he ever worked with? *Julian Jackson, Hong Kong, SAR of PRC*
John Ebbrell springs to mind.

Dave Watson

Do the current Everton squad practise defending corners and free kicks? Really practise them, I mean! *David Catton, Sheffield, England*

I don't know what you mean by 'really' practise them, but we dedicate one afternoon a week to it.

Was Danny Williamson any good? *Mark Edwards, Crosby, Liverpool*

Danny had a lot of ability, but I don't know whether he had the desire to play football at the highest level.

Which players really can't take a joke? *Lee Farrell, Glasgow, Scotland*

The foreign contingent. Whether it's because they can't understand it fully, I don't know.

How come you manage to look like such a really nice bloke despite being a bit of a ruthless tackler? *Jeremy Wyke, Wigan, England*

Not very many people think that I look like a nice bloke.

You have no doubt had contact with mad Evertonians wherever you and the team have gone on pre-season tours. I'd like to take you back to Standard Liege on 2 August 1998. I was there in the front row, seven-year-old lad in tow. After the match you told me to hand my son over the railing to you and you walked him around and introduced him to the rest of the players on the field. My question to you is: why didn't you keep the little swine? Seriously though, that has to be one of the highlights of my Everton-supporting life and I am eternally grateful. Did you get my thank-you letter and, if so, why didn't you respond? *Ken Myers, Long Beach, California, USA*

I can't remember getting a letter, but I put myself in other people's shoes at times and if I was there with my kid I'd like the same to be done to him. I'm glad it made your day and hopefully it's something your lad will never forget either.

When you were first-team coach did you have direct responsibilities for coaching the defence? *Nick Williams, Warrington, England*

No, my role was first-team coach, not just defensive coach.

When you start at Tranmere as manager who will have a greater influence on your managerial style, Kendall or Smith? *Matt Traynor, Finchley, north London*
Both men have great qualities. I worked with Howard a lot longer than with Walter so I've learnt a few more tricks from him.

Do you despair at the apparent near complete absence of loyalty in today's game? *Rob Hamilton, Melbourne, Australia*
Totally.

What are his feelings about the match interruption at Arsenal and did Walter and Archie understand what it was all about? *John Walton, Dubai, United Arab Emirates*
I think everybody could understand the frustration, but it's certainly something I couldn't condone or agree with.

What is the secret to your longevity as a player? *Ken Myers, Long Beach, California, USA*
I've kept going for so long because I've got a wife and four kids and I need to survive.

How hard was it to leave Everton after all these years? Are you secretly hoping that the manager's job at Tranmere is a stepping-stone, towards coming back and managing Everton? *Andy Howarth, Long Beach, California, USA*
It's my ambition to manage Everton one day. It was very difficult to leave but you have to move on in football and there have been better players than me who've left Everton. I see my job at Tranmere as a starting-point and how well I do there will determine how well I do in the future. I had the time of my life at Everton and I couldn't have wished for a better career as a player. I'll never forget it, the people are magnificent, the club is fantastic and the fans are the most loyal in the land. Thanks for having me.

GORDON WEST

Born 24 April 1943
March 1962 – October 1975
£27,500

Although he had only played 31 games for Blackpool, there were already whispers about the Yorkshire lad who could stop any shot and then throw the ball with deadly accuracy to the halfway line. In March 1962, backed by the might of Sir John Moores' chequebook, Harry Catterick headed north to see for himself. The millionaires' club had a simple remit: success.

Parting with a world record fee of £27,500, 'The Cat' returned with his prize – a strapping teenager whose frame belied his incredible agility and speed. The fans couldn't believe their luck, as the lad with the face of a movie star took his place in the nets and Albert Dunlop was consigned to the record books. And there was something else afoot at Goodison Park: it was the buzz of excitement amongst the Royal Blue faithful because they could sense that, at long last, Everton's time had finally come.

> I was so frightened when I had to come here on my own, but my dad
> was a coal miner in Barnsley and I knew my alternatives only too well.

So please, throw your hats in the air and give a rousing cheer for the man who transformed goalkeeping into an art form. I give you the magnificent Gordon West.

He was tipped as the best prospect for England and I remember a photograph of Westy in full acrobatic motion as a Blackpool player that was awarded sports photo of the year. *Kenny Jones, Tel Aviv, Israel*
I remember that too. I was 17 years old when I made that save against Arsenal and it was out of this world. The reason I remember it so well is that it won an award for the photographer, Adidas used it for an advert, it was in all the

papers and it cost me nearly a fiver to get four copies of it. I had to send off and get them too. My son, Stephen, has still got it though, so I suppose I got my money's worth.

I remember his first game for us – does he? *David Catton, Sheffield, England*

It was Wolves at home and we won 4–0. I was only 18 and frightened to death. The sports coverage wasn't as it is now but there was this cameraman in the dressing-room and a fella called Wally Barnes who started off with the BBC on *Match of the Day*. He was taking my photo and I was almost wetting myself, I was so frightened. I was just a lad from Barnsley and I didn't want the fame, I wasn't interested in the cameras. I wanted to get it over with, win and go home.

Who did he most dislike, as an opponent? Who did he most respect? *Iain Cooke, Basel, Switzerland*

My most respected opponent has to be Bobby Charlton, I played against Manchester United many a time and I admired him very much indeed. As for whom I disliked, well, the answer has to be the entire Leeds team, and I mean that, they were terrible. They'd go over the top all the time and they were so good at it. Every time you'd go for a ball you were fouled and they always got away with it. I used to hate playing against Leeds.

Was his extraordinary throwing ability something he learnt and practised, or could he just do it? *Phil Bowker, Brussels, Belgium*

When I was an apprentice it was different than it is now. I was at Blackpool and my main job was to sweep all the stands and clean the ground up. When that was done I was allowed to train, but not with the players. I was 15 at the time and I would come back in the afternoon and talk to the groundsman about Bert Trautmann. He had a fantastic throw and that was why I started practising it. It just came naturally, I was a big fella and I could throw the ball quite far.

Somehow he stopped a volley from Alan A'Court in 1962 when the ball buried itself in his body from about three yards. His positioning was brilliant, but apart from this did he know anything about the save? Personally, I don't know how he even managed to hold onto it, never mind clear it. *David Tickner, Bowring Park, Liverpool*

I remember that too. He was a few yards out when he hit and it stuck in, shall we say, my stomach. You had to get on with it though; there was none of this getting stretchered off malarkey like you see now. The ref wouldn't even blow the whistle and if he had done, I don't know what they'd have given, maybe a bounce-up about a yard away. I felt it for a week or so and just remembering it now brings tears to my eyes. I don't know which was the worst pain, that or a kick in your ear, especially if it was cold. Your ear would sting for the whole match and they were the sorest things ever.

Did he really throw up before games? *Jim Lynch, Brentwood, England*

No, that's been exaggerated. I couldn't throw up because I was too nervous to eat anything in the first place. I did feel sick with nerves though. Everybody's nervous and if you're not, you shouldn't be going out onto the pitch. I remember playing for Blackpool in the same side as Stanley Matthews. He used to walk around with just his shirt on and he was permanently weeing, he was so nervous. When I was in the Blackpool first team, I had a brilliant run and I helped get them out of relegation at Birmingham. After the game, I got into the big communal bath and could hear the champagne corks popping in the dressing-room. The next thing, there was a tap on my shoulder and it was Stanley Matthews with a glass of champagne. He said: 'There you are, son, you deserve this.' It was the first drink I'd ever had in my life, but I've made up for it since.

I missed his debut and had to wait for Monday's *Liverpool Echo* for a report on him. It went into great detail on his astonishing 'throwing' ability. I witnessed this on a number of occasions that season, but following that it was used less and less. Ask him why he stopped the long, long throws? *John Quinn, Tewkesbury, England*

Did I stop it? I don't think I did. I snapped my thigh muscle and I played right to the FA Cup final with it, but I couldn't kick the ball. They kept saying there was nothing wrong with me and I was playing so well that the players took my goalkicks, and it worked out all right.

The thing about throwing the ball is that there's got to be somebody there to receive it. If he's marked up, there's no point and it's just a waste, but the only time I kicked it was when there was nobody to throw it to.

Who was the better player, Jimmy Armfield or Tommy Wright? *Phil Pellow, Waterloo, Liverpool*

I played with both of them and Tommy Wright was a good player, but Jimmy Armfield was a great player.

I remember Gordon talking to a policeman during the 'Eddie Cavanagh' interlude. What did he say to him? *David Tickner, Bowring Park, Liverpool*

That was the equaliser, I just told the policeman to leave him alone. Eddie was one of us and I didn't want him to get arrested or go to prison or anything like that. He just couldn't stop himself, he started running and nobody could catch him. It was marvellous to witness and I'm so glad it was captured on film. I went to his funeral and I don't know what kind of circles he moved in, but the turnout was unbelievable. The closest I've seen to that was the Krays' funerals. There was the hearse, then another huge car full of flowers, and then about ten big cars behind that. I saw people there I knew from my playing days and they did him proud.

What was his greatest save? *Jim Lynch, Brentwood, England*

I remember a few saves, but most of all I remember my mistakes. People tell me about saves I made, or saves their dads have told them about, and they're always on about the one against Wolves from Ernie Hunt. We signed him after that. I don't really remember it myself. I know I had a good game, but I never really had time to pat myself on the back.

Harry Catterick – what are Gordon's memories of The Cat? *Phil Pellow, Waterloo, Liverpool*

Harry Catterick was very fair, and if you did nothing wrong he was all right. He was really strict and he would even tell the trainer to pass on the message to get your hair cut. It had to be short, and if you didn't do it he would fine you £10. There was a book at Bellefield, I was number four, and you had to sign your name alongside your number. At ten o'clock the book would be taken away and if your name wasn't in there you got fined a tenner. I think Frank D'arcy must have owed the club money some weeks. The same people grumbled all the time, and they were the ones who were constantly late. I was never late. One day, Catterick asked me what I thought about him taking the book away. I told him it didn't matter because it didn't affect me, and that was exactly his point. He said that people in the real world worked nights, or on the docks, and they started work much earlier and a lot of players didn't realise that. Harry said if you couldn't get in for ten o'clock then you deserved to be fined.

Is it true that during one game that we were coasting (it might have been against Southampton) Alan Ball turned in midfield and belted the ball at your net, forcing you into a scrambling, yet

athletic save? And is it also true that you chased him all over the pitch trying to wallop him for his cheek? *Mark Murphy, Horsham, England*

There's no truth in that whatsoever. I don't know where that came from. I don't know what the story is with Alan Ball and me, I'm not sure what I'm supposed to have done. I think I once said he was a great player, but I wouldn't have a drink with him, and I'm sure he'd say the same about me.

How did he react to the Sandy Brown own goal? *Steve Fairclough, Toronto, Canada*

I remember the ball coming over and thinking: 'Is it mine, is it theirs?', and the next thing it was in the back of the net. I just turned to him and said: 'Good goal, Sandy.' There are two things I'm remembered for most of all, Sandy Brown's goal and that bloody handbag! I've got two Championship medals, two FA Cup final medals, I've played for England and had 400 games for Everton, and all I'm remembered for is Sandy Brown's goal and my handbag.

This handbag lark from the Kop – what was behind all that? *Tim Gunnion, Frankfurt, Germany*

I played my first game at Anfield, but I didn't know what Everton and Liverpool games really meant. So, I made my way down to the Kop and there were 25,000 people giving me rude gestures and hurling abuse. It really hurt my feelings and I couldn't understand why they would be doing it to me, I'd never done a thing wrong in my life other than collect birds' eggs.

A year later, I'd learnt that we hated each other and I thought I would shut them up. Gordon, the miner's son and conker champion from Barnsley, was going to shut the Kop up! So I sauntered along, showed them my bum then blew some kisses. A year later, I got the handbag. It shut me up – it stuck with me the rest of my life! A couple of years ago, the *Echo* ran a 'sports photograph of the century', not the year, the century. Somebody knocked at my door and told me I'd won it. Number one was me accepting the handbag! I'd won it and I didn't even want to.

Did you keep any of them, and were any of them good quality? *Tim Gunnion, Frankfurt, Germany*

Nah, they were rubbish, but the lipstick was good.

When we brought the FA Cup back in '66 there was a joint celebration with Liverpool who had won the league near St George's Hall. As the Everton bus drew up a Liverpool fan

signalled 5–0 to West, to which he replied: 'Not me.' (I think it was Andy Rankin who let the five in.) What did he think of his record against Liverpool? *Michael Dudley, Long Island, NY, USA*

I thought it was very poor actually; I beat them seven times, drew seven and lost five. But I did play in that 5–0 defeat. I didn't have a good game and I was gutted about it. I came home that night and the phone rang and a voice just said: 'Thank you very much indeed.' It was quite sinister and I went ex-directory after that. I would often get phone calls in the middle of the night. Derek Temple had one just before the FA Cup final, and so did I. I forget what he said now, but it was quite unnerving. But that was me, the 5–0, I was very upset and I must have been just passing the blame on to Andy Rankin.

How come Catterick, Mr Conservative, allowed the cameras into the dressing-room in the '66 FA Cup final? *George Lee Stuart, Lismore, Australia*

He must have got paid! I don't know really, it was something you never thought about or questioned, it just happened. In my day, you never questioned anything; you just did as you were told. Although I'd left school, it was like I was still at school in my career because I was told what to do all the time. If they told you to get your hair cut, you did. You had to be punctual or you were fined. If you went abroad, they took your passport and gave it to you before you went through to board the flight. Everything was done and you never asked why. If you did you were in trouble.

After winning the league the season before the 1970 World Cup, Everton didn't capture the same form the following season. Had the World Cup taken it out of the players who had been to Mexico? *Tony Kennedy, Loughborough, England*

I don't know, I blame myself for it. We knew we'd won the Championship in 1969–70 with roughly ten games to go. We played at Burnley and there was a 50-50 ball with Brian Labone, Steve Kindon and me. There was only ever going to be one winner and that was me, but my knee caught Labby in his kidneys and he missed the last eight games. Alan Ball was made captain and we won seven and drew the last game 0–0 at Roker Park. The following season Catterick made Alan Ball the permanent captain and that was the worst thing that ever happened to Everton. Bally was fanatical and if we didn't win he would be in tears saying: 'What's my dad going to say? He'll kill me.' Nobody wanted to lose, but he would be devastated and it's hard to respect your captain when he's crying like a baby.

Gordon West

When you sat watching the 1970 World Cup quarter-final and saw Peter Bonetti making such a holy show of himself did you feel any pangs of regret that you'd turned down the chance to go to Mexico? *Ian Roberts, Wallasey, Wirral*

No, I didn't actually, I felt sorry for him. He went out there to play his very best. Bonetti was a decent keeper and nobody wants to make mistakes. All I could think was: 'Thank God it isn't me.'

I heard on the radio today that, contrary to popular belief, Man United and Liverpool players are quite friendly. When you were playing how did you get on with players from other clubs, particularly the red you-know-whos? *Michael O'Connell, Galway, Republic of Ireland*

I got on very well with them because we all drank in the Punchbowl Hotel. I always went there and lived nearby. In fact, I'm still friendly with Ian Callaghan to this day. Labby's big mates with him too, and sometimes goes to Anfield with him. We were winding him up at his own birthday party the other week saying he watches Liverpool more than Everton, but with Labby it's something for him to do. He likes to fill his time. He goes for lunch and makes a day of it. I can cook and look after myself, but not Labby, he hates being on his own.

What do you miss most from your playing days? *Michael O'Connell, Galway, Republic of Ireland*

Probably the money, and I wasn't even paid well. I remember going to Everton from Blackpool, I was a world record signing at £27,500 and my wages went from £20 to £30 a week. I had a signing on fee of £20 and we won that week, so I got a bonus. I went home to Blackpool on the train with £58 and I stood up all the way, with my hand on my pocket in case I lost it. I'd never had so much money in one go in my life. A docker was earning about £12 in those days, so it was an enormous amount of cash. Later on in life I had two cars. I used to fill them both up for £5, get the week's shopping in for another £5 and the rest was spare.

Ask him if his hands ever stung when saving a hard shot not wearing any gloves? *Gary Fulton, Northwich, Cheshire, England*

No, they didn't, because I never got a hand to any of them! Nah, seriously, they didn't hurt at all. You had to go and buy your own gloves and bring the chitty back to get reimbursed. I'd go to Greenwoods or somewhere like that, 4/6, and I'd ask for a receipt for 7/11. It was a great scam because you made a few bob and you could buy about three or four pints with that! I would hold my hands up and show them that they were full of holes and they would tell me to turn them over! I used to turn them inside out and get a few more games out of them. Mine were just ordinary woollen gloves like you'd wear for walking to school. The gloves they sell these days are about 60 quid and if I'd had them I'd still be playing now.

Are today's fluorescent keepers as good as the greats of the '60s, like West, Yashin, Banks and Jennings? *Mike Owen, Childwall, Liverpool*

I think the modern-day goalkeepers are flashy. You can kid people on, I mean, look at Barthez, he makes these supposedly spectacular saves and he's no reason to dive, he could just catch it. But he's there with his legs up and they're all applauding him. I only rate two keepers in the league now, David Seaman and Nigel Martyn. That bloke from Newcastle, Harper, he's kidding them all. They go on about how fantastic his saves are, but they're not really, even though they do look out of this world. Andy Rankin, when he took over for a while, was a bit flash, his legs were up in the air and he was launching himself around. A normal keeper would have just caught it, but he wanted to look the part.

Who were Everton's best three outfield players in his day? *Mike Owen, Childwall, Liverpool*

Everybody in their own right was brilliant; I don't know if I could even pick three. I suppose the obvious answer would be Harvey, Ball and Kendall, but what about Alex Young and Tony Kay? They were all magnificent.

What really happened when he was sent off up at Newcastle? *San Presland, New Brighton, Merseyside*

It was when the three-step rule came in and this bloke, Albert Bennett, wouldn't get out of my way. There were a few words between us and I had a rule that if they didn't do as I'd said, I'd floor them. So I threw the ball, followed through and gave him a dig. I always did it, but this time he went down. The linesman flagged the foul, I got sent off and Catterick fined me a tenner. I've done it to Summerbee and Jeff Astle too. I got the ball and told Jeff to piss off, but he wouldn't, so I flattened him. After that we came to a compromise, he would go to the left and I'd go to the right, but at Newcastle I got caught out and I'm guilty as charged.

My question to Gordon would revolve around the reasons that the team of the early '60s did not establish themselves more – one league title and one FA Cup was scant reward for a team and

club that had everything going for it, including Sir John's money.
Paul Rigby, Connecticut, USA

The thing is, in '66 we were in the FA Cup final and in '67 we were knocked out in the quarter-finals. I was playing brilliantly, but I missed that game because I broke my hand, so Andy Rankin came in. He let three goals in, and with me playing so well before my injury the finger was pointed at him. We should have gone to the Cup final that year too. But we did well, two leagues, two cups and a few semi-finals. Your name's got to be on the cup for you to have won it, but we were close.

Why does he think it is that notable outfield players remain broadly comparable with the 'best' of yesteryear, while goalkeepers seem to have gone the other way and are now mostly total crap? *Mark Wilson, Warrington, England*

I think that's right. In my day, there were so many good goalkeepers. Name the club and I'll name the keeper, that's how it used to be. Fulham had Tony Macedo, Chelsea had Bonetti, Peter Springett was at Sheffield Wednesday and at Man City there was Bert Trautmann, who I played against when I was 17.

Does he think the various rule changes, like not handling back passes, has made their job any harder? *David Catton, Sheffield, England*

When I first started, the goalie used to run all over the 18-yard line. As long as you bounced the ball every three yards you were OK, although you looked stupid. To be honest, I don't think I could handle it now. It was bad enough when the three-step rule came in. I have to ask my son what the rules are, they change so often. Now they get the ball and they run; if I'd have done that I'd have been sent off.

That FA Cup match at Wolves was one of the best goalkeeping performances I've ever seen, especially the save from Ernie Hunt. Does he rate it his best? *San Presland, New Brighton, Merseyside*

Everybody tells me it's the best, so I guess it was. Whenever you had a good performance you'd buy the paper the next day, but you wouldn't bother when you'd had a bad one. I bought all the papers that week and got ten out of ten in each one. I can still remember one journalist saying he'd never seen a display like that before.

What really was the story behind his theatrical leaving of the field after the European Cup tie against Keflavik in 1970? *Jim Lynch, Brentwood, England*

I didn't actually leave the field, but things weren't going right and the crowd was getting on my back. The ball came to me, everybody was jeering and there was a fella behind me who got on the pitch. I was so angry that I gave the crowd the V-sign and I shouldn't have done. Labby was sub and Catterick sent him to ask if I wanted to come off. I stayed on, but I got dropped after that. I deserved it, I suppose, but when you go through a bad time you're aware of it and you don't need the crowd to tell you.

You kept Andy Rankin on the bench for so long. How was your relationship with him? *Steve Fairclough, Toronto, Canada*

Very good actually, we got on great. When I joined Everton in '62 I took over from Albert Dunlop, who was nearly thirty. He gave me a dog's life. I was only a kid, virtually straight from school, and I remember he used to kick the ball as hard as he could from about four or five yards and almost knock me over. I wanted to tell him not to, but he really was so horrible to me that I thought it would make him worse because he was a recognised keeper and I was this slip of a lad. Anyway, he left after 18 months or so. When we made it to the FA Cup final in '66 there were loads of good luck letters and telegrams. I opened mine before the match and there was one from Albert. It said: 'Dear Gordon, I've finally plucked up courage to apologise for what I did to you all those years ago and I realise what a great keeper you are now. Please accept my apology.' I was made up.

Having come from behind in '66 what went wrong for us in the '68 FA Cup final against supposedly inferior opposition? *Phil Bowker, Brussels, Belgium*

Two months before the Cup final we played West Brom and beat them 6–2 away. We got to the final and in our team meetings we were told that their keeper was no good so we should cross the ball. On the day he caught everything, we missed everything and if we were still playing that same game today it would end 1–0. That's football, that's why people win the pools and that's what makes the game what it is. It was a good day for the West Brom fans though.

How does he rate himself alongside Neville? *Colin Smyth, Ormskirk, England*

Neville was brilliant. If he was better than me then good luck to him. I was just so proud to be an Evertonian and I always played to the best of my ability.

Alex Young recently said: 'I should have done better, personally, and we should have won more than we did with the team we had.' Could he have been any better? *Neil Wolstenholme, Muswell Hill, north London*

Alex was a great player, but he didn't really do it when we played away. Catterick didn't like him much because he wanted consistency. Alex was lovely to watch, but it's like Duncan McKenzie, they sometimes have to be carried. They have their minute and it's marvellous, and beautiful to watch, but they don't do much for the rest of the match. I want to mention somebody who I think is an unsung hero from the '63 side, he never gets a plaudit and I don't know why: Dennis Stevens, he was a bread-and-butter player. He was signed the day after me for about £25,000 from Bolton, he played inside-forward and all he did was run and run like a modern-day half-back. Nobody liked him at Everton because he didn't have any 'School of Science' flair, but I'll tell you what; he was constantly doing all the work for all the others.

Was there ever a chance of Sandy Brown claiming your starting goalie job? *Steve Fairclough, Toronto, Canada*

We used to have a lot of fun with Sandy and take the mickey out of him a bit. When we played Newcastle away and I got sent off, the ref gave a penalty and it was 0–0. In those days there was no substitute, so Sandy got my jersey and went in goal. On the way back on the bus I said to him: 'You bastard! You ruined the game for us, it was 0–0 when I went off!' He went mental and was ranting all the way home in that mad Scottish accent of his.

Why did he throw the ball so much? Did he get stick for not kicking it? *Peter Jones, Dorking, England*

I never got stick. If you could throw the ball it was better and it got us on to the attack.

I remember a rumour about Westy not going to the 1970 World Cup because his missus would not let him. Is this true or is my memory going completely? *Reg Pearson, San Francisco, California, USA*

It's true. I'm not telling tales, but here are a couple of stories about Ann, my ex-wife. We got divorced in 1974 and we have two fabulous sons. Our first child was due and we were playing Birmingham away. On the Friday she said she didn't want me to go and I was to tell Catterick I couldn't play in the match. I told her I couldn't do that and we had a terrible argument. About ten to three I was called into the manager's office and my wife was on the phone. She told me we'd had a boy and we called him Stephen.

Our next son, Mark, was also born on a Saturday, the day we played Liverpool in the Cup, which was a night match. I went to the hospital to see them in the afternoon and spent a few hours there. We lived in Southport then and it was the same story, she said I was to tell them I wasn't going. I went and she went ballistic. The press came into the dressing-room after the match and they were taking all the photos and I told this guy I'd had a son earlier that day. He told me not to tell anyone else and he took a photograph. It was the front page of the *Daily Mirror* the next day.

Only three caps for England. Any regrets about giving up the chance in 1970? *Steve Fairclough, Toronto, Canada*

Brian tells the story that my wife said if I went to Mexico she'd divorce me, so I didn't go and she did anyway! It was all about my wife and I'd do anything for a bit of peace. I regret it now, I should have gone, but I'd have lost everything. The way it worked out I did anyway, so it made no difference. Brian's wife, ex-wife, Pat, was even worse than mine. I still love her to death, but she was. I'm his best mate so I won't say anything else.

Gordon West, a great keeper. Does he think keepers in the modern game get too much protection or does he wish the same interpretation of the laws had been in force when he played? *Neil Wolstenholme, Muswell Hill, north London*

Players were allowed to barge into you then, but I didn't mind because I was 14½ stone and not many could get the better of me. The keepers get away with murder now and wouldn't have lasted a match in my day.

He always wore black shorts and then the rule came in that the goalie had to wear the same colour as the rest of the team (very important rule that). Anyway, did it put him off his game? *George Lee Stuart, Lismore, Australia*

The rules were so funny, but you're right, I couldn't wear the black shorts and had to wear white like the rest of the team. I thought the black shorts looked better, but it made no difference. Another time I can remember going out with a jersey on and it was just a little bit different, it was still green but it had a tiny row of black around the neck. I was told to take it off because it wasn't all green! There were no names or anything in those old days. In the 1966 FA Cup final Catterick wouldn't even let us have a badge on our shirts. He said that everybody knew that blue shirts and white shorts were Everton; we didn't need any writing to tell them who we were.

Is his wife's name Rose (I think it may be) and does he have any bodies buried under the patio? *San Presland, New Brighton, Merseyside*
Her name is Ann, but I won't be checking under the patio – she was capable of anything!

I was chatting with a couple of Blues the other day who were reminiscing about a save he made against West Brom – 'better than Banks from Pele'. Does he remember it? Does any one save stand out amongst the thousands? *Neil Wolstenholme, Muswell Hill, north London*
I don't really remember a lot of saves. I will say that Banks made that save and it was fantastic, but he was on the telly. I've made better saves than that, but it's not been televised, so it's only what people can remember. Back then, they only covered a couple of games a week, but there are cameras everywhere now.

My darkest day as a kid was travelling to Sunderland for a cup tie (there were no motorways in those days). Gordon played appallingly, even letting a goal go through his legs. A few more errors and it was 3–0. The following Wednesday we played at home he was jeered and heckled consistently by most of the crowd, and it was months before he was forgiven. My question: how did the crowd's jeering affect him over the subsequent weeks? *John Quinn, Tewkesbury, England*
I remember that game because I remember all the bad games. I was terrible and there was nothing I could do about it. I was so glad when it was over because I just wanted to go home. We stopped near Newcastle on the way back for something to eat and I stood in the foyer. The next thing, these fans came in, went over to Brian and said: 'What we want is a new keeper!' I felt terrible and I can still remember it like it was yesterday.

The bus dropped Brian and me off in Maghull. I walked from Kirby's garage about a mile home and I was in tears all the way. It does affect the players and it certainly affected me. I didn't want to play badly, but that's football, sometimes you just have a bad game. I was terrible, I admit that, but I didn't need anyone to tell me.

Still Talking Blue

During a game against Real Zaragoza in the Cup Winners' cup away he was chased behind the goal by at least two of the opposition players. I wasn't at the game, but it's a memory that has stuck with me. What happened? Did he get them after (or even during) the game? *Mike Wood, Zurich, Switzerland*

I can't remember how it began, but there was an altercation and they ran after me. I had to run because if I had started fighting I would have been sent off, so they just carried on chasing me. They were tiny too, the cheeky monkeys. Nothing happened after the match, it was a heat-of-the-moment type of thing, but it must have looked funny.

Does he hate Jeff Astle as much as I do? *Tony Field, Loughborough, England*

No, he was just doing his job. I remember this fella asking me if I'd seen him on that Baddiel and Skinner show. I watched it one night and I almost died for him, he was singing. I would never do that, I don't care how much they offered me.

Any regrets about retiring early? *Steve Fairclough, Toronto, Canada*

Yes, plenty, but it's too late now. I've had a lot of time to think about what might have been, but you can't undo what's been done.

Does he, like me, believe that Brian Labone was a more influential figure in the 1970 team than the midfield three? *Phil Pellow, Waterloo, Liverpool*

Brian was a great player and a brilliant captain, but those three got the credit for everything, didn't they? I only found out the other week that Labby was on a fiver a week more than me. He showed me his contract, the bastard! The thing is, I was happy; I didn't care how much anybody was on, but Labby? I was choked.

The wage structure was very simple. When I signed in '62 I was on £30 a week. We won the Championship and Mr Catterick called us into the office. We didn't ask for more money, he told us we would get a £5 increase. I didn't question anything, I just signed. The next year I was on £40 a week and that was how it increased all my life. I had one year at £100 a week right at the end and when I was playing for England.

Before we won the Championship, Roy Vernon, God bless him, was the captain and he went to ask Catterick what bonus we were going to get. He took us all into a room while he explained how it was going to work and he was rubbing his hands together. He said we would get a pound per thousand over 35,000, in other words, if there were 37,000 we'd get a bonus of £2. But we were getting crowds of about 50,000 then, so it was an extra £15 a week. I would run onto the pitch behind Labby and he would scan the stands and say: 'Nice one, there's seven quid there, Westie.' That was how we were thinking all the time. We knew if we could give a good performance then they would come back again next week.

Did he really hate Ian St John (and if not, why not?) and did he land a punch in the cup tie derby game in '67? *Jim Lynch, Brentwood, England*

It was a full season before I realised how intense the rivalry was. By then, I'd had it instilled into me that Liverpool were evil and bad, and I just hated them. As for St John, he never hit me, he threw a punch, but he only came up to my chest so I wouldn't have felt it even if he'd made contact – I took a dive to try and get him sent off anyway.

Was he aware that the fans nicknamed him Handbag? *Tony Field, Loughborough, England*

Hopefully, that was only Liverpool fans.

How did he feel when clowns like Andy Rankin and David Lawson were brought in to replace him? *David Tickner, Bowring Park, Liverpool*

Andy Rankin replaced me because I was playing badly in '63, but I got my form back and got back in. When they signed David Lawson it was one of my best seasons at Everton and I couldn't believe it. A journalist phoned me at home and said we'd signed David Lawson and I asked him what position he played! He was from Huddersfield and we paid £80,000, which was a hell of a lot of money, so they thought they would have to play him – even though he was having a bad run. If they'd have put me back I'm sure I'd have come good. In those days they just kept you instead of letting you go. They kept me for over three years. It was sad.

Did he ever tell Andy Rankin to get his hair cut? *Mike Owen, Childwall, Liverpool*

Yes, many a time.

My dad says he always used to dive with his head back and his feet

tucked tight to his (no doubt impossibly handsome?) backside for the cameras. Now THAT'S showbiz! *Neil Mckeown, Woolwich, south-east London*

That was the picture that won the sports photo of the year. I didn't do it on purpose, but it did look pretty good.

Does he feel that he should have challenged Gordon Banks on a more regular basis, or did he feel that Banks was the best? *Tony Field, Loughborough, England*

Gordon Banks was the best and it's as simple as that. I played three games for England and I could have played more but for my marriage. I was sub a few times, but there's no doubt at all that Gordon Banks was the best.

What's the real story about not going to Mexico with the England squad? Was it really family reasons or was there a personality clash? *Phil Bowker, Brussels, Belgium*

The only personality clash was between my wife and me!

Does he think that the 1970 side was the best he has seen? *Ray Finch, Havant, England*

I was in the 1962–63 Championship side and the Cup Winners of '66, the '68 Cup final team and the 1970 Championship side. The best team of the lot was the 1969–70 one and its no wonder we were champions – that team was magnificent. I used to look at that midfield of Ball, Harvey and Kendall and would wonder what on earth I was doing there, and I was playing for England at the time! That was the best Everton side ever, and it's never been bettered to this day.

Does he still have the handbag? *George Lee Stuart, Lismore, Australia*

No, I never kept any of them.

What was it like to be absolutely brilliant? *Mike Owen, Childwall, Liverpool*

I never thought I was brilliant. I knew when I'd had a good game, but playing brilliantly was our job. In the olden days at Goodison Park there used to be a big clock and when it got to twenty to five, all hell would break loose. We were usually winning and I would just be waiting, begging for the ref to blow the whistle because if I let a goal in then it would spoil my weekend. I wouldn't even dare to go out if we hadn't won because we drank in pubs and you would always see the fans. As soon as the whistle blew I knew I was in for a great night.

Sorry for all the barracking we gave him at the end of his career.
George Lee Stuart, Lismore, Australia
That's OK, that's life.

I have so many memories of his heroics. Sadly, my memory has seen better days and tends to transplant years and matches with ease, but I seem to remember Mike Lyons's testimonial at Goodison. As the second half started Gordon was carried onto the field on a stretcher and deposited on the goal-line. His weight had ballooned and I felt really sad watching him until he suddenly dived to make a great save and all the years dropped off him.
David Tickner, Bowring Park, Liverpool
It was my idea to do something like that. I said they should carry me on because I couldn't get my breath even then! The next thing, there was a shot and I made a fantastic save. The crowd went berserk and it was brilliant.

It's always great to go back to Goodison and hear the crowd I just love it. Last time I went was with Blueblood, the former players' charity, at the Spurs game. It was a reunion of the 1970 Championship side, which was over 30 years ago now. We went out in numerical order, so that meant me first. They called out my name and the crowd went mad. I was so proud and the cheering went on and on and on. I couldn't believe I'd been good enough to warrant such applause, but when I turned round I realised that all the others were following me. I was gutted, I thought it was just for me.

What was his best-ever moment as an Everton player? *Phil Bowker, Brussels, Belgium*
Winning my medals was great, but my proudest moment was when I was picked for England in December 1968. I'd played for the Under-23s before but this was with the Big Boys. We played Bulgaria at Wembley and we won 2–1. I was from a mining village in Yorkshire and to get capped for my country was beyond belief.

You don't get your cap at the time, it gets sent to you in the post. Every day I would go upstairs and look for mail, really casually, but I was dying to get my hands on this cap. It didn't arrive for about three months, and then suddenly it was there. I ripped the packet open and put my cap on and that was my proudest moment in my life.